SUPREME CO

and Supreme Law

edited by EDMOND CAHN

GREENWOOD PRESS, PUBLISHERS

NEW YORK   1968

Reprinted with the permission of
the Indiana University Press

First Greenwood reprinting, 1968

Library of Congress catalogue card number: 68-55629

The following publishers and authors have kindly granted permission to quote from the books and articles indicated:
Farrar, Straus and Young: *The Science of Culture*, copyright 1949 by Leslie A. White; Harvard University Press: Eugen Ehrlich, *Fundamental Principles of the Sociology of Law* (1936); Hollis and Carter, Ltd., and The Viking Press: G. E. Fasnacht, *Acton's Political Philosophy* (1952); Houghton Mifflin Co.: Ruth Benedict, *Patterns of Culture* (1934); Iowa Law Review: A. S. Abel, "The Commerce Power: An Instrument of Federalism" (1950); The Macmillan Co.: Alfred N. Whitehead, *Adventures of Ideas* (1937); New Republic: Harold Laski, "The Obsolescence of Federalism" (1939); New York University Press and Professor Edmond Cahn: *The Sense of Injustice* (1949); New York University Press and Professor Karl Loewenstein: *Constitutions and Constitutional Trends Since World War II* (Zurcher ed., 1951); The Philosophical Review: W. V. O. Quine, "Two Dogmas of Empiricism" (1951).

Printed in the United States of America

With the gracious consent of the contributors, New York University School of Law, sponsor of this volume, dedicates it to

ARTHUR T. VANDERBILT
Chief Justice of the Supreme Court of New Jersey

in recognition of his distinguished contributions to legal education and judicial administration.

PREFACE

WHAT PRACTICAL, working differences does judicial review make in the contemporary American scene? Has the Supreme Court exercised its power to determine constitutionality too extensively or too narrowly, with wisdom or imprudently? By passing on the validity of laws and executive actions, in what directions does the Court turn the dynamic force of the Constitution?

These are the questions to which this enterprise is addressed. Our book is the outcome of meetings held at New York University School of Law in 1953 by way of observing the hundred and fiftieth anniversary of *Marbury v. Madison.* What we undertook was to take stock of the institution of judicial review in its major functioning aspects. In short, we did not attempt either to attack or to defend the institution, but for once to differentiate, comprehend, and evaluate it.

Perhaps it would be helpful to say a word or two about the method by which the book is organized. After chapter I, which serves as an introduction, there follow two chapters devoted respectively to the scope of judicial review and the principles of constitutional construction. These chapters (II and III) are based on short papers which were read, then quite spontaneously discussed at our meetings. The discussion appears here as it was recorded by a stenotypist, the speakers having been afforded no opportunity to polish or revise their remarks. The chapters present questions of policy and judicial statecraft that are enormously important because they cut sectionally across the entire corpus of constitutional law. My colleagues, by dint of discussing the doctrinal issues, seem eventually to have reached an impressive and, I must add, rather unexpected measure of agreement among themselves—which may illustrate the advantages to be found in conference and exchange when men begin with mutual respect.

Chapters IV to VII follow a quite different plan. In each of them, one of the contributors was charged with personal responsibility for describing judicial review's cumulative impact on a specific and fundamental principle of the Constitution—the principle of federalism, the principle of individual liberties, the principle of distribution of powers, and the principle of majority rule. These four chapters, to which their distinguished authors devoted several months of intense study and reflection, together fulfill the main design of our enterprise.

It is pleasant to acknowledge my indebtedness and extend my hearty thanks to the many kind persons who have assisted in our undertaking. Among them, let me mention Dean Russell D. Niles of New York University School of Law for his warm and encouraging support; Herbert M. Wachtell and James C. Kirby, Jr., senior students at the School of Law, for very valuable aid in regard to my editorial burdens; and Bernard Perry, Edith Greenburg, and others on the staff of Indiana University Press for their talented and skillful cooperation.

In 1776 George Mason, one of America's great prophetic voices, warned his countrymen that they could preserve their liberty only by "a frequent recurrence to fundamental principles." Since that time, we have striven so earnestly to heed the admonition that Dicey felt constrained to call us "a people of constitutionalists." The doctrine we have inherited is a good one and we are not likely to forsake it.

THE EDITOR

CONTENTS

SUPREME COURT AND SUPREME LAW

I.
AN AMERICAN CONTRIBUTION

by Edmond Cahn

BEGINNING WITH Oliver Cromwell's "Instrument of Government" adopted in 1653, the modern history of written constitutions covers a period of some three centuries. At the precise half-way point in 1803, John Marshall delivered his judgment in *Marbury v. Madison.* Now after the lapse of another century and a half we propose to take stock of the various consequences his doctrine has brought about; and by way of prologue this chapter will suggest why the decision itself represented an important departure in the progress of American government.

For some time it has been fashionable to disparage *Marbury v. Madison* on the ground that there was nothing particularly new about it. Recent American scholarship grants that the decision raised the Supreme Court's prestige from a very low plane and that it linked John Marshall's powerful personality to the institution of judicial review; in all other respects the case is usually dismissed with a rather patronizing shrug. Legal historians have pointed to earlier judgments in the state courts, precedents in the British Privy Council on appeals from the colonies, and passages in the *Federalist* papers—as demonstrative proof that John Marshall borrowed and did not invent. But unless our philosophy of government is to be controlled by the rules of a patent office, novelty can hardly be accepted as the sole or decisive test of merit. In point of fact, a mature understanding—far from identifying the important with the novel—would attribute greater value to *Marbury v. Madison* precisely because it formalized and installed political conceptions which had already gained some measure of general support.

It is interesting to note how American treatises on the theory of constitutionalism have been influenced by the British experience of the seventeenth century. To this day our scholars tend to concentrate on supremacy of law as the central problem of the subject. The basic antithesis, as most of them see it, remains substantially what it was in the period between Coke and Locke, that is, the antithesis between government by laws and government by men, between legal precept and executive prerogative, between wise rules and exercise of wise discretion. In this sense the issues of constitutionalism are fully as old as Plato, whose thought moved in successive stages from the unfettered discretion which he favored in *The Republic* to the particularized statutes which he set down in his final work, *The Laws*.

However, the self-same struggle against the Stuarts which focused attention on this classic problem of constitutionalism also inspired resort to the expedient of a written constitution. Thus there arose a cognate yet competing problem in the philosophy of government, a problem with antecedents even older than Plato. Its origins can be traced to the period in Greek philosophy when men like Parmenides were preaching that all was sameness and unity and men like Heraclitus were insisting that all was flux and change. In short, it was the antithesis between *permanence* and *change* that became one of the characteristic and magistral problems of constitutionalism as soon as men attempted to embody the constitution in a written document.

There is nothing abstruse about the way this antithesis presents itself in concrete experience. Let us suppose that, in a time of great public disturbance, the leaders of the people determine that certain fundamental institutions are indispensable to the survival of their political principles. Accordingly they compose a written constitution which describes the framework of government, defines the several political organs, and establishes certain lines of relation not only between one organ and another but also between the government and the citizenry. This is the fabric they desire to endure, this is to be the fundamental and permanent structure of government. But even if no extraneous cause should intervene to destroy the structure, the lapse of time most assuredly and inevitably will. For though we assume that the founders' wisdom has been entirely adequate to the needs of their society and the sentiments of their fellow-citizens, nevertheless social, economic, and technological changes will sooner or later make what was appropriate obsolete, what was modern archaic, and what was enlightened oppressive. If the constitution is drafted in loose and flexible terms, it may last somewhat longer, but the framers hardly dare draft it in terms so elastic as to imperil their own purposes. The minimum degree of rigidity necessary for the preservation of social order eventually becomes a political strait-jacket.

In the experience of the Anglo-Americans from the middle of the seventeenth century down to the time of *Marbury v. Madison,* written constitutions proved very short-lived. Of course, many adopted since 1803 have likewise fallen into history's wastebasket. But the naked fact that the United States Constitution has survived for more than a century and a half implies that something special was accomplished between 1787 and 1803 to make it an exception. Somehow or other, a sufficient balance was attained in the tension between the principle of permanence and the principle of change. If such was the case, the American solution, although it may or may not be suitable to the government of other countries, certainly merits careful study. It may constitute a major contribution to the technique of successful government. Let me therefore suggest the outlines of the historic turn which I see initiated in 1787 at the Constitutional Convention and consummated in 1803 by *Marbury v. Madison.* It was a turn in the theory of the written constitution, which may be summarized:

	As to Objective	*As to Content*	*As to Sanction*
from	perpetuity	immutability	appeal to Heaven
to	efficacy	adaptation	appeal to the courts

II

Suppose we take ourselves back to the Constitutional Period (1787–1803) and consider the concept of a written constitution as it must have appeared to educated Americans of the time. Surely, it presented a strange, almost baffling history, streaked with confusion in theory and utopianism in practice. In point of fact, if the leaders of American thought had felt a wholehearted respect for the indications of that history, they might never have attempted a written charter. As it was, they were astute enough to consult the history mainly for negative purposes: from it they ascertained some of the things a wise draftsman should *not* do.

Rarely in any department of human interest has theory been so obscured by errors and ineptitudes of practice. Among the ancients, for example, a few keen observers like Plato, Aristotle, and Polybius seem to have perceived that a "constitution" should be identified rather by its content and political function than by the source which promulgated it. Their works offered highly instructive reading on the level of theory. When, however, one turned to the concrete texts in the various ancient polities, what did one find? Code after code, without exception, deemed to be a fundamental law for no other reason than its inspired, preternatural, or divine authorship. The authoritative differentia was not the content but the source, not the function but the charisma of the legislator. Hence only a confirmed heretic would feel disposed to suggest that this command deserved a higher rank than the other; that this prohibition could be enforced by jural sanctions and that could not; that certain provisions had only ceremonial value; or that dispositions fixing the general fabric of government might be distinguished from conventional, transitory, and particularized regulations. To everyone but the heretics, it seemed fairly obvious that if these classifications and distinctions had been worth making, the divine or divinely inspired legislator would have made them.

It is easy to smile at the vagaries of ancient political practice, and to reflect with pleasure on modern superiority—but perhaps not wholly justified. For we are about to see a strange phenomenon: the typical political theorist of seventeenth century England proceeds in a sensible fashion to secularize and naturalize the process of drafting a fundamental law; he transmutes the obsolete supernatural code into a product of human ingenuity and intellect; yet—the moment the draft has been formulated—incontinently he assumes the prostrate attitude of the ancients, invests the document with the same reverential awe he feels for its source, and declares—in terms suitable for a doxology—that every part and the whole of it shall remain immutable forever and in perpetuity!

Here again, our reluctance to criticize can be overcome only by the exigencies of our theme and the obligation to deal justly with the accomplishments of the Constitutional Period. In the first place, we know that we stand on a height of vantage which three intervening centuries of historical experience have provided for us. There are propositions that have become so obvious in the course of these centuries that we are likely to confuse our own fund of empirical information with a superior endowment of wisdom and judgment. For example, when in his last years Mr. Justice Brandeis remarked, "A code of law that makes no provision for its amendment provides for its ultimate rejection," [1] he merely asserted, in a neat rhetorical form, what the modern history of written constitutions has taught Americans to accept as palpably evident, if not truistic; but who of us has sufficient pride of intellect to claim that he could have excogitated this simple maxim *a priori*, without knowing anything about our ancestors' efforts and failures? In the second place, the American indebtedness to England's Classical Republicans, to the statesmen of the "Glorious Revolution," and especially to John Locke is so enormous that any disparagement—however justified—suggests an unworthy ingratitude or, at best, a chauvinistic attempt to minimize our national obligation. When of all men it is John Locke that I feel compelled to single out for criticism, my consolations seem hardly adequate. Yet even they have been provided by him, for he too cared more for truth than for John Locke's stated opinions and, when he would discover error in his own work, he did not hesitate to acknowledge it and to recast his thinking. [2]

Locke's example is the one we must select, not only because his intellectual eminence is beyond cavil but also because he drafted his written constitution with the conscious expectation that it would be put into prompt and practical effect. Unlike various other charters—intended rather for edification than for application—his was designed to serve the day-to-day government of a specific country, covering a specific area, inhabited or to be inhabited by colonists of known origins and customs. This was no figment of a willful dream, destined to live only in the still air of a philosopher's study. Quite the contrary; when the young Locke drafted and redrafted his "Fundamental Constitutions," [3] he knew very well that they were commissioned expressly for the government of Carolina.

There is no need to comment on the detailed provisions of the fantastically baroque document that Locke concocted. The Carolina colonists of the time commented more or less conclusively by resisting adoption of the plan for nearly fifty years until, despite continued support from the lords proprietors, it was finally abandoned in its entirety. If we turn back to Locke's text today, the scheme proposed seems bizarre and unrealistic almost beyond belief. It is like one of the White Knight's inventions in *Through the Looking-Glass*, which he described to Alice:

> "Now the cleverest thing of the sort that I ever did," he went on after a pause, "was inventing a new pudding during the meat-course."
>
> "In time to have it cooked for the next course?" said Alice. "Well, that WAS quick work, certainly!"
>
> "Well, not the NEXT course," the Knight said in a slow thoughtful tone: "no, certainly not the next COURSE."
>
> "Then it would have to be the next day. I suppose you wouldn't have two pudding-courses in one dinner?"
>
> "Well, not the NEXT day," the Knight repeated as before: "not the next DAY. In fact," he went on, holding his head down, and his voice getting lower and lower, "I don't believe that pudding ever WAS cooked! In fact, I don't believe that pudding ever WILL be cooked! And yet it was a very clever pudding to invent."

But could not the Carolina colonists have been induced to experiment with Locke's document and then remedy its defects by resorting to a prescribed method of amendment? We have no way of telling. For although the draft of the "Fundamental Laws" went through various revisions at Locke's own hands, it concluded by providing categorically that:

> These fundamental constitutions, in number a hundred and twenty, and every part thereof, shall be and remain the sacred and unalterable form and rule of government of Carolina forever.

I wish Locke had done no more. If he had been content to ordain that no one must ever alter his handiwork, he would merely have followed the accustomed path of seventeenth and eighteenth century framers. (For instance, in the 1689 Bill of Rights, without a pretense of discrimination between general and specific, lasting and temporary provisions, it is laid down that "All . . . shall stand, remain, and be the law of this realm for ever . . .") But since Locke was a philosopher of the new enlightenment, he surpassed the lawyerlike parliamentary draftsmen—even in the dimensions of his error. Apparently, immutability and perpetuity were not enough to claim; he felt impelled to kick harder against the pricks of history's teachings. And so, imitating the fatuous example of Justinian, who had attempted in vain to prohibit commentaries on his *Corpus Juris,* our great democratic philosopher inserted an additional clause reading:

> Since multiplicity of comments, as well as of laws, have great inconveniences, and serve only to obscure and perplex, all manner of comments and expositions on any part of these fundamental constitutions, or on any part of the common or statute laws of Carolina, are absolutely prohibited.

As the physicians of Locke's time would have expressed it, there must be something about sitting down to prepare a constitution which induces the "humors" to become excessively sanguine. Indeed, the most modest instance I have come upon was that of ancient Solon, who was satisfied to state that his legislation should endure for only a hundred years. (Of course, like so many others, he lived to see it subverted after a decade or so.) In the seventeenth and eighteenth centuries, eminent draftsmen would accept nothing less than a provision for unqualified perpetuity.

Yet some of these were very wise and thoughtful men, at least in many other respects. I do not feel we ought to leave them here in a posture that borders on the ridiculous. We ought, on the contrary, to take note of the premises implicit in their thinking; for if we do, we shall readily see that—given the premises which were generally accepted in those times—a claim of immutability and perpetuity was neither so implausible nor so pretentious in their eyes as it appears to us. We should remember that although they succeeded to a considerable degree in secularizing the process of constitution-making, they were intimately familiar with the Bible and the series of solemn covenants and compacts reported in it. Understandably, therefore, they were led to assume that fundamental arrangements of this kind would have to be immutable and perpetual. The religious influence continued in the background of their thinking.

In the foreground there were cogent factors derived from the law, the politics, and the philosophy of the situation. In its legal appearance, the early modern written constitution followed the technical form of a charter or land-grant; it resembled the customary deed of real property, which was assumed to be binding on the grantor and his heirs forever. Politically speaking, the charters had served, as far back as the time of Magna Charta, to provide rallying points for the assertion of various civil rights; whether in England or America, the men who claimed "imprescriptible rights" would be prone to insist that the documents had eternal validity. And in the philosophic aspect of the matter, a written constitution was deemed to possess superior dignity and force because it mirrored the principles of the natural law, which everyone agreed were fixed, immutable, and permanent. All these assumptions were exceedingly easy to credit at least during the seventeenth century and the greater part of the eighteenth. Soon the full impact of the Industrial Revolution would be felt; soon the paw of accelerated technological change would brush aside everything that appeared so continuous, disciplined, and static in those simpler days; but at the time even the most gifted and enlightened statesmen might fairly suppose that the social relations with which they were familiar would continue or could be made to continue indefinitely without material disruption.

When the American Continental Congress undertook in 1777 to consider "Articles of Confederation and Perpetual Union," the assumptions we have just described were still in full vigor and more or less unchallenged. Obviously, in that particular setting they must have seemed valid and expedient in the highest conceivable degree; else why had the Americans resolved to revolt at the risk of life and honor? Immutability of charters and rights under them was one of the American maxims against George III, just as it had been an English maxim against Charles I and later against James II. But in 1777 the

Americans had additional good reasons to impose immutability on their "Articles of Confederation and Perpetual Union." From the positive aspect, they knew that they had no chance of military success unless the new-born States would act unanimously, that is, they must without exception "hang together or hang separately." From the negative aspect, no delegation, no State trusted the others sufficiently to commit itself to an instrument of confederation which might be amended without its approval.

In the Articles of Confederation these considerations, theoretical and practical, political and military, all converged to induce a reiteration of the weary yet magical word "perpetual" (What wry smiles that word must bring to the lips of heavenly observers!) as well as a prohibition of "any alteration at any time hereafter" except by *unanimous* consent of the thirteen States.

It was in the teeth of these provisions, of course, that the members of the Constitutional Convention proposed a completely new charter in 1787. What they did amounted to nothing less than a *coup d'état* —an overturn not merely in the form but likewise in the theory of American government. For suddenly, the States were told that the principle of immutability had been abandoned. No longer would a single State be able to veto the process of growth and adaptation, because Article V of the new Constitution provided boldly that amendments binding on *all* could be adopted by action of *three-fourths* of the States.

It seems that in England during the preceding century one statesman had been endowed with such a happy combination of practical wisdom and intellectual modesty that he had hit upon the prototype of this remarkable device. When William Penn in 1682 issued his "Frame of Government of Pennsylvania," he wrote a preface explaining the purposes and objectives he had in mind.[4] It is clear that he had reflected long on the subject. His reflections taught him that, in the long run, change and chance will not be subdued by any static framework the mind of man can devise. Therefore, having said in his preface, "I do not find a model in the world, that time, place, and some singular emergences have not necessarily altered . . . ," he went on to provide that his charter might be amended whenever the Governor and six-sevenths of the freemen in the Provincial Council and

General Assembly would consent. Thus to William Penn we owe the invaluable expedient of permitting amendment by a vote less than unanimous yet large enough to insure extended deliberation and lasting approval.

In the fall of 1776, Pennsylvania adopted its first constitution as a new State. Guided by Benjamin Franklin, the State convention not only accepted but considerably elaborated the device it had inherited from Penn. It framed a plan for the periodic election of "censors," who would be charged simultaneously with (1) seeing that the State Constitution was obeyed scrupulously and (2) recommending any amendments that might appear to be necessary.[5] Here was a sure omen that American statesmen were beginning to recognize the inherent relation between efficacy and progressive adaptation in the life of a constitution. But, as we have seen, an attempt at that juncture to apply this perception on the level of federal government would have met enormous and probably insuperable obstacles. In relation to federal structure, Penn's guidance was required to wait another decade for a riper and wiser gathering—held, fittingly, in Penn's own city.

To the men at Philadelphia in 1787 an amendment clause must have seemed an absolute necessity. Behind the closed doors of their convention they had struck one ingenious compromise after another in order to achieve approximate unanimity among the delegates. All of them realized that because of these compromises the document they had signed probably contained a number of imperfections. Most of them must have speculated at least privately whether the compromises would work to their satisfaction in actual practice and whether experience would show that one interest had yielded too much or the other had acquiesced in an unrealistic solution. In arguing for ratification, even Hamilton was not willing to say more than "that the system, though it may not be perfect in every part, is, upon the whole, a good one [and] is the best that the present views and circumstances of the country will permit." [6] I suspect the statesmen of 1787 would be astonished to learn that at this remote date the Constitution remains in force at all and would scarcely believe that since 1804, when their generation finally rested content with the document, it has been amended only ten times. (From these ten, two may be subtracted because the Twenty-first Amendment did little if anything more than repeal the Eighteenth.) Could we consult them today, I think the framers would inquire why we have not exercised the power of amendment more frequently and extensively.[7]

If they looked upon the amendment clause as a necessity, what a virtue they forthwith made of it! It became one of the standard arguments in the campaign for ratification, a big gun which was reserved for use after every other debating weapon had failed to repel the opposition, then wheeled systematically into place, loaded with the ammunition of ostensible reasonableness, and discharged point-blank in the adversary's face—to his discomfort at least, often to his devastation. Does this or that provision in the draft seem unwise? Does the gentleman persist in his objection? Very well, since the times do not admit of delay, let us proceed to ratify in haste, then we can go about amending at leisure.

When Madison wrote *Federalist* No. 43, he was satisfied to expound Article V and to find in it "every mark of propriety"; but by the time Hamilton was ready to compose No. 85, which would serve as the peroration and ultimate epitome of the whole federalist case in New York, he found himself compelled to endow Article V with supreme practical importance. For his opponents had largely consolidated behind the argument that the process of corrective amendment should precede, not follow, the act of ratification. Then did Hamilton prove his virtuosity. He took Article V out of its modest position, burnished it until it fairly shone, and displayed it to America as an incomparably easy and expeditious arrangement for the remedying of errors, compared to which an attempt to improve the instrument before it was ratified would be desperately difficult, inept, and divisive.

The Virginia scene was not different. Objecting vehemently to the lack of a bill of rights in the document Madison had sent overseas to him, Thomas Jefferson acknowledged that the draftsmen's mistake could be corrected by resorting to the amendment clause.[8] And in the Virginia ratification convention,[9] which largely determined the destiny of the Constitution, the federalists repeatedly pointed to Article V by way of answer to Patrick Henry's and George Mason's indignant criticisms. Yet even after the federalists had solemnly promised to support amendments which would supply the missing bill of rights, the motion for ratification squeezed through by the very barest of margins; it is therefore an understatement to say that without Article V the Constitution would never have been adopted.

What a fascinating reversal we have here! How the tune has changed in that brief decade from 1777 (when a power to amend without unanimous approval was denied by way of reassurance) to 1787 (when just such a power made it possible for the new pattern of government to come into existence)!

Once the Constitution had been ratified, Article V was given immediate exercise. By the time Marshall rendered his judgment in *Marbury v. Madison*, the first ten amendments had been added to establish a bill of rights, the Eleventh had been adopted to reverse a decision of the Supreme Court, and the Twelfth was under way to correct defects in the original plan exposed by the presidential election of 1800. It is fair to conclude that, by 1803, the American theory of a written constitution (1) had begun to subordinate perpetuity to practical efficacy (2) had completely discarded the false notion of immutability, and in its place (3) had approved a policy of seeking stability through progressive adaptation.

Much however remained to be done. The slow and cumbersome mechanism of Article V can at most produce a needed change in the literal text of the Constitution; the goal of adaptation requires more than that, the goal of efficacy requires considerably more. How can we discover just what the broad, sweeping phrases of the text signify as concrete legal mandates unless they should be interpreted by some authoritative organ? How can their meaning reflect the shift and flux of social conditions, economic interests, and political ideals unless the organ which interprets should likewise be equipped to reinterpret? And finally what pragmatic value can either the text or the successive interpretations retain unless the process of adapting the Constitution should be somehow combined with a concomitant process of effectuating it by force of law? These concernments lead us to the import of *Marbury v. Madison*.

III

If the objective and content of the written constitution were transformed during the course of the Constitutional Period, there was an even sharper turn in theory on the subject of effectual enforcement. No political problem perplexed the leading American statesmen so deeply and continually. To them it seemed inevitable that from time to time one official organ or another would attempt to infringe the Constitution; they were perfectly familiar with the way power brings out arrogance and ruthlessness in men, and the way personal ambition or fanatical enthusiasm can exacerbate the process. They knew that often the most redoubtable enemies of a free society are very sincere individuals obsessed with a belief that destiny has singled them out and anointed them to protect liberty by defining its limits. Clearly, against dangers and inroads like these, "parchment barriers" [10]—to adopt Madison's phrase—would be futile without effective sanctions.

The sanctions they found available when they consulted previous history can be grouped under the heading of "appeal to heaven." In ancient times—Livy, Herodotus, and similar sources tell us—the technique for enforcing fidelity to a treaty, compact, or charter consisted in exacting a sacramental oath from the person who undertook the obligation. (These were strictly promissory oaths, relating only to acts to be performed in the future. They should not be confused with iniquitous "test oaths" which relate to one's past conduct and past opinions.) When a vow was taken in ceremonious circumstances, it involved a great deal more than merely promising to perform. It amounted in effect to a sort of conditional imprecation, because the oath-taker agreed either expressly or by religious implication that his promise might be considered as having been made to the celestial powers, who, if he should violate it, would evince their displeasure in some characteristically divine fashion. In seventeenth and eighteenth century England, statesmen set great store on the precise wording of all official oaths; what the king would or would not be willing to swear might well determine whether he or some other candidate would be found present at the coronation. The constitutional sanction consisted in invoking *lex coeli*, the law of heaven.

Not long after the close of our Constitutional Period, Jeremy

Bentham wrote a devastating critique of this belief in the efficacy of promissory oaths. In it he said:

> . . . *The arm pressed into service is that of the invisible and supreme ruler of the universe.*
>
> *The oath being taken, the formularies involved in it being pronounced, is or is not the Almighty bound to do what is expected of Him? Of the two contradictory propositions, which one do you believe? If He is* NOT *bound, then the security, the sanction, the obligation amounts to nothing. If He is bound, then observe what follows: the Almighty is bound, and by whom? Of all the worms that crawl about the earth in the shape of men there is not one who may not thus impose conditions on the supreme ruler of the universe.*
>
> *And to what is He bound? To any number of contradictory and incompatible observances, which legislators, tyrants, madmen, may, in the shape of an oath, be pleased to assign Him.*[11]

As usual, Bentham was correct. For sheer, unmitigated insolence, men who presume they have God's power at their beck and call to enforce their paltry engagements can hardly be surpassed—except perhaps by men who purport to "demonstrate" syllogistically that God exists.

Yet likewise as usual, Bentham was not quite wholly correct. There is a genuine moral cogency in an oath of office when it is taken in solemn form by a man of radical integrity. In the forum of conscience, he feels committed, no longer free as he was before but tethered to the obligations he has assumed. Thus it was that when in 1766 Edmund Pendleton—sitting as a judge in the colony of Virginia—resolved intrepidly to disregard the Stamp Act because he considered it unconstitutional, he referred very simply and movingly to his "having taken an oath to decide according to law." [12] So also if one turns to *Marbury v. Madison* and reads Marshall's justification of judicial review: it all seems inspired by Hamilton's analysis in *The Federalist*—until one comes to the conclusion. And there with rather eloquent indignation Marshall insists on the oath he has taken to discharge his duties "agreeably to the Constitution." [13] These factors seem to have changed very little since his day: I have known quite a register of trial and appellate judges but never one who doubted that the solemn assumption of office had somehow fettered his will. Even in the case of executive and representative officials this is sometimes true, particularly where the influence of some professional or corporate tradition can be felt. However, these considerations have no pretentious connection with appeals to heaven or conditional imprecations. The official oath is now only a solemn type of promise, the penalties involved in a breach are strictly secular. Perhaps without intending to, we of the twentieth century manifest a more seemly reverence in this regard.

I do not mean to imply that the issue presented itself in any such aspect during the Constitutional Period. Quite the contrary: when the American statesmen of the time decided they could not put their trust in oaths as the working warranties of the Constitution, it was simply because human experience, including their own, had established beyond question that an oath would be a sadly feeble kind of tether. Their generation had first sworn fealty to King George, then they had sworn it to the cause of independence; they had vowed a perpetual allegiance to the Articles of Confederation, then they had agreed to disregard them at the Philadelphia Convention. If egregiously honorable men like themselves were susceptible to awkward shifts like these, how could they expect a mere oath to restrain the ordinary run of politicians who might succeed them, much less the morally perverse? The Constitution clearly could not be left dependent on the efficacy of ceremonious oaths.

"Appeal to heaven" had, however, a second and possibly more familiar connotation to the founding fathers. John Locke had taught them to associate it with a people's resort to revolution.[14] If major provisions of the constitution should be violated arbitrarily and persistently, the people were entitled to consider that the political compact had been dissolved, that they had been thrown into a state of nature in relation to the sovereign, and that their taking up arms in defense of their rights constituted an appeal to *lex coeli*. Of course, the framers of the Constitution were constrained to endorse everything in these propositions; how else could they justify their own participation in the Revolutionary War? But now that an American government was in contemplation to restore confidence and stabilize the social order, Locke's maxims, however valid they may have been when they were needed, must be laid aside as irrelevant. In '76 there had been a time to tear down; that time had passed. In '87 "the good people," "the right-minded people" agreed that the time to build up had long since arrived. In their judgment, "appeal to heaven," having served its historic purpose, had nothing to offer toward meeting the need of the new era, *i.e.*, the day-to-day enforcement of a written constitution. (Consider moreover the infamous behavior of this Daniel Shays!)

In respect of sanctions, it was clear that *lex coeli* could never provide an acceptable solution. What was needed was a change to the law of the land or *lex terrae*, a change from higher-than-positive law to higher, positive law. This, of course, is the very change that Marshall consummated in *Marbury v. Madison:* by legitimizing the appeal to the courts he presumedly bastardized any possible "appeal to heaven."

Where did he learn the method of solution? I should like to suggest that his indoctrination in judicial review came several years prior to the issuance of *The Federalist*—to be precise, on November 2, 1782. If I am correct, then Marshall's intellectual debt to Hamilton was considerably smaller than most of us have assumed. Hamilton's arguments in the 78th *Federalist* did in all likelihood provide Marshall with a ready-made model of exposition for the *Marbury* opinion; and considering the intrinsic qualities of the model, its prestige as a factor in bringing about ratification, and the superbly ironic twist that the present defendant—Jefferson's own Madison—had collaborated actively with Hamilton in writing *The Federalist*, Marshall would have been either more or less than human if he had not availed himself of such a tempting opportunity. Since he was intensely human, he did adapt and paraphrase Hamilton's line of presentation. But his understanding of judicial review and his faith in its efficacy he owed to others.

I have found no indication that Marshall became acquainted with judicial review before November 1782. His formal education in the law consisted in attending George Wythe's lectures at William and Mary College "for perhaps six weeks" beginning about May 1, 1780, during which time the jottings in his notebook show he was profoundly preoccupied with thoughts of the young lady whom he was to marry in January 1783. The notebook records Wythe's lectures, but these appear to have related to topics of private law only. Then, in 1782 having been elected to the Virginia legislature, Marshall came to Richmond for the purpose of taking his seat and establishing a law practice in the city.[15]

For lack of a quorum, the opening of the House was delayed for eighteen days until November 9, 1782, and Marshall seems to have been entirely at leisure during this interval.

Now, anyone arriving in Richmond in the fall of 1782 would have found the city agog over one of the most dramatic and celebrated cases of its history.[16] Three alleged traitors had been convicted and condemned to death. The Virginia Assembly had passed a bill pardoning them, but the Senate had refused to concur. They were respited just as they were about to be hanged. (I may say here at the outset by way of easing the reader's mind that if any of them was eventually hanged, it was not because of the crime of treason.) The issue of the validity of their pardon was finally remitted to the Virginia Court of Appeals. One of the great questions in the case was whether the legislation passed by the House had conformed to the requirements of the Virginia Constitution governing the subject of pardons. At the unprecedented invitation of Edmund Pendleton, who was presiding over the Court of Appeals, many leading lawyers in the State of Virginia voiced their opinions in order to assist the judges.

On November 2, 1782, each of the judges delivered his views to the assembled public. There was Pendleton. (It will be remembered that when he was a colonial judge he had not feared to declare the Stamp Act unconstitutional.) Now he could be heard to emphasize the desirability of avoiding affront to a co-ordinate branch of the government; he could also be heard to declare if he were ever compelled to face the issue, he would not shrink from the performance of his judicial duty. There was Judge Mercer, who flatly pronounced the legislation unconstitutional—the first such occasion in the annals of the State of Virginia. And on the same bench there sat none other than Marshall's only law teacher, George Wythe, revered for the profundity of his scholarship and the brilliance of his reasoning.

Wythe proceeded to hold the pardon invalid without having to reach the question of constitutionality. But these are the words he spoke concerning the obligations of judicial office:

> I have heard of an English chancellor who said, and it was nobly said, that it was his duty to protect the rights of the subject against the encroachments of the crown; and that he would do it at every hazard. But if it was his duty to protect a solitary individual against the rapacity of the sovereign, surely it is equally mine to protect one branch of the legislature and consequently the whole community against the usurpations of the other: and whenever the proper occasion occurs, I shall feel the duty; and fearlessly perform it. Whenever traitors shall be fairly convicted by the verdict of their peers before the competent tribunal, if one branch of the legislature without the concurrence of the other shall attempt to rescue the offenders from the sentence of the law, I shall not hesitate, sitting in this place, to say to the general court, Fiat justitia, ruat coelum; and to the usurping branch of the legislature, you attempt worse than a vain thing; for although you cannot succeed, you set an example which may convulse society to its centre. Nay more, if the whole legislature, an event to be deprecated, should attempt to overleap the bounds prescribed to them by the people, I, in administering the public justice of the country, will meet the united powers at my seat in this tribunal; and pointing to the constitution, will say to them, here is the limit of your authority; and hither shall you go, but no further.[17]

It seems safe to conclude that on November 2, 1782 the principles were first planted [18] which would bear fruit twenty years later in *Marbury v. Madison*, and that Wythe, Pendleton, and Mercer deserve to rank with Hamilton as Marshall's intellectual coadjutors in installing the institution of judicial review. On him destiny conferred the role it reserves for its special favorites—the role of converting essence into existence. In the *Marbury* case, applying his mentors' teachings, Marshall equipped the United States Constitution with an efficacious sanction. Thus he gave it an opportunity to maintain its legal vigor and preserve its identity through all subsequent vicissitudes. I think even those of us who are not fond of Marshall's personality or his politics must recognize that he received little more than a piece of parchment and finally transmitted a viable organism.

In terms of our theme, it is exceedingly important that when we call judicial review an efficacious sanction, we detect the bivalence of the word "efficacious." Judicial review is always more than pure and simple enforcement of the Constitution; in addition, it always comprises express or tacit interpretation of the Constitution, or—in other words—a continual process of adjusting and adapting the fundamental fabric. The sanction which Marshall installed in *Marbury v. Madison* should be seen as having served both purposes; it has maintained the Constitution not only by giving it legal force but also by providing in a substantial measure for continual reshaping and development. That is why our theme has linked Article III concerning the judicial power with Article V concerning the power of amendment. I believe their functions link them of necessity.

Yet when we have reached this point in our analysis, it is strange to discover that what William James used to call "the sentiment of rationality" seems somehow to elude us. We have traced the turn from perpetuity to efficacy, from immutability to adaptation, and from heavenly to judicial sanctions; yet some element, some strand appears to be missing without which there is only an abstract pattern. Oddly enough, it seems as though we have lost sight of the country while describing its government. If our account was adequate and satisfactory, why has there been little or no room in it for the American *people*?

The *Marbury* opinion has a comment to contribute on this very subject. In a paragraph [19] that has attracted comparatively little notice, Marshall refers to the people's exercise of their right to establish a constitution as "a very great exertion; nor can it nor ought it to be frequently repeated." The people, he reiterates insistently in the same paragraph, "can seldom act." A rather enigmatic sort of reference, this; what might Marshall have intended by it?

IV

I think the meaning—in an objective sense, of course—should not be difficult to reach, if only we place ourselves in the circumstances of the time and recall that the *Marbury* opinion represented an attempt on Marshall's part to rebuke his arch-adversary, Thomas Jefferson. Under the thin guise of an impersonal utterance, the Chief Justice was really engaged in admonishing the President and challenging his political creed. At least that is the way the opinion was understood by contemporary readers in both camps.[20] In the setting of February 1803 where Jefferson was far and away the outstanding advocate of popularism, to say—as Marshall did—that "the people . . . can seldom act" was equivalent to firing a shot in his direction. Which is, I think, the right direction for us.

To follow it, one must begin with an accurate picture of Jefferson's contribution to the development of judicial review, which has often been distorted by anachronisms of emphasis. For example, it has become usual to quote from an informal letter he addressed to Mrs. John Adams in 1804,[21] where, justifying the pardons he had granted to persons convicted under the Sedition Law, he asserted that the judges were entitled to decide on constitutionality "for themselves in their own sphere of action" but not for the executive and (presumably) not for the legislature. This remark did constitute a portion of Jefferson's doctrine; it has subsequently been vindicated at least to the extent the Supreme Court has refused to adjudicate so-called "political issues"; [22] nevertheless, just because it dealt only with power relations inside the structure of government, it remained a more or less subordinate element in the Jeffersonian philosophy. It was hardly the kind of contention that would put John Marshall in a febrile state.

Jefferson's more fundamental doctrine was the outcome of long and thoughtful study. As early as June of '76, he had tried his hand at drawing up a constitution for the emerging State of Virginia. In a few weeks' time he produced three successive drafts.[23] The first of them prohibited amendments except with the unanimous consent of both legislative houses. Then Jefferson's thinking advanced very rapidly: the second and third versions permitted adoption of amendments by a majority vote of the people in two-thirds of the State's counties. Unfortunately, although the State convention made considerable use of Jefferson's draft, it ignored his amendment section.[24] As adopted the Virginia charter contained no provision on the subject.

In Jefferson's intellectual advance, these steps proved to be merely preliminary. Lodging in Philadelphia until September and conversing often with men like Franklin, he enjoyed a fine opportunity to observe the preparation of the Pennsylvania State constitution of 1776. This, as we have seen, was the constitution which provided for a periodic choice of "censors" who would report on breaches of the constitution and on desirable amendments.

Though he must have been intrigued by the Pennsylvania device, Jefferson apparently let his ideas incubate for as long as seven years, or until the advent of peace afforded a more propitious occasion to improve Virginia's charter. In 1783 he composed a new plan.[25] For the pertinent clause of this plan [26] he set out to build upon the model that Pennsylvania had furnished, but since his philosophy would not permit him to touch anything—any institution, expedient, or arrangement—without democratizing it, he finally produced a clause that was altogether Jeffersonian because it was so firmly bottomed on the people's good judgment and their right of ultimate decision.

In effect, the 1783 draft provides that whenever any two of the three branches of government shall determine (by two-thirds vote) that "a Convention is necessary for altering this Constitution or correcting breaches of it," delegates shall be elected by the people, to convene within three months and to exercise the same powers as the convention that adopted the original constitution. Thus where Pennsylvania had recognized the connection between enforcing a charter and amending it, Jefferson went a great deal farther: he converted the Pennsylvania device into an effectual nexus between the operations of government and the desires of the governed. According to his plan, final jurisdiction over every constitutional controversy would reside in the minds of the people. In regard to fundamental issues, the people would be more than the passive source of the constitution, they would intervene actively and enforce or construe or amend it as they might see fit; in short, it would at all times remain theirs and express their genius.

It is very important to discern Jefferson's position clearly. Far from objecting to judicial review of constitutionality, he frequently proposed that the judiciary share with the executive in exercising the veto power. If his proposal had been accepted, the judges would have been concerned not only with questions of constitutionality but also, quite avowedly, with the desirability and wisdom of legislative acts. And, as we saw, he conceded the courts' right and duty to pass on constitutionality at least "in their own sphere of action." It was not judicial review that he opposed, but the assumption that its results would be final and beyond further appeal. Not so, he submitted; if the judges should err so egregiously that the executive and legislature might have cause to fear for the constitution, then there must be provision for a further appeal—to the whole people as ultimate arbiters. This looks like a stride beyond the Declaration of Independence. In the Declaration he had described governments as *deriving* their powers from the consent of the governed; in 1783 he would further require that the very fabric of government be subjected to continual re-assessment and reshaping in conformity with the judgment of the governed. For the balance of his days, Jefferson was to preach that the Constitution of the United States belonged only to the living generation.[27]

The federalists felt no difficulty in accepting what Jefferson had written in '76; in point of fact, so consistently were they persuaded of the people's status as the sovereign fountainhead of legitimacy that they were willing to invite opposition to the Constitution by beginning it with "We the People" instead of "We the States." But they found Jefferson's subsequent, more advanced attitude entirely unacceptable. It would leave a constitution tentative like a power of attorney issued by an officious and meddlesome principal; they understood that a constitution should be rather like an irrevocable and immutable grant or, if the need of some slight possibility of amendment must be admitted, then like a nearly irrevocable and immutable grant.

One of the authors of *The Federalist* (whom we shall call by his pseudonym "Publius" because it is not certain whether the relevant passages [28] were Hamilton's or Madison's) was astute enough to recognize that Jefferson's 1783 proposal might epitomize the entire philosophy of popular rule. He appears to have given much care to the strategy of refuting it. The means employed were well chosen: Publius began by lavishing compliments on the author of the proposal; abstained from any suggestion of false or improper motives; conceded the proposal's plausibility and consistency *in theory*; showed however that it was idealistic to a fault, utopian, and impractical; [29] and finally, having analogized it to the device in the Pennsylvania constitution, went on to demonstrate that Pennsylvania's experience with periodic conventions had been very unsatisfactory. Two complete papers (Nos. 49 and 50) of *The Federalist* were devoted to this refutation—which indicates the importance Publius attached to it.

With considerable adroitness he manipulated his readers' anxieties, pointing out that "frequent appeals" to the people would deprive the government of "veneration" and would involve a "danger of disturbing the public tranquillity by interesting too strongly the public passions." Sadly he added that "it must be confessed that the [constitutional] experiments are of too ticklish a nature to be unnecessarily multiplied." "The *passions*, therefore, not the *reason*, of the public would sit in judgment." Things would, of course, be different in "a nation of philosophers." But as matters stood, the people's decision "could never be expected to turn on the true merits of the question." There was therefore no possibility of enforcing the Constitution by "occasional appeals to the people."

Now, Publius' eloquent and ingenious argument in the 49th *Federalist* would of itself sufficiently explain what John Marshall was referring to when he insisted redundantly that "the people . . . can seldom act." If the balance of the *Marbury* opinion derived its inspiration from *Federalist* No. 78, the phrases we have been tracing seem unmistakably to echo not only the reasoning but also the emotional overtones of No. 49. And considering the events and developments between 1788 (when No. 49 was issued) and 1803 (when Marshall drew upon it), the only wonder is that the Chief Justice was able to exercise so much restraint. The mere thought of popularly elected conventions would cause him to suffer; thirty years after *Marbury v. Madison* he still described the process of ratifying the Constitution as though it had been an almost traumatic experience.[30] To him, Publius' "too ticklish" must have appeared an extreme understatement.

The frequent use of Article V to amend the Constitution may well have troubled the Chief Justice; [31] he could scarcely have regarded the Eleventh Amendment, which reversed a decision of the Supreme Court, with complete equanimity. But these matters appeared like child's play when he recalled certain other events—as recent as February of 1801. At that time, despite the popular mandate expressed in the tumultuous campaign of 1800, Marshall's party had come exceedingly close to frustrating Jefferson's victory; the electoral stalemate they had decided to contrive seemed reasonably certain; and there was considerable talk (or perhaps a concerted plan) that, since no President would be elected by the end of Adams' term on March 3, 1801, the Congress could choose a sort of Provisional President, a Federalist of course, who would necessarily assume semi-dictatorial powers. Many of Marshall's persuasion thought that a firm, Federalist hand could yet bring the country back to sanity. And then—

And then the searing bolt had fallen. Let me describe the climax in Jefferson's words, written while the outcome still remained uncertain:

> . . . If they could have been permitted to pass a law for putting the government into the hands of an officer, they would certainly have prevented an election. But we thought it best to declare openly and firmly, one and all, that the day such an act passed, the Middle States would arm, and that no such usurpation, even for a single day, should be submitted to. This first shook them; and they were completely alarmed at the resource for which we declared, to wit, a convention to reorganize the government, and to amend it. The very word convention gives them the horrors, as in the present democratical spirit of America, they fear they should lose some of the favorite morsels of the Constitution.[32]

Within two days, Jefferson was duly elected President of the United States. The Federalist rank and file had at last agreed to emulate the example of Henri IV; they had concluded that the Constitution was well worth stomaching a "democratical" President. At worst, dangerous though he was, he presented a lesser menace than amendment or revision by a popularly controlled convention.

Two brief years after this feverish melodrama, was it not natural that Marshall should attempt in the *Marbury* case to foreclose consideration of "appeals to the people"? He did make the attempt and, by doing so, he joined the most fundamental issue affecting the concept of a written constitution and the process of judicial review.

Jefferson had proposed that whenever indications of a constitutional crisis might arise, the development and reshaping of the charter should be confided to the discretion of the people. In opposition, Marshall declared for the Court as the ultimate place of judgment, permitting exception only by means of the formal and cumbrous machinery of Article V. The *Marbury* opinion would have been vastly important to constitutional law and political theory if it had done no more than place this elemental conflict at issue and thus invoke the arbitrament of the future. Indeed, without anticipating my colleagues' analyses, I venture to predict that, in every ensuing chapter of our stocktaking, the reader will be able to discern various subtle manifestations of the two opposing philosophies, and that at some points he may be tempted to wonder whether Jefferson's system, which the builders thought they had refused, has not become the headstone of the corner.

Marbury v. Madison has proved to be one of those very special occurrences that mark an epoch in the life of the republic. Culminating the great achievements of the Constitutional Period, it accomplished the transition from perpetuity to efficacy, from immutability to adaptation, and from heavenly to judicial sanctions. Finally, it introduced an unending colloquy between the Supreme Court and the people of the United States, in which the Court continually asserts, "You live under a Constitution but the Constitution is what *we* say it is," and the people incessantly reply, "As long as your version of the Constitution enables us to live with pride in what *we* consider a free and just society, you may continue exercising this august, awesome, and altogether revocable authority."

II.
CONDITIONS AND SCOPE OF
CONSTITUTIONAL REVIEW

1. by Ralph F. Bischoff STATUS TO CHALLENGE CONSTITUTIONALITY

THIS SUBJECT being well worn with discussion and debate, I believe we can begin with certain assumptions. My purpose is to suggest that the general rules governing litigable interest should not be applied so zealously as they have been recently where the issue in the case involves an alleged civil right. I would like to illustrate this thesis by three cases decided by the Supreme Court in the spring of 1952.

First for the assumptions: Once the Court had created or declared its power to call laws unconstitutional in *Marbury v. Madison* [1] and *Martin v. Hunter's Lessee*,[2] the question of how to obtain jurisdiction became of increasing importance. In addition to the "case or controversy" requirement of Article III of the Constitution and the limitations set down in the Judiciary Act, the Court has itself established certain rules, some formal and others informal, whereby it has limited its own power. As enumerated and described by Mr. Justice Brandeis in the *Tennessee Valley Authority* case,[3] the central purpose behind these rules is to avoid, wherever possible, exercising the power to declare laws unconstitutional. The requirement of standing, the idea that the plaintiff must have a litigable interest, is derived from the necessity of a controversy and from this principle of self-denial. A definite foundation stone of the doctrine is, of course, that the case must be a good faith action and that the plaintiff must not be just an actor on the stage. Usually the question of standing to sue is raised where there is cause to doubt whether the plaintiff asserts a pocketbook interest or a direct invasion of some personal or property right. Mr. Justice Frankfurter said in the recent *Adler* case:

> We cannot entertain, as we again recognize this very day, a constitutional claim at the instance of one whose interest has no material significance and is undifferentiated from the mass of his fellow citizens.[4]

Here Mr. Justice Frankfurter cites the *Doremus* case [5] decided on the same day. In the latter decision the doctrine is expressed by the Court in a direct quotation from *Massachusetts v. Mellon*,[6] which decided that the interest of a federal taxpayer in a federal appropriation is too indirect to provide him with standing to challenge the appropriation. The pocketbook test was emphasized even in the recent civil rights cases.

The three cases which I wish to discuss are *Adler v. Board of Education, Doremus v. Board of Education*, and *Zorach v. Clauson*.[7]

In the *Adler* decision the Supreme Court affirmed the judgment of the New York Court of Appeals that the Feinberg Law was constitutional. To implement the civil service law of New York in so far as it pertained to teachers in the public schools, the New York legislature passed the Feinberg Law, which aims to eliminate subversive persons from the staffs of public schools. After a legislative finding that subversive groups have infiltrated the school system, the State Board of Regents was given the power to promulgate rules and regulations for the enforcement of the existing law which forbade the employment of persons who advocate the overthrow of the government. In addition, after inquiry and appropriate notice and hearing, the Board was empowered to list organizations which advocate overthrow of the government and to provide that membership in such an organization would be *prima facie* evidence of disqualification to teach. The Board of Regents designed an elaborate machinery, but enforcement was held in abeyance by the pendency of the *Adler* case. Some forty plaintiffs brought an action for declaratory judgment and injunction praying that the law be declared unconstitutional, and the case was heard on motion for judgment on the pleadings. The trial court dismissed the action except for eight of the plaintiffs on the basis that the others had no standing to sue under New York law. Of the eight, two asserted an interest as parents of children in the schools, four were teachers, and all alleged that they were taxpayers. Although the trial court found that the interest as parents was inconsequential and that the interest of the teachers was insufficient under the Supreme Court doctrine of *United Public Workers v. Mitchell*,[8] it did find that under New York law the eight, as taxpayers, possessed standing to bring suit against a municipal agency to enjoin the wastage of funds. When the case reached the United States Supreme Court, eight Justices found themselves in agreement with this conclusion, so much so that it is discussed only in Mr. Justice Frankfurter's dissenting opinion. Conceiving himself the watchdog of the Court's function in our democracy, Mr. Justice Frankfurter submitted that no showing had been made that expenditures under the Feinberg Law would be other than inconsequential or *de minimis*. The fact that New York deemed the plaintiffs' interest sufficient could not, he insisted, control the Supreme Court.

With three dissents, the Court in the *Doremus* case dismissed the appeal on the basis that the plaintiffs lacked standing. At issue was New Jersey's statute which provides for the reading, without comment, of five verses of the Old Testament at the opening of each public-school day. The action for a declaratory judgment that this statute violated the Federal Constitution was brought by two plaintiffs, each alleging an interest as a citizen and taxpayer and one of them alleging, in addition, that he had a daughter in school. On the basis of pleadings and a pre-trial conference, the trial court held the statute constitutional. This result was affirmed by the highest court of New Jersey, which expressed doubts as to the standing of the plaintiffs but "nevertheless concluded to dispose of the appeal on its merits."

Since the child had graduated from the public schools before appeal was taken, the majority of the United States Supreme Court held the interest of the father was moot. The Court granted that the interest of a taxpayer in the application of municipal (as distinguished from federal) funds was direct, but it found no allegation in the case that the practice of Bible reading had any direct effect on the taxpayer's pocketbook. Justices Douglas, Reed, and Burton in dissent declared that the interest as taxpayer was sufficient, since the plaintiffs were alleging that public money was being deflected to an improper purpose.

In the third case, *Zorach v. Clauson*, no problem of jurisdiction was posed. The appellants, objecting to New York City's released time program, alleged that they were taxpayers and residents of New York City and that their children attended its public schools. Although the Supreme Court divided six to three in favor of constitutionality, all the Justices agreed that the plaintiffs had standing as parents of children attending schools subject to a released time program.

These three cases focus on the two different aspects of standing, *i.e.*, allegation of a pocketbook interest and assertion that a personal or property right has been directly affected. No quarrel is possible with the Court's refusal to accept a moot issue, as in the *Doremus* case where the father no longer had a child in a public school. Many of the cases involving personal interests are also improperly pleaded, as was true in the well-known decision of *Tileston v. Ullman*.[9] There a physician claimed that a statute forbidding the dissemination of contraceptive information endangered the life of a patient but failed to allege that any interest of his own was violated. Similarly, in the *Doremus* case, the New Jersey Supreme Court was by no means certain that the plaintiff was claiming that the Bible reading conflicted with the convictions of mother or daughter. But quite aside from these individual instances of mootness or inadequate pleading, the question still remains: how much of a litigable personal interest should be required where the substantive issue is the police power of the state versus a civil right?

Granted that the Court must use its power in this and other areas moderately, has it not required too much of a litigable interest, with the result that decisions on genuine controversies are often unnecessarily delayed and individuals are left in doubt about the status of their civil rights? Although a decision on the Feinberg Law was reached by the pocketbook method in *Adler v. Board of Education*, the case serves as an illustration of what I believe is a too rigid requirement of personal interest. The trial court had the following to say about the jurisdictional issue:

> The plaintiffs are a heterogeneous group. Among them are the teachers' union, other unions, parents, parent-teacher associations, citizens, a social worker, the head of a religious group, teachers and taxpayers. The answer denies that any of them have the right to maintain this action.[10]

The mere recital of this list of plaintiffs grants validity to the conclusion of the trial court that only the claims of the teachers and taxpayers had substance. To quote Mr. Justice Frankfurter, "it is like catching butterflies without a net to try to find a legal interest" in most of the forty plaintiffs. But the trial court denied the right of four teachers to bring the action only because it felt bound by the Supreme Court's decision in *United Public Workers v. Mitchell*. Where the teachers claimed that the very existence of the law against subversive teachers brought uncertainty and threats to their rights, the Court interpreted the *Mitchell* decision to require more. On this reasoning, until a list of subversive organizations is promulgated and a teacher can be accused of being a member, no one has been hurt. If the trial court had been free it would clearly have accepted the interest of the teachers as a justiciable one. The effect of denial is to require the teacher to disobey the statute by being a member of a proscribed organization and thus to risk discharge in order to raise the issue of constitutionality.

This dilemma is the one Mr. Justice Douglas had underlined in the *Mitchell* case. There, twelve plaintiffs sought an injunction and a judgment declaratory of the unconstitutionality of the Hatch Act, which made unlawful certain political activities of federal employees. Except for one of the plaintiffs who had already violated the Act, the majority of the Supreme Court found no justiciable controversy. The assertion of the others that they wished to engage in political activities was labeled a hypothetical threat and similar to a request for an advisory opinion. Only Mr. Justice Douglas and Mr. Justice Black held that the damage to the other plaintiffs was imminent and real and that the majority was forcing the plaintiffs to first incur a penalty, thus making any legal remedy illusory.

Whatever the proper decision where the Court is faced with a congressional enactment and the issue of separation of powers, as was true with the Hatch Act, the *Mitchell* doctrine should not apply to a claim of civil right against a state. If the plaintiff is not just an actor on a stage, if he is honestly affected by the existence of a statute such as the Feinberg Law, the Court should take jurisdiction.

As for pocketbook actions, it would seem to me that here again, in the area of state regulations and civil rights, the general public interest requires taking jurisdiction and settling a question, at least where it is clear that there is a genuine controversy and that the action is in good faith. Mr. Justice Frankfurter's argument of *de minimis* in the *Adler* case and the majority's inference in *Doremus* that the taxpayer interest was feigned are products of the type of thinking which went into *Massachusetts v. Mellon*. That decision, however, involved something quite different, a federal appropriation and a federal taxpayer. In the *Mellon* case the Court agreed that the interest of a taxpayer in the application of municipal funds is direct and not unlike the relation of a stockholder and a corporation. But a federal taxpayer shares his interest in the moneys of the treasury with "millions of others," and to decide a case where the plaintiff asserts such a vague interest is "to assume a position of authority over the governmental acts of another and co-equal department . . ." [11] In all three of our cases, the state courts found the requisite interest; the question of the comity due to a state was therefore eliminated; nor was the Court confronted with the possibility of declaring an act of Congress unconstitutional. Granted that the Supreme Court should not be bound by a finding of standing in the state courts where the issue is one of federal constitutionality, at least due deference should be paid to such findings. The Court's conception of litigable standing needs to be reformed.

DISCUSSION

CHAIRMAN CAHN: *Mr. Curtis, will you open the discussion?*

CURTIS: *I would like to ask if we ought not to go a little further into the reasons why the Court has limited its own power in this way, and I suggest three of them. One is a matter of caution in the exercise of a great and a very hazardous power and the need of preserving the Court's power of timing its decisions.*

The second is keeping at least the pretense of being nothing more than a court of law. And the third is to keep very far away, as far away as possible, from undertaking the duty of what really amounts to giving advisory opinions where the request does not even come from the President (we know the Court refused an advisory opinion requested by President Washington) but from a private citizen.

I suggest that those three reasons may not amount to enough to justify the present practice, but they ought to be duly weighed before it is enlarged.

FRANK: The only doubt I have from the standpoint of the social utility of Professor Bischoff's thought is whether it does any good to have the Court take the cases, because it decides them wrong after it gets them. That is to say, in each instance mentioned, the case of the United Public Workers, the case of Adler v. Board of Education, and the case of Zorach v. Clauson, each of those three cases, it seems to me, was wrongly decided on the merits.

If we are going to have judicial review, we might as well really have it and let the Court take the cases without requiring, as in the case, for example, of United Public Workers v. Mitchell, that somebody actually walked the plank and fell into the water before he could find out whether it was necessary to make the trip at all.

FREUND: My first point is that, if you enlarge the area of Supreme Court review in cases that appeal to one's heart's desire, it seems to me that you are in danger at least of breaking down restraints that have been very carefully and laboriously erected in the interest of general legislative policy.

I think we would all be happy if we could establish as a preliminary jurisdictional question the answer to how the Court will decide the merits. I think we have got to recognize the danger of a decision that will not please our heart's desire.

Now, we lose the benefit of the concreteness of a record, the concreteness of experience, of judgment not from speculation but from experience with reality, when we fail to insist on all the concreteness and particularity of a traditional controversy. I think in the teachers' oath case that is particularly true.

There are technical doctrines about exhaustion of administrative remedies. I am not interested in the technical requirement but I am interested in the policy behind it. It seems to me that if we had a record showing what the regents had done, showing to what extent these fears had or had not materialized—and perhaps they would materialize—then you would have a record not only to persuade the Court in this case but, in the event the Court went wrong from your standpoint, a record to which to appeal for self-correction in the future and for professional and public criticism.

It seems to me a great strength of our system as compared with, say, the Canadian and Australian systems where constitutional questions of all kinds are presented and decided abstractly by reference. The great strength of our system is that it does provide an appeal to the record facts after the decision, if necessary.

I think the self-reversal by the Supreme Court in the New Deal period owes much to the fact that there was exposed on the record the history of labor stoppages in the NLRB cases and the like. Now it seems to me that we ought to consider at least whether we are not sacrificing a good deal in those realms when we tend to invite early (and to me) somewhat abstract decisions, even in areas that we call civil rights.

HURST: Agreeing with Mr. Bischoff's general position, I would like to state my agreement simply with emphasis on two points of technique. It seems to me that the Court in many of these cases has been guilty of one of the prime sins of craftsmanship of men of ideas, that of not being conscious of what they are doing.

I think that many of these decisions on standing are born of a typical nineteenth-century American concern with tangibles. This is very much out of place in twentieth century America which is more and more characterized by organization and administration as the very structure of society.

One of the marks of the extent to which the Court in some of its decisions is captive of an outworn set of ideas is the astonishing neglect of the implications of the great common law doctrine of libel and slander, which certainly affords a vast reservoir of almost untapped resources for the definition of legally protectable interest in intangible human relationships.

Secondly, I would like to criticize some of these decisions from a technique standpoint on the ground that they represent the Court's apparently unconscious violation of one of its most fundamental principles, and that is not to decide a constitutional issue if they can avoid it.

I fail to see in many of these interest or standing cases why the issue could not be handled in terms of the burden of proof and not in terms of standing at all. Why doesn't the Court protect itself against situations it would be unwise to venture into simply by being hardboiled about the amount of factual proof and factual definition of the factual interests at stake? Instead of denying the existence of interests, if it feels it wishes to reject a given litigation, why doesn't it put the denial on the basis that the party claiming interest has simply failed to sustain his burden of proof in making out the interest?

FRANK: Could I put a question to my colleagues here to find out how we stand on the one precise issue of the Doremus case? Let me refresh the recollection of the audience as to the case, which was fully stated by Mr. Bischoff. That was the case involving the challenge to the validity of the New Jersey law in respect to Bible reading.

The action was—so far as pertinent here—brought by a taxpayer of New Jersey. The law clearly holds that if this had been a federal statute and a federal taxpayer, then under the doctrine of Massachusetts v. Mellon, the case could not have been brought; but it wasn't, and the Doremus case, therefore, is the first case on the books, so far as I know, in which it has been held that where a state court is willing to let a taxpayer bring an action the Supreme Court will nonetheless refuse to decide that case on the merits.

Now it seems to me that the rule had been in sound balance before that time in that the practice had invariably been to follow the state courts' practice in this; if they were willing to have taxpayers' suits the Supreme Court would accept the case and decide the issue.

I take it that Professor Bischoff agrees that the law was more satisfactory under the practice prior to Doremus than since the innovation of this decision. I would like the opinions of the other three gentlemen with respect to that case.

CURTIS: You suggest that the Supreme Court ought to be bound by the state court as to what is a case or controversy? Or, in other words, if it is a case in the state court it ought to be a case in the Supreme Court?

FRANK: No; I don't want to take that position because a state court might hold all sorts of things cases which the Supreme Court might not. Until 1952 when Doremus was decided, the one area which had been left to the states, and the only one I mean to speak to, was on the sole question whether a taxpayer could bring a suit or not.

CURTIS: I vote that a taxpayer whose interest is "undifferentiated from the mass of his fellow citizens" ought not to have standing.

FREUND: I welcome the line taken by Doremus. I think it does not go far enough. In Doremus, as I understand it, the Court said, regardless of what the state court thinks about a taxpayer's suit as a vehicle for raising this constitutional question, we will not accept the case on review.

I think it is a needed change to make standing to raise a federal constitutional question, itself a federal question, so that it will be decided uniformly throughout the country. I disagree with the Doremus case in so far as it lets the state judgment stand and merely declines review. It seems to me the Court should have gone the full way, holding that standing to raise a constitutional question is itself a federal question, that there was no standing and, therefore, the petition should stand dismissed in the state court and the decree vacated so that it would not be a precedent even in the state court.

HURST: I would vote that Doremus was not a good taxpayer's action, but I mean to limit the vote very much.

I agree with Mr. Freund. It seems to me these questions of litigable interest are constitutional issues. I agree with him that there should be a uniform doctrine on that.

CAHN: Given a uniform federal doctrine, should that doctrine make the distinction that is made in Massachusetts v. Mellon? That is, a distinction based on recognizing a more direct economic interest in a municipal taxpayer for the purpose of raising these issues?

HURST: No.

CAHN: I understood that you were endeavoring to get away from limitation to economic relations as the sole basis for the presentation of these issues.

HURST: *That is true, and I think that a taxpayer's effort to bring a lawsuit is inherently an economic issue. In the Doremus situation there would be proper interest in a parent. On the other hand, it does not seem to me that it was a proper taxpayer's suit.*

2. by John P. Frank   POLITICAL QUESTIONS

THE TERM "political question" is applied to a species of the genus "non-justiciable" questions. It is, measured by any of the normal responsibilities of a phrase of definition, one of the least satisfactory terms known to the law. The origin, scope, and purpose of the concept have eluded all attempts at precise statement.

General definitions of the term are so general as to be non-descriptive, as for example the pronouncement of the Court of Appeals for the District of Columbia that "political questions . . . are such as have been entrusted by the sovereign for decision to the so-called political departments of government, as distinguished from questions which the sovereign has set to be decided by courts." [12] As that same court observed two months later, "It would be difficult to draw a clear line of demarcation between political and non-political questions. . . ." [13] Although certain problems, such as whether or not a foreign government is recognized by the United States, or whether a given state of the Union has a republican form of government, are universally defined and treated as political issues not subject to judicial determination, the Court of Appeals' approach highlights the fact that "political questions" is a legal category more amenable to description by infinite itemization than by generalization.

Thus the puzzled makers of the Digest System, for want of any clear notion of the boundaries of the concept, lump together under this title a perfect hash of unrelated cases. And the District of Columbia opinion first mentioned above, after making no progress by means of comprehensive statement, finally resorted to a listing of ten major sub-categories. These were: the recognition of foreign governments and republican form of government issues; conditions of peace or war; the beginning and end of war; whether aliens shall be excluded or expelled; government title to or jurisdiction over territory; status of Indian tribes; enforcement of treaties (in some aspects only); existence of treaties; and constitutional powers of representatives of foreign nations.[14]

Because its boundaries are so hazy, blending off in various directions with such different concepts as that of the final authority of Congress over the public lands,[15] or the conventional (if dubious) principle that courts of equity will not protect purely political rights of no property value,[16] the origin of the doctrine cannot be clearly determined. The familiar leading case of *Luther v. Borden*,[17] which declined to consider whether Rhode Island had a republican form of government, was regarded by the Justices themselves as presenting a question of first impression, and in a narrow sense it was. But it was antedated by *Ware v. Hylton*[18] in 1796, holding that the Court would not pass upon whether a treaty had been broken, and this in turn had been antedated by the refusal of the Justices to advise George Washington on certain general legal aspects of foreign policy.[19] *Luther v. Borden* was also antedated by *Martin v. Mott*,[20] holding that the President had exclusive and unreviewable power to determine when the militia should be called out. Any of these could have been considered "political questions."

If the origin and scope of the concept are unclear, what of its purposes? Conceptual analyses have been made: that the doctrine is applied to avoid judicial embarrassment where no rules of law exist; that it applies to protect the area of issues reserved for decision to the people themselves; that it is required by the separation of powers. But as Professor Post's useful book shows, none of these theories will withstand close scrutiny.[21]

As Post says, the term "political questions" is a magical formula which has the practical result of relieving a court of the necessity of thinking further about a particular problem. It is a device for transferring the responsibility for decision of questions to another branch of the government; and it may sometimes operate to leave a problem in mid-air so that no branch decides it.

But while the conceptual justifications for this particular avoidance are unsatisfactory, the functional case in its behalf has real strength. Practical grounds for the doctrine may be divided into four categories which overlap and which frequently buttress each other:

1. *The need of quick and single policy.* Especially in the field of foreign affairs, it is frequently more important to answer a question definitively and promptly than to answer it "correctly," even assuming there may be a wholly correct answer. Recognition of foreign governments, as in *United States v. Pink;* [22] determination of the means of carrying on war and disposing of prisoners captured in battle, as in the case of *Yamashita;* [23] the question whether the property of a foreign government should be granted sovereign immunity, as in *Ex parte Peru:* [24] these are good, fairly recent examples. But foreign affairs are not the only instances in which finality of decision is important. It would be calamitous to have the validity of constitutional amendments brought into serious question long after their promulgation; even if, for example, someone could now bring in absolutely conclusive proof that the Thirteenth Amendment had never been validly adopted, he would, happily, not be heard to raise the issue.[25] On this very practical ground the Supreme Court in *Pacific States Tel. & Tel. Co. v. Oregon* [26] also reaffirmed the principle that the existence of a republican form of government was for the exclusive determination of Congress; to decide otherwise would have been to jeopardize every law passed by the Oregon legislature.

2. *Judicial Incompetence.* This ground operates where a particular problem is in fact soluble only by a legislative solution which a court is totally incapable of providing, or where action requires information which a court cannot have or get. For example, in *Coleman v. Miller,* [27] the Court was asked in effect to decide how long was a reasonable time for the pendency of a constitutional amendment before the states. As Chief Justice Hughes said, ". . . the question of a reasonable time in many cases would involve, as in this case it does involve, an appraisal of a great variety of relevant conditions, political, social, and economic, which can hardly be said to be within the appropriate range of evidence receivable in a court of justice and as to which it would be an extravagant extension of judicial authority to assert judicial notice . . ." Similarly the opinion of Justice Frankfurter in *Colegrove v. Green* [28] (though the application of the prin-

ciple in that case will be criticized below) that the Court would not upset the apportionment of congressional districts within a state rests on this ground, for it emphasizes that only a legislature could substitute a sound districting system for one destroyed by judicial decision. And in *Chicago & Southern Airlines v. Waterman Steamship Co.*,[29] a majority refused to review a Civil Aeronautics Board decision affecting international air transportation, because of a belief that a wise solution would depend upon knowledge of foreign relations unavailable to the courts.

3. *Clear prerogative of another branch of the government.* This category includes cases in which courts do not pass upon claimed rights because someone else has a clear and unequivocal responsibility to make the particular decision. These are cases not of judicial discretion but of legal requirement.

For example, it is up to Congress to pass upon the qualifications of its own members; the Constitution says as much, leaving nothing for the judges to do.[30] Almost as clearly, the duty of determining when the Constitution is amended is not a judicial responsibility.[31] As Justice Frankfurter says, with several examples, in *Colegrove v. Green*, "The Constitution has left the performance of many duties in our governmental scheme to depend on the fidelity of the executive and legislative action . . ." [32]

4. *Avoidance of unmanageable situations.* Courts are, in many respects, the weakest division of government, dependent for their effectiveness upon the acquiescence of the other branches and upon popular support. They are understandably reluctant to give orders which either will not be enforced or are practically unenforceable, and on occasion may be hesitant to precipitate situations which may outrage the popular attitude.

Professor Post is very persuasive in his thesis that the status of Indian tribes became a political question because John Marshall realized that Andrew Jackson and the State of Georgia had no intention of letting the judiciary solve the problems of the Cherokees.[33] If the Illinois Supreme Court had not decided that the doctrine of political questions precluded it from issuing mandamus to the state legislature requiring it to redistrict the state, that Court might have been in the awkward position of committing an entire legislature to jail.[34] Perhaps Justice Frankfurter was moved by related considerations of judicial prestige when he said in *Colegrove v. Green*, that the Court has traditionally held aloof from immediate and active relations with party contests.[35] The Supreme Court might have invited armed conflict if it had decided the merits in *Luther v. Borden*.

When allowance has been made for all these factors, it nevertheless seems to me that the doctrine of political questions ought to be very sharply confined to cases where the functional reasons justify it, and that in a given case involving its expansion, there should be careful consideration also of the social considerations which may militate against it. The doctrine has a certain specious charm because of its nice intellectualism and because of the fine deference it permits to expertise, to secret knowledge, and to the prerogatives of others. It should not be allowed to grow as a merely intellectual plant.

The sound approach is that of Judge Charles Clark in *Banco de Espana v. Federal Reserve Bank:* [36]

> *The courts will leave for the Executive the determination of all "political" issues; in the international field this means such matters as the recognition of new governments or the making of treaties, not the direct determination of questions of property. . . . A broader interpretation of "political" questions is unnecessary to the effective conduct of diplomatic relations with other countries and is undesirable as subjecting issues of private property to the changing circumstances of international politics beyond what is inevitable in any event.*

Courts adopting the *Banco de Espana* approach will look to the reasons for the rule as to political questions, and therefore balk at applying it when the reasons are not present. In the four matters about to be mentioned, I believe that the Supreme Court has undesirably expanded the rule:

1. The political apportionment cases, of which *Colegrove v. Green* is the leading example.[37] In these, the issue is whether the courts can do anything to encourage redistricting when a state is outlandishly maldistricted. Thus in *Colegrove*, had the plaintiff prevailed, the state would have been forced to elect all its representatives at large or redistrict. It presumably would have done the latter.

None of the four practical grounds for the political question doctrine required that the Court deny plaintiffs their remedy in this situation. There was no imperative need for a single, final decision; even though the judiciary had no power to achieve a completely satisfactory solution (because it could not redistrict by itself), it could scarcely make the problem worse by forcing elections at large; though Congress has abundant power to act, its authority is not exclusive; and no unmanageable situation would result. Unlike the situation in the Illinois state case which I have mentioned, the issue of congressional redistricting does not involve risk of a direct clash with a state legislature because the legislature is not compelled to do anything. To put it affirmatively, maldistricting is totally incompatible with democracy. Direct political methods are not adequate to correct the evil, for they require the assent of those whose advantage will be surrendered by the correction. If creative jurisprudence is needed to meet this arch-enemy of democracy, the Supreme Court should provide it without undue preoccupation with the political-question doctrine.[38]

2. A second example of what seems to me excessive deference to the concept of political questions is *Chicago & Southern Airlines v. Waterman Steamship Co.*[39] The case is too complicated to be worth restatement here; suffice it to say that the issue was whether the courts could review orders of the Civil Aeronautics Board in respect to foreign air transportation. These orders had been made by the Board, but had been specially approved by the President. Five Justices thought that review of the order would require also review of the President's order, which would involve a political question because his decision might rest on special information. Four Justices thought that the order of the Board, which covered conventional matters of the competence of the applicant line to do business, could be reviewed without entering into the sphere of the President's judgment. As it seems to me, to hold so much of this order unreviewable as could well have been reviewed is to expand the area of lawlessness by a gratuitous extension of the political question doctrine.

3. The point at which war begins or ends is a conventional political question for international purposes, but there is no good reason why it must be similarly unreviewable for domestic purposes. An example of a needless extension of the doctrine is *Ludecke v. Watkins.*[40] The

ultimate issue in the case was the extent of the power of the Attorney General to order removal of enemy aliens without judicial review. Under the statute, this power was to continue until the war was terminated. The Court (5-4) held that the question of termination in this application was "a political act." The case came to the Supreme Court three years after the close of the war with Germany and as the dissent said, "Of course it is nothing but a fiction to say that we are now at war with Germany. Whatever else that fiction might support, I refuse to agree that it affords the basis for today's holding that our laws authorize the peacetime banishment of any person on a judicially unreviewable conclusion of a single individual." [41]

The *Ludecke* decision serves none of the purposes which call for the application of the political question doctrine. There is no particular harm in regarding the war as over for some purposes and not for others. And there is no perceptible harm in variations of policy in respect to deportation. The only issues that the judiciary were called upon to decide were within the judicial competence, there was no clear prerogative of the Attorney General to be considered, and no great hazard of embarrassment would have faced the judiciary if it had entered this field. By these tests *Ludecke* is a needless extension of the doctrine.

4. The last case to be especially mentioned is *Harisiades v. Shaughnessy.*[42] The issue was the validity of a provision in the Alien Registration Act of 1940 providing for the deportation of aliens who may ever have been Communists even though they left the party long before the passage of this act. In the most extreme case, the petitioner was a member of the Communist Party for a few years in his late teens and early twenties, left the party in 1929 because of lack of sympathy with it, and never had any subsequent association. The Court held that under the act he might nonetheless be deported. One issue was whether the principle against retroactivity protects aliens under these circumstances. In upholding the act, the Court paid at least some deference to the concept of political questions, saying that "any policy toward aliens is vitally and intricately interwoven with contemporaneous policies in regard to the conduct of foreign relations, the war power, and the maintenance of a republican form of government.

Such matters are so exclusively entrusted to the political branches of government as to be largely immune from judicial inquiry or interference." [43]

Just how the Court used the doctrine of political question in the *Harisiades* case was unclear even to it—it said that the proposition just quoted is not "controlling" but is "pertinent." Let me argue on the contrary that in this case the political-question doctrine is not pertinent at all. The Court either has a duty to review or it does not. If it does not have that duty, then it should excuse itself for some clearcut and categorical reason and not for some misty notion about the distribution of power. Here we have an alien who is being turned from the home in which he has lived for thirty-five years because of conduct which offended no law when it occurred and which had been repented twenty-three years before the decision. To find a shade of a shadow of a scintilla of a reason for thus treating a human being because of anything in *Luther v. Borden* or in the *Waterman Steamship* case seems to me all wrong.

I conclude that the doctrine of political question is currently undergoing a most undesirable expansion. Because it may well exclude important claims of individual liberty from any judicial review, it is contrary to the spirit of our institutions and ought to be confined to situations in which it is imperative.

DISCUSSION

FREUND: *I have more trouble with the redistricting cases than John Frank seems to have from the standpoint of judicial competence to handle the problem. What are the constitutional claims that are presented in the maldistricting case?*

I suppose that the right of voting in a federal election, if you are a qualified voter under state law, is diluted to the extent that your district is much larger than another district. That kind of right has been recognized in the criminal law to justify federal legislation punishing ballot-box stuffing. I take it that even one bogus ballot would run afoul of the law because to that extent it violates the guarantee of the right to vote. I am sure, however, that a disparity of one in the size of election districts would not be regarded as violative of that constitutional provision.

Second, there is the equal protection of the laws, which I assume would be applicable to both state and federal elections but, again, what is going to be the measure of equality? The Court could, I suppose, set up some arbitrary figure like ten per cent, fifteen per cent, or twenty per cent as the limit of disparity in districts. That somehow does not seem the conventional judicial function. Congress could take care of it.

There is more to be said for excluding the judicial function here because of the grant of power to Congress together with the practical problems I have mentioned than there is in the case of regulation of commerce by the states. As to the latter, Justice Black has felt that because Congress has power to regulate interstate commerce, the Court should not. It seems to me here, if anywhere—certainly more strongly than there—the grant of power to Congress is a more formidable argument for excluding the judicial function, and it is curious that Justice Black is on opposite sides on those issues.

FRANK: What I had meant to say was this. I think if the view is sound that I expressed about Colegrove v. Green, then the practical effect would be to abolish the existing election districts in, say, the State of Illinois, which would confront the state legislature with a choice. It could either set up a new system of districts or it could let all the congressmen be elected at large. What the Court would do would be to give them that choice.

HURST: I think the doctrine of political questions has suffered from too much of the absolutist approach to what ought to be treated as a very practical problem in inter-agency relationships. Paul Freund is concerned with the problem as to how you test whether an apportionment is equitable or not. I would appeal to the lesson of experience there. There are better than a score of cases in which state supreme courts have tackled the problem and have resolved it satisfactorily in the sense that no fundamentally embarrassing political conflict ensued in passing on the substantive merits of the equitable or inequitable character of state apportionment.

Secondly, I think the question of the exact frame of the lawsuit is very important here and is often ignored in some of these political question issues. On this apportionment matter I would agree with John Frank's criticism in the case with respect to Illinois. There was a situation where the Court had a chance to strike a blow in favor of perhaps the most fundamental of all civil liberties, the right to a fair vote, without getting into any of these embarrassments of enjoining or mandamusing a whole legislature, because all they had to do was to sustain an injunction against one member of the executive branch, the secretary of state, from sending out election notices. While perhaps it might be unfortunate if you had to put the Secretary of State of Illinois in jail, I don't think it would lead to any irreparable political damage.

State courts have said very clearly that they will not even enjoin the secretary of state from sending out election notices under existing apportionment acts. They will only enjoin him from sending out election notices under new apportionment acts, because if they enjoined his proceeding under the existing act, they would leave the state without the means of getting a new legislature. It seems to me that here again the handling of the Illinois case is open to the objection of absolutist techniques because, as John Frank pointed out, the consequence would not be to leave Illinois without congressional representation. The consequence would simply be to shift its congressional representation from one apportioned by districts to one of congressmen at large.

I think as a matter of political history there is a good deal to be said for the position that the quality of the House of Representatives has frequently benefited very much by the addition of representatives at large.

CURTIS: It troubles me. There are John Frank and Willard Hurst and the dissent in the Supreme Court in both those cases talking very seriously of imposing our standards of what is proper with regard to the democratic process. Now if they can improve it, more power to them, but it gives me great pause to have either of them or the United States Supreme Court trying to improve the political morals of Illinois.

I was trying to remember who it was that said the proper remedy for the errors of democracy is more democracy.* Who was that? Thomas Jefferson?

* The source of this aphorism is M. I. Ostrogorski.—EDITOR.

CAHN: *I don't know, but Charles Evans Hughes said the cure is not more democracy, but more intelligence.*

CURTIS: *Which is the better representative process in democracy, general elections or this districting or some other districting? It gives me pause.*

HURST: *I don't think it is we who are setting a standard. I think the standard has been set by many wise men over 150 years ago and that you are depriving the people of the state of their fundamental rights if the legislature does not undertake to reapportion after each federal census.*

FRANK: *I would summarize what I think about it in the light of the discussion and make a brief response in this fashion. It seems to me that the basic objective of a plan of government ought to be to put the responsibility for the decision of questions some place, and that the political question doctrine is useful when it operates to put responsibility at the best place, and is harmful when it puts the decision no place.*

Now, applying this to the election cases, I would like to express my complete concurrence with the view of Mr. Curtis that the best remedy for the ills of democracy is more democracy, and that this is peculiarly compelling in the election field.

The practical result of that mandate, it seems to me, is that it ought to be the duty of every judge all the time to try to achieve at least a greater possibility of the operation of the machinery of democracy. Now what happens in the redistricting cases is that the responsibility, if not taken by the court, is transferred to a body which has a completely vested interest in the maldistricting.

As a result, it becomes totally impossible ever to achieve democracy through the action of the people themselves. This is so terrible an evil in our society that it becomes imperative that anybody should strike at it whenever and wherever he can, and if the Supreme Court has that opportunity it ought to do it without regard to notions of political questions.

FREUND: *I might say that I don't think the state supreme court precedent is quite on the level with the national redistricting problem. I think in the state the alternative is either the state supreme court* doing it or nobody but the very body that benefits from maldistricting. But I think Congress, although it may be the beneficiary of maldistricting, is somewhat more removed from maldistricting in any particular area or to any particular degree.

FRANK: I would like to note for the record that on this redistricting point the question is far closer in my own mind than perhaps I have made clear. The arguments that Mr. Freund makes seem to me so compelling that my thinking on that one quesiton is at about the 60–40 per cent stage. It is very tough because the bad consequences might outweigh the good ones, but on balance it seems to me the desire to cure this evil ought to overshadow the losses which would be taken.

3. *by Paul A. Freund* REVIEW OF FACTS IN CONSTITUTIONAL CASES

AT THE risk of descending to pedantry, a discussion of the review of facts in constitutional cases must make some distinctions. The first is the difference between adjudicative facts and legislative facts—a difference comparable to that found in administrative law between the adjudicating and rule-making functions. A law forbidding the sale of beverages containing more than 3.2 per cent of alcohol would raise a question of legislative fact, *i.e.*, whether this standard has a reasonable relation to public health, morals, and the enforcement problem. A law forbidding the sale of intoxicating beverages (assuming it is not so vague as to require supplementation by rule-making) would raise a question of adjudicative fact, *i.e.*, whether this or that beverage is intoxicating within the meaning of the statute and the limits on governmental action imposed by the Constitution. Of course what we mean by fact in each case is itself an ultimate conclusion founded on underlying facts and on criteria of judgment for weighing them.

A conventional formulation is that legislative facts—those facts which are relevant to the legislative judgment—will not be canvassed save to determine whether there is a rational basis for believing that

they exist, while adjudicative facts—those which tie the legislative enactment to the litigant—are to be demonstrated and found according
to the ordinary standards prevailing for judicial trials. (I am not considering at the moment problems of federalism.) This formulation,
like most categorizations, will have to give a little at the seams. It
puts exclusive emphasis on the formal aspects of law-making. It is
valid insofar as the legislature does indeed indulge in a generalization
when it acts; but to the extent that the legislature particularizes it
approaches the judicial arena. The due process clause and the guarantee against bills of attainder may help to keep the legislature within
bounds; but there are cases where the legislative act may not be invalid and yet may resemble the judicial function in its application of
standards to particular persons or groups, and should be so judged on
review.

Who is to try the facts? The judge is the appropriate trier of legislative facts, for if these were left to a jury with no further effective
review, a statute might remain constitutional on the east bank of the
Mississippi and unconstitutional on the west, thus confirming the rela-
tivism of the ancient sophists: truth on one side of the Pyrenees, false-
hood on the other.

In the realm of adjudicative facts, there is an issue not clearly
resolved—whether on review of the decision of a state court the Supreme Court will reassess the basic facts. The issue has arisen in confession cases, if not in the holdings at least in the divergence of the
language employed in the opinions. Perhaps the Court has gone
furthest in weighing conflicting evidence on basic facts in the Scottsboro case, where one of the issues turned on the presence of names of
Negroes on the jury roll.[44] In the face of a finding of the trial court
that the names had been included in regular course, the Supreme
Court determined that the names had been added after the event;
but it is not clear that the decision of the Supreme Court really turned
on this revision of the finding. In confession cases the ultimate question is phrased as one of coercion, which of course is not a basic fact
but a legal judgment. Indeed, it is a moral judgment, since the law,
wisely ignoring problems of free will and determinism, and unable to
draw a scientific line between "voluntary" and "involuntary" conduct,
really treats some forms of inducement as morally legitimate and

others as so ethically improper that different legal consequences are attached to the conduct which has been induced.[45] But it is not quite clear whether the Supreme Court will go behind the basic findings, such as period of detention, character of treatment, and the like. Perhaps the best solution here is again to eschew ironclad rules and to recognize that where constitutional guarantees turn on the nature of the underlying facts, the guarantees cannot be evaded by state courts through plainly untenable findings of fact. This ought to be true no less in confession cases than in cases involving the existence of a contract which has been impaired by state legislation.

In the realm of legislative facts, the great invention was of course the so-called "Brandeis brief." [46] Of that device certain criticisms could be made. Even though the data adduced are presented not to demonstrate the truth of the facts but only to establish a respectable body of opinion holding them to be true, it would seem that upon challenge the data ought to be presented on the record, giving an opportunity to discredit or refute the body of opinion so offered. Moreover, it may be thought that to open up the legislative judgment in even this limited way is to weaken the presumption of constitutionality. But to this objection there is the answer that the presumption is indulged by a court more comfortably when buttressed with some evidence; and besides, the amassing of the legislative facts becomes part of the process of education, self-scrutiny, and if necessary self-correction in which the courts, the profession, and the public are participants.

A more serious limitation of the Brandeis brief is that it is designed to support legislation rather than to undermine it—to vindicate an experiment, not to veto it. Consider, for example, the attack on the so-called death sentence provision in the Public Utility Holding Company Act. In one of the test cases the utilities offered an extensive study made by a professor of economics purporting to show that after the enforcement of the control provisions of the act, before the death sentence was to become effective, subsidiaries of holding companies were at least as efficient and free of abuses as were independently operated utilities.[47] The Government insisted that this study was irrelevant, since at most it left the subject where Congress found it, namely in the area of legitimate debate. Furthermore, even if the study could conceivably undermine the conclusions of Congress regarding the need for the death sentence in the interest of efficiency and honesty, there would remain a question of political judgment whether reliance should be placed indefinitely on the administration of the control provisions of the act or whether the subject should not be remitted to a larger extent to the state authorities through the simplification and geographic integration of utility systems. Obviously no professor operating an I.B.M. machine, even in an age of cybernetics, could furnish the answer to such a question.

Today, when legislation restricting civil liberties is under attack, the possible role of the Brandeis brief on the side of negation is again to the fore. If it was right to exclude the economic study in the holding company case, would it be right to exclude studies showing the scientific fallacies in miscegenation laws or the psychological damage flowing from segregation in the public schools? Or at least is it right to require such studies to do more than make a preponderant case, to require in short that they impeach the case for the proponents of the legislation as patently irrational?

Thus we are brought by one of many avenues to the thorny problem of the double standard in judicial review. Before dealing with it further, it may be well to turn to an area where legislative facts are concededly subjected to weighing in the judicial scales. I refer, of course, to the cases of state interference with interstate commerce. It is not clear whether a state law which regulates interstate trains or trucks is to be given the benefit of a presumption of constitutionality. Mr. Justice Stone in the South Carolina trucking case seemed to think that the presumption operated, but Mr. Chief Justice Stone in the Arizona train-length case seemed to think that it did not.[48] At any rate, some weighing is done by the courts, for otherwise each state would be the arbiter of the legitimate balance between its own local welfare and the national interests protected by the commerce clause.

May there be found in these commerce cases an analogy for the First Amendment cases? To the extent that a free market in ideas is a basic process upon which representative government rests, as a free market in goods is a basic process on which our federal system rests, there may be ground for judicial intervention in the two areas alike. Does the guarantee of equal protection of the laws fall in the same category? Should the standard of review in enforcing that clause be the same whether the discrimination alleged is against chain stores or against Negroes? In answering this question it would be idle to close one's eyes to the fact that the equal protection clause, however greatly it has expanded, was designed immediately for the protection of a racial group. In that sense, those who adopted the Fourteenth Amendment may be said to have expressed a relatively focused judgment, which is to be overcome only by assuming the burden of persuasion on a given form of discrimination. This, at all events, is the kind of problem of standards for review of constitutional facts which is most vexing and most urgent today.

DISCUSSION

HURST: *I agree with everything that Paul Freund has said here. I would annotate it by putting it in a slightly different frame of reference.*

I think the Court has bungled this matter of the presumption of constitutionality by its failure to use it as a technique for disciplining the bar. You don't have to read very many briefs in constitutional issues to feel that there is probably no type of lawsuit in which lawyers more miserably fail in their supposed functions as officers of the Court. There is no type of case in which the Court receives less assistance from the bar. A lawyer who would consider himself seriously remiss in his duty to his client in an automobile accident case if he had not got out of his office and looked at the scene and found people to question, will consider, when he is confronted with an issue of substantive due process, that all he is called upon to do is to tilt back his chair, put his feet on the desk, call in the stenographer, and let fly. It is apparent that that has been the process of intellectual construction.

I think the Court too often covers up for the bar when it says the statute must be presumed valid. What they should say is that the lawyer attacking it has not shown enough evidence to destroy it, therefore we uphold it. I would suggest there is perhaps no area in which one could be more justly critical of what John Marshall started than in the lost opportunity implicit in the presumption of constitutionality.

CURTIS: I think the notion the paper brings out is of such importance that it must be pursued and enlarged. The similarity between the free national market in goods and the national market in ideas is of primary importance.

Yet I am not wholly clear what Paul Freund means by facts. Take a body of belief which a Brandeis brief has offered to the Court. As Freund himself has pointed out in his book Understanding the Supreme Court, the "fact" is the body of belief, the existence of that body, not the minute details upon which that body of belief rests. This I take it is what he means by legislative fact.

I don't think the legislative fact is anything more than such a body of belief compounded with a hope or a desire to have future facts happen in a certain way. Ordinarily, to adjudicate a fact is something quite different. It is to reach something wholly in the past and which cannot be in the future. That is the only reason why the legislative facts have to be expressed in generalities and adjudicated facts have to be expressed in concrete detail.

FREUND: I think there is an ambiguity here. What I mean by legislative fact is the underlying fact, for example, whether filled milk is deleterious or whether a peacetime draft is necessary, and the Brandeis brief gives evidence to support that fact. The difficulty arises of course when you are attempting to veto, so to speak, or to undermine the legislation rather than support it, and that is a problem that Brandeis never really faced as far as I can see from the standpoint of the Brandeis brief.

CAHN: I take it that with respect to the fact of clear and present danger in a matter relating to freedom of speech you would have the issue disposed of, within the scope of the Supreme Court's review activity, in the same manner as a state enactment affecting interstate commerce?

FREUND: Yes, that is what it comes down to. In that area—this is something of an embroidery on the theme—it may be that there ought to be two judicial scrutinies of the fact: (a) the legislative fact—that is to say, whether organized advocacy of overthrow creates a clear and present danger of overthrow or sabotage or espionage, which would be for the judge, under my suggestion, with the probative balance as you indicate; and (b) whether the defendants in this case created a clear and present danger by their acts, which analytically might be equivalent to determining whether they came within the statute as interpreted. This would be an adjudicated fact for the jury. Thus you might get a double test of clear and present danger, one from the general standpoint of legislative policy and the other from the standpoint of the acts of these defendants.

FRANK: The vital thing about the subject we are now discussing is that it is quantitatively and by any other measure the most important matter we have before us. That is to say, the questions which Mr. Bischoff discussed could be disposed of either way and it would not quantitatively make a great deal of difference. He criticizes two or three cases and I criticize three or four, but quantitatively it is perhaps more interesting than significant. The matter raised by Professor Freund, on the other hand, affects deeply every single case which comes before the Supreme Court in the field of constitutional law.

It seems to me a matter of deepest regret that the argument Professor Freund makes, which is so compelling to me, does not represent the law as it is but rather the law as it ought to be. In two notable respects practice deviates altogether at the present time from what Professor Freund thinks ought to be done, and my sympathies are entirely with his view of it.

First with respect to the matter of confessions. In the confession cases there ought to be a rule that plainly untenable conclusions of fact as to whether a confession was voluntary should be reviewed. As I understand what the Court is presently doing, it is rejecting that point of view. The case of Gallegos, for example [Gallegos v. Nebraska, 342 U.S. 55 (1951)], seems to hold that we are not going back into the facts at all even where, as found below, they may be untenable, if we can find that they were disputed below. This becomes a go-ahead sign to prosecutors to raise a dispute as to any questionable fact and thus put it beyond the scope of judicial review.

This policy is all wrong, it seems to me. If the Court cannot review confession cases, it should look them over to see if there is anything wrong or preposterous about them. I would go further by buttressing the rule in the confession cases with a series of fixed presumptions as to what police can do to people in their custody.

Turning to the other branch of Professor Freund's analysis, it seems to me the very best idea I have heard in a very long time, that is, we should borrow from the commerce cases and make some use of them in the free speech cases. What is wrong with the free speech decisions (the Dennis case is a good example) is that we are in a peculiar situation which I shall elaborate on—the circular buck-pass. Congress passes the problem over to the Court with the happy assumption that the Court somewhere is going to examine the matter closely and come to a decision; and the Court passes it back again and says that Congress has decided all the relevant factual issues, hence we can stamp it through.

In the Dennis case there is no evidence in the record on the very vital questions to be decided. The decision rests basically on some intuitions of Judge Medina, Judge Hand, and a majority of the Supreme Court based on their notion of what is in the air. Now it may well be that if a factual record were made they might come to the same conclusions, but the point is that none was made.

If the commerce-clause approach had been used, there would have been an abundant record, on the basis of which a sensible judgment might have been made. I think it would be a great advance if you could persuade the Supreme Court to do the very thing you think ought to be done.

III.
THE PROCESS OF CONSTITUTIONAL CONSTRUCTION

1. by Willard Hurst   THE ROLE OF HISTORY

THREE DECISIONS of the Supreme Court of the United States bring into focus some problems involved in the resort to general history as a guide in construing the Constitution.

First, consider *Pensacola Telegraph Co. v. Western Union Telegraph Co.*,[1] where the Court had to decide whether, under the commerce clause, Congress could license interstate telegraph lines so as to protect them against state laws designed to give local companies a monopoly on telegraph business coming into the state. For a majority of the Court, Mr. Chief Justice Waite declared:

> *The powers thus granted are not confined to the instrumentalities of commerce . . . known or in use when the Constitution was adopted, but they keep pace with the progress of the country, and adapt themselves to the new developments of time and circumstance. They extend from the horse with its rider to the stage-coach, from the sailing-vessel to the steamboat . . . and from the railroad to the telegraph, as these new agencies are successively brought into use to meet the demands of increasing population and wealth. They were intended for the government of the business to which they relate, at all times and under all circumstances. As they were intrusted to the general government for the good of the nation, it is not only the right, but the duty, of Congress to see to it that intercourse among the States and the transmission of intelligence are not obstructed or unnecessarily encumbered by State legislation.*

In *Missouri v. Holland*,[2] Mr. Justice Holmes spoke for the Court in ruling that it was within the treaty-making power of the Federal Government to enter into an agreement with Great Britain for the international protection of migratory birds. To the argument that this would in effect permit the central government to encroach upon areas historically those of state police power under our federal division of power, Holmes replied in a paragraph which has become a classic of constitutional law:

> . . . when we are dealing with words that also are a constituent act, like the Constitution of the United States, we must realize that they have called into life a being the development of which could not have been foreseen completely by the most gifted of its begetters. It was enough for them to realize or to hope that they had created an organism; it has taken a century and has cost their successors much sweat and blood to prove that they created a nation. The case before us must be considered in the light of our whole experience and not merely in that of what was said a hundred years ago. The treaty in question does not contravene any prohibitory words to be found in the Constitution. The only question is whether it is forbidden by some invisible radiation from the general terms of the Tenth Amendment. We must consider what this country has become in deciding what that Amendment has reserved.[3]

Hawke v. Smith[4] raised the question whether a state may require that ratification of an amendment to the Federal Constitution be submitted to popular referendum, consistent with Article V's provision for ratification by state "legislatures." The Court dismissed this contention with a short answer: The word "legislatures" "was not a term of uncertain meaning when incorporated into the Constitution. What it meant when adopted it still means for the purpose of interpretation."[5]

Plainly, in the light of these decisions, the general political, economic, and social history of the United States is legally competent and relevant evidence for the interpretation of the Constitution. If we add to the list such a case as *Thompson v. Utah*,[6] with its ruling that "jury" means a body of twelve men, as that body was known to the generation of the constitution-makers from English history, we may say also that the general history of English legal institutions before the adoption of our Constitution may be competent and relevant evidence for the construction of constitutional terms that have reference to that history.

Cases like the *Thompson* and *Hawke* decisions naturally suggest the next question. We are interpreting a document which has a very definite origin in time, between 1787 and 1788. Granted that we may resort for its interpretation to the general history of the times, what times are these? Perhaps we are limited to the history of events up to 1787–1788, and to the historic cross-section of the society as of the adopting years. Where the Constitution uses language like the terms "jury" or "legislature" which had precise, historically established meaning as of 1787–1788, this is the rule; for this purpose, history stops then. But as one looks at the cases where constitutional meaning has been strictly held to the 1787–1788 meaning, almost all of them prove to involve the definition of particular legal agencies or particular legal procedures; these are not cases dealing with the interpretation of grants of substantive power to be used in an indefinite future, nor cases defining phrases which set standards of official conduct.

This is a distinction which emerges from the pattern of decisions, more than it is made explicit in the opinions. The underlying, inarticulate policy seems sound. If the idea of a document of superior legal authority is to have meaning, terms which have a precise, history-filled content to those who draft and adopt the document must be held to that precise meaning. On the other hand, when the document speaks in generic terms, to outline substantive power and to announce standards for the use of power, "we must never forget, that it is a constitution we are expounding." For no intent is more basic to the Constitution than the design that it provide a framework within which life may move on in ordered fashion into an indefinite future. Nothing is plainer in our social history than the fact that to the men of 1787 that future was seen as an expanding one; they expected their society to grow; they were not a generation minded to put legal fetters on growth.

Holmes, in *Missouri v. Holland*, pushes this argument as far as it can go; in effect, he says that when all other evidence of the constitution-makers' intent fails, we must yet be guided by what we know to be their most general objective—to provide a structure within which the future may settle its own problems. This is good doctrine by criteria which Thomas Jefferson as well as John Marshall set for us. And it is common sense; no generation can in fact evade the responsibilities of choice which resistless change will surely thrust upon it.

Yet the fact that we are talking about a constitution must always remind us to pay heed to the balance of power in the community and among its official agencies. Constitutionalism and balance of power are close to being synonyms. Holmes' bold formula implicitly includes a vastly expanded range of judicial discretion, as compared with the strictness of *Hawke v. Smith*. Waite speaks within a much more confined frame of historic reference in the *Pensacola* case, but even so his opinion expresses a wholly different breadth of judicial power from the sharply focused historic reference of *Thompson v. Utah*. Any resort to general history, as compared with the history crystallized in particular decisions or authoritative documents, means wider scope for judges' policy choices.

This is not contrary to the constitutional ideal. Constitutionalism means, not a vain effort to foreclose choice, but rather the insistence that responsibility be defined, and that it be exercised as objectively as possible. Holmes of *Missouri v. Holland* is also the Holmes who insisted that we think things and not words. And hardheaded, factminded Waite looks at the way contracts are made, goods ordered and shipped, government administered at a distance, for his conclusion that history has brought the telegraph into the mainstream of interstate commerce. If we are to invoke history, it must not (to borrow Lincoln's story about the Illinois jury) be just the judge's "notion." This means that for a reasonably safe resort to general history in constitutional interpretation, as indeed for the safe conduct of any high policy-making through the courts, we must depend upon a challenging standard of advocacy at the bar. The history in the context of which we read the Constitution must be an appraisal of the record not just as it is read by any one mind or even any one generation, but as it emerges in many-sided reality from the best consensus of many minds and many years.

DISCUSSION

CHAIRMAN CAHN: *Before we begin the discussion, would you mind telling me Lincoln's story about the Illinois jury; I don't know which one you mean.*

HURST: *The foreman asked the judge if he could help him out with respect to a question that he had, and the judge said that is what he was there for; he would be very glad to give any help he could.*

The foreman said, "Well, judge, the jury wanted to know: Was that there you tol' them the law or just your notion?"

BISCHOFF: *I am interested in how you would decide the general question whether the Fourteenth Amendment adopted the specific procedures of the Bill of Rights. My own point of view on that seems to get close to Justice Black's, that if history is going to guide us, the Fourteenth Amendment should ipso facto take all the first ten Amendments and apply them against the states.*

HURST: *I think an answer to that suggestion would be that the first ten Amendments, where they speak of specific institutions and procedural guarantees, are speaking with very specific reference, whereas the Fourteenth Amendment was adopted by the men who framed it and pushed it through with the deliberate idea of creating a general standard of some deliberate vagueness. If we import any Bill of Rights limitations into the Fourteenth Amendment, it is sound judicial practice to say that we are importing them in so far as they are indicative of basic standards of decency in government. Therefore in importing them we are not necessarily limited to all the specific semicolons and commas of the framers of 1790.*

BISCHOFF: *Suppose the Federal Government proposed to adopt prosecution by information in place of grand jury indictment. As of now, after 150 years, would you say that just because of the specific mention of grand jury in the Fifth Amendment the Court itself rather than Congress could not adapt federal procedures to something which most of us recognize as pretty good?*

HURST: *I would say so, yes. I would say if you have an authoritative document which you know in some respect has an historically precise* meaning, it would offend my notion of the proper separation of powers to allow the judges the scope of policy discretion involved.

FRANK: What would you do, Professor Hurst, with the mass of historical data that we do have on the intention of the Thirty-ninth Congress when it adopted the equal protection clause in respect to segregation? How would you use it and what weight would you give it?

HURST: I think that question has to be read in the light of the constitutional phrase you are construing. I think we must start by recognizing that it is a very different kind of provision from the provision which guarantees a trial by jury. It is different in that it is a deliberate, self-conscious effort to set a standard. Therefore by definition the most basic intention of the Fourteenth Amendment was to delegate what you might call a rule-making power to somebody to spell out what the standard would mean in application throughout an indefinite future.

Now it is pretty plain that the actual framers thought they were delegating the rule-making power to Congress, being confident as men so often are that they and like-minded people would always be the Congress. It is quite plain that the Supreme Court of the United States took the ball away from the Congress; but the fact remains that the basic intent was to set a broad and vague standard and to allow the standard to be defined as particular situations might call for definition. I don't think you can sensibly distinguish in that respect between the power of judges and the power of Congress even though Thaddeus Stevens meant primarily to give the power to Congress.

I would say that taking the concrete history of any policy which was discussed in the Congress which formulated that Amendment, one is historically justified in considering whatever the record shows as at best a guide for specific application. But the overriding intention was always the intention to create a flexible standard for the enforcement of decency in the application of governmental power.

Secondly, I would say that one should view the historical record with skepticism where you find substantial conflicting testimony and that one should not limit a broad standard of power by a counting of heads or by adopting the position which seems to have been taken by fifty-one per cent of the speakers. But I would come back always to **the historic fact that we are dealing with a standard.**

FREUND: *I would like to start by summarizing what I think Charles Curtis' position is because I want a chance to quote from his book* Lions Under The Throne. *In discussing the role of the framers in constitutional interpretation he says, "We do not sit in their councils. We invite them to sit in ours."*

It seems to me that sums it all up. Now I find myself in agreement with the reasonable position that Professor Hurst has taken. The difficulties come in assigning particular constitutional provisions to the category of the "jury" or the category of "due process of law."

I think some of the provisions have a deceptively precise historic meaning which should not mislead the courts. I think this is particularly true of the guarantee of the privilege of the writ of habeas corpus. The Supreme Court has had a tendency throughout to regard habeas corpus as that form of remedy which was known in 1787 on the basis of a congeries of English statutes, practices, and traditions. My point is that there is involved in such institutions or practices a dynamic element which itself was adopted by the framers.

There is an analogy here of course to the adoption of the common law. The organic element in an institution ought to be taken into account, and so as to habeas corpus I would say that whether or not a specific wrong could be redressed by habeas corpus or whether the order of a court of competent jurisdiction could be attacked on habeas corpus as of 1787 is not controlling, because the whole history of habeas corpus shows that the courts in England were capable of developing the writ, and we did not adopt an institution frozen as of that date.

There is just one other point that I would like to make. Pursuing what I gather Dean Bischoff opened up, does it make a great difference in Professor Hurst's view whether we take Justice Black's theory of the incorporation of the Bill of Rights into the Fourteenth Amendment or whether we take the other view that the due process clause simply guarantees some fundamental rights which are illustrated by the first eight Amendments?

Professor Hurst has said he thinks the establishment of religion had a fairly precise meaning in the First Amendment. If we take the view of the majority of the Court about the Fourteenth Amendment, is it possible to test state legislation by conceptions prevailing in 1868 rather than in 1787? I think the difference is significant when you look at the materials referred to, say, in the opinion of Mr. Justice Frankfurter. On that issue, he used materials which appeared between 1787 and 1868 and, indeed, some subsequent to 1868. Does it make a difference in that somewhat academic controversy which view you take from the standpoint of your attachment to an historic position?

CURTIS: Didn't Frankfurter even use Elihu Root's statement made in 1894?

HURST: It seems pertinent to say that a basic fact in American history is that we committed a new act of constitution-making at the time of the Civil War, and that one of the key elements in that new period of constitution-making was a deliberate assertion of an expanded range of policy for the agencies of the Federal Government. So it seems historically sound to start certain lines of thinking from the Fourteenth Amendment and not be concerned that they appear novel in the light of 1790.

FRANK: I would like to add a comment on this Fourteenth Amendment problem. It seems to me that one of the factors which has to be taken into consideration in deciding what is the role of history is to realize that there are a variety of parts of history. Error can become history, too, and it can become vested with the same weight that perhaps an original intention had. In the Fourteenth Amendment situation it is possible that as of 1868 it was in fact intended to make the Bill of Rights applicable to the states. Let us assume arguendo that that is so, that there is some evidence to that effect. We have grown from a country of 30 million to 160 million in the intervening period. Our way of life has grown up with an opposite point of view.

It would now be simply grotesque (no other word can be used, it seems to me) to apply the requirement of a petit jury to all state litigations, thus destroying all the municipal small claims courts and the like, and it would be more absurd to free every criminal in the country who had been indicted by a state using the information procedure. When there has been so much experience it seems to me that we are forced to make as much allowance for the last seventy-five years as we are for whatever we may have had in mind in the first place. Hence, the desirable solution to that problem is the one that

Professor Freund advocated in his book, namely, compromising the whole difficulty by expanding the list of rights which are applicable against the states, and then let the rest of the controversy go.

CAHN: Does anybody want to comment on the question: Whose history? It may appear to you as somewhat peculiar that, in a country which contains such a high proportion of individuals who do not share Anglo-Saxon origins, the only history regarded as relevant, not merely for the purpose of defining specific terms like "jury" but likewise for the purpose of defining basic national traditions, should be Anglo-Saxon history. It is assumed that the Volksgeist the Supreme Court is supposed to consult is Anglo-Saxon. Do you want to comment on that?

HURST: I think the history of the peoples who made up the United States must be considered in some respects broader than Anglo-American history, and I think that has been done in fact when dealing with the clauses involving the great grants of power.

I would say, for example, that for the Supreme Court to permit the full use of the federal power to combat the downswing of the business cycle might be said to be a reflection of the contribution to our history of those parts of our people who came from the Continent as distinguished from those who came from the British Isles. I think that drawing upon the accumulated wisdom of various peoples as to what they should want from their legal order is legitimate when you are interpreting parts of the Constitution which were designed to keep the door open to a flexible dealing with the problems of the future.

FRANK: I would like to put this question to Professor Hurst. It is for me one of the hardest problems to decide. I know where I want to come out and I would like his help to get there. To me the vital problem is the question of the application and scope of the First Amendment. Now there my end-result is that that Amendment ought to mean at a minimum what it meant to James Madison, its author, and that it should not be allowed at any point to call for less than that and that we should not allow it to be condensed below that.

The first job in history is to find out what Madison had in mind in dealing with the problems of free speech but, at the same time, it is perfectly apparent that there are any number of possible ways of limiting free speech which occur in our generation but which never occurred in Madison's. Thus in respect to the matter, for instance, of loyalty programs and how they should be appraised under the First Amendment, Madison probably had nothing in mind. The question I would put to Professor Hurst is this: Is it rational, fair, and logical to say that you want a rigid historical interpretation of the First Amendment as to its minimum meaning but you also want some expansions to go on in other situations? If you can have the expansions, then why can't you likewise have contractions in order to meet current situations?

HURST: I don't find any particular difficulty with that because the First Amendment's reference to free speech is on the historic record very clearly one of these constitutional provisions which undertake to set a standard and not to define a particular institution.

It goes essentially to the faith of the Parliamentary revolutionary period, the faith of John Locke in the idea of the social desirability of a wide dispersion of power through the community so that there would be a large number of centers of decision-making. I think you are dealing with what in the historic record was clearly intended as a standard to set the whole framework for the adjustment of tension, trouble, and conflict in the community; and I would appeal to Thomas Jefferson instead of Madison.

2. by Charles P. Curtis   THE ROLE OF THE CONSTITUTIONAL TEXT

I LIKE TO think that what Marshall did was offer us, the people of the United States, in whose name the Constitution was written, the opportunity to sign it, adding our names to those of the Convention. This may be fanciful, but it's none the worse for that. It is a metaphor, and "A world ends," MacLeish says, "when its metaphor has died." [7]

Let me show you how good and true my metaphor is by what happens when it is denied. In the Dred Scott case [8] Chief Justice Taney, giving the opinion of the Court, quoted from the Declaration of Independence, "We hold these truths to be self evident: that all men are created equal. . . ." Then he said:

> The general words above quoted would seem to embrace the whole human family, and if they were used in a similar instrument at this day would be so understood. But it is too clear for dispute, that the enslaved African race were not intended to be included, and formed no part of the people who framed and adopted this declaration; for if the language, as understood in that day, would embrace them, the conduct of the distinguished men who framed the Declaration of Independence would have been utterly and flagrantly inconsistent with the principles they asserted; and instead of the sympathy of mankind, to which they so confidently appealed, they would have deserved and received universal rebuke and reprobation. . . .
>
> No one, we presume, supposes that any change in public opinion or feeling, in relation to this unfortunate race, in the civilized nations of Europe or in this country, should induce the court to give to the words of the constitution a more liberal construction in their favor than they were intended to bear when the instrument was framed and adopted. Such an argument would be altogether inadmissible in any tribunal called on to interpret it. If any of its provisions are deemed unjust, there is a mode prescribed in the instrument itself by which it may be amended; but while it remains unaltered, it must be construed now as it was understood at the time of its adoption. It is not only the same in words, but the same in meaning, and delegates the same powers to the government, and reserves and secures the same rights and privileges to the citizen; and as long as it continues to exist in its present form, it speaks not only in the same words, but with the same meaning and intent with which it spoke when it came from the hands of its framers, and was voted on and adopted by the people of the United States. Any other rule of construction would abrogate the judicial character of this court, and make it the mere reflex of the popular opinion or passion of the day. This court was not created by the constitution for such purposes. Higher and graver trusts have been confided to it, and it must not falter in the path of duty.

Commenting on Douglas' support of this position, Lincoln replied: [9]

> Chief Justice Taney, in his opinion in the Dred Scott case, admits that the language of the Declaration is broad enough to include the whole human family, but he and Judge Douglas argue that the authors of that instrument did not intend to include negroes, by the fact that they did not at once, actually place them on an equality with the whites. . . . I think the authors of that notable instrument intended to include all men, but they did not intend to declare all men equal in all respects. They did not mean to say all were equal in color, size, intellect, moral developments, or social capacity. They defined with tolerable distinctness, in what respects they did consider all men created equal—equal in "certain inalienable rights, among which are life, liberty, and the pursuit of happiness." This they said, and this meant. . . . They meant to set up a standard maxim for free society, which could be familiar to all, and revered by all; constantly looked to, constantly labored for, and even though never perfectly attained, constantly approximated, and thereby constantly spreading and deepening its influence, and augmenting the happiness and value of life to all people of all colors everywhere. . . . They knew the proneness of prosperity to breed tyrants, and they meant when such should reappear in this fair land and commence their vocation they should find left for them at least one hard nut to crack.

Though Taney and Lincoln were talking about the Declaration, they were both construing the Constitution. The difference between them is not only that Taney was wrong and Lincoln right. It is that Taney was ascribing to the words what he thought their authors intended, and Lincoln was giving the authors credit for what their words meant. Men intend, words mean, though our language uses both terms indiscriminately. Lincoln saw the difference; Taney did not.

Moreover, meaning and intention can each exist quite well without the other. The English courts conscientiously abstain from giving any thought to what Parliament or the Sovereign intended. When the Companies Act of 1900, which Lord Halsbury had drafted, came up for interpretation before the House of Lords after he had become Lord Chancellor, he said:

> *My Lords, I have more than once had occasion to say that in construing a statute I believe the worst person to construe it is the person who is responsible for its drafting. He is very much disposed to confuse what he intended to do with the effect of the language which in fact has been employed. At the time he drafted the statute, at all events, he may have been under the impression that he had given full effect to what was intended, but he may be mistaken in construing it afterwards just because what was in his mind was what was intended, though, perhaps, it was not done. For that reason I abstain from giving any judgment in this case myself; but at the same time I desire to say, having read the judgments proposed to be delivered by my noble and learned friends, that I entirely concur with every word of them. I believe that the construction at which they have arrived was the intention of the statute. I do not say my intention, but the intention of the Legislature. I was largely responsible for the language in which the enactment is conveyed, and for that reason, and for that reason only, I have not written a judgment myself, but I heartily concur in the judgment which my noble and learned friends have arrived at.[10]*

To whom is the Constitution addressed? To whom are We speaking? Barring the egregious Dred Scott case, up to 1868 all the acts of Congress which the Supreme Court held unconstitutional related to the organization of the courts.[11] The Constitution was speaking directly to the Court. Since then, the Court has been concerned with other parts of the Constitution which are addressed to other agencies of our government. Here the Court has been exercising a secondary judgment, on a meaning which has already been given to the Constitution by someone who had likewise sworn to support it and who therefore had also a right to construe it.

To be sure, the Court has its own opinion as to what the constitutional words mean, but when they are addressed to someone else, the Court uses its own meaning only for the purpose of comparing it with the meaning already given it by that other. The Court is only a critic who compares a picture for its likeness to the object.

This is one reason why only present current meanings are pertinent. We cannot have our government run as if it were stuck in the end of the eighteenth century, when we are in the middle of the twentieth. It is idle to think that we shall become either better or wiser than we are, or have nobler aspirations than our best, just because our forefathers hoped we would or even intended we should. "What's past is prologue, what to come in yours and my discharge."

This comparative function of the Court's own meaning is also the reason why the Court respects what the Congress, or the governmental agency, or the official, thought the proper meaning to be. As much deference is due as is deserved, and it is due as a matter of fact, not as a presumption of law. The deference depends on the dignity, the local or expert knowledge, and the known wisdom of the official, agency, or legislative authority whose meaning has been brought before the Court for judgment. This makes it all the more inappropriate, even offensive, to judge their meanings by any but current standards.

It is plain, therefore, that any theory of the Court's interpretation of the Constitution must be the same theory on which the other government agencies act, consciously or unconsciously, when they interpret the Constitution for their purposes. The Court cannot fairly compare its own interpretation with theirs unless they are both made to the same pattern and based on the same principles. So we are looking for at least the rudiments of a general theory of meaning. It must be current, because the interpretations on which the Court is passing judgment are now and immediate. It must be practical, because these official interpretations concern our lives, and meaning and life are intertwined if not inextricable. At the same time and for the same reason, there is no possibility of its being easy to operate. Life is not simple nor do we really want it to be, certainly not simple enough to be verbally intelligible.

We may as well start with Aristotle. We nearly always have to. But we will take him through the scrutiny and better understanding of a modern logician. Quine says:

> The Aristotelian notion of essence was the forerunner, no doubt, of the modern notion of intension or meaning. For Aristotle it was

essential in men to be rational, accidental to be two-legged. But there is an important difference between this attitude and the doctrine of meaning. From the latter point of view it may indeed be conceded (if only for the sake of argument) that rationality is involved in the meaning of the word "man" while two-leggedness is not; but two-leggedness may at the same time be viewed as involved in the meaning of "biped" while rationality is not. Thus from the point of view of the doctrine of meaning it makes no sense to say of the actual individual, who is at once a man and a biped, that his rationality is essential and his two-leggedness accidental or vice versa. Things had essences, for Aristotle, but only linguistic forms have meanings. Meaning is what essence becomes when it is divorced from the object of reference and wedded to the word.[12]

This is what we must do—divorce the Aristotelian essence from the thing we are talking about, the particular piece of behavior or the course of conduct which is claimed to be unconstitutional, and marry essence to the words we are applying, which then becomes their meaning. The essence of a thing consists in those of its qualities or properties without which it would cease to be itself. That's metaphysics, and "muddle-headed" anyway, Bertrand Russell says. The meaning of a word, on the other hand, consists in those properties which the word connotes, that is, those properties which, when we apply the word to anything, we imply that the thing possesses. That's linguistics.

The transformation is none the less radical for being easy to perform. Simply put the word in quotation marks. There is a good example in the opinions in *Eisner v. Macomber*,[13] where the Court held that a stock dividend was not income under the Sixteenth Amendment. The opinion of the majority speaks of "the characteristic and distinguishing attribute of income" . . . "considering its essential character" . . . "[h]aving regard to the very truth of the matter. . . ."[14] All quite Aristotelian. Holmes, with Day, dissenting, says, "I think that the word 'income' in the Sixteenth Amendment should be read in a sense. . . ."[15] Holmes and Day were talking about a word. The majority was talking about a thing.

The practical objection to ascribing essences to things instead of meanings to words is not that it's metaphysics, muddled or not. The objection is that we are thereby led to think that the properties which make up the essence of a thing change only as the thing itself changes. The marriage of essence to things is Platonic; it is also indissoluble except by death or adultery. If things did have essences, I suppose this would be true. The advantage of a divorce and the remarriage of the essence to words, by which it becomes their meaning, is that it puts the properties within our reach and under our control, as, of course, the properties of things are not. As soon as we recognize that the essences which Aristotle taught us belonged to things are really the meanings of our own words, we see that interpretation is a handicraft and not a speculation. This may make interpretation all the more difficult.

The trick is to pick out the properties which the word connotes. For some words this is usually pretty easy. The properties which we imply by calling a number even or odd, or by saying that there was a quorum present, can be singled out and distinguished from other properties as easily as picking coals out of a snowdrift. In the vocabulary of human affairs, on the other hand, connotations are not so neat a matter of black and white.[16]

Lawyers, who deal with the words which are at once the most familiar and at the same time the most complicated and vexatious i.e., those which concern the conduct of their fellow human beings, need not be appalled, or even impressed, by the difficulties. The art of the relevant and a sense for the important are the peculiar virtues of lawyers and judges. The Court is well fitted to find the meaning of the Constitution where it belongs, in its words. This is a lawyer's usual and familiar vocation. It may be easier, but I won't agree that it is nobler, and I know it is not wiser, to chase the meaning of our Constitution through the basement door of our ancestors' intentions. The justices are at their best when they measure their respect for the opinions of their fellows and co-workers in our government against the meaning of the words, instead of against a reverence for the past.

DISCUSSION

FREUND: Let me say that as I listened to this really profound discourse on the meaning of meaning, I thought of that quip about the poet, Robert Browning, who was asked whether he meant such and such by his poem and he said, "I may not have meant it when it was written but I mean it now."

CURTIS: I will adopt anything you say.

FREUND: I think that may sum up in a sense what Mr. Curtis was saying. I agree with him that we ought to be post-Aristotelians. I am a little doubtful about employing the terminology of essences even though we transfer essences from intention to meaning, from things to words. I suggest rather that in interpreting the text our choices are between definition by essences and definition by consequences. I will be post-Aristotelian but I would like to be a little William Jamesian at the same time.

I am thinking of what the Privy Council does with respect to the Canadian and Australian constitutions, which is to look to the pith and substance of the law and see under what category of the constitution it falls. We experienced that kind of interpretation in the mid-nineteenth century when the Supreme Court, faced with state laws dealing, for example, with inspections of pilots or seamen, attempted to classify the law by its essence. Is it a regulation of commerce or is it a health measure? Some said it is one and some said it is the other in essence. Now, of course the truth was that it was both, and the problem for the Court was to classify by consequences. What were the consequences of the law in aid of health, what were the consequences of the law in detriment to commerce, and—weighing one off against the other—what would a viable federalism require or support?

It may be a matter of terminology. I am just a little fearful of introducing the concept of essence. If we have learned anything in constitutional interpretation it is that a pragmatic view is the safest and most viable. I know that pragmatism is an unpopular philosophy in many quarters and in some parts is even considered unholy. I am perfectly agreeable to inventing or choosing another word for that—

operationalism, perhaps, but somewhere in that area it seems to me we find our safest rules of interpreting the constitutional text.

FRANK: I suspect that the audience like me finds Mr. Curtis an extraordinarily stimulating man. If he were as persuasive on the subject as he is stimulating, I would have nothing to say.

Solely, therefore, for definitional purposes, I would like to direct his attention to three concrete questions and ask him how, in his view of the proper approach to the matter, he would decide those questions or how he approaches them.

In order to test his technique, I will ask him to accept my assumptions as to what the law is or as to what the documents will show. First, take the cruel and unusual punishment clause in the Constitution. It is clear that the punishment of whipping was used almost universally in the eighteenth century and it was a common practice when that clause was adopted. However, at the present time only two states have whipping and only one has it for general purposes.

I would like to know whether in his view the practice of whipping should be held unconstitutional on the ground that it may not have been a cruel and unusual punishment in the eighteenth century but it is now.

CURTIS: Indeed, yes.

FRANK: Let me give you all three because it is a comparison that I want to get. Secondly, let us suppose that we have on the face of the First Amendment an ambiguity which I think is clearly there, and that is: Does the protection of freedom of speech mean to allow for those exceptions which existed in English common law or doesn't it?

This is a disputable point. Let us assume that by no amount of analysis of the words of the First Amendment will we know for sure what was intended (if we care what was intended) in respect of the English common law exceptions. But we do have a complete, detailed, contemporary writing of Madison which shows without any doubt at all that the Amendment was intended not to allow for the English common law exceptions. Do we look to what Madison had to say and to what extent are we bound by it?

Finally, in connection with the impairment of contracts clause, let us suppose that a particular enactment of mortgage moratorium is offered and we know for sure that this is the kind of mortgage moratorium the founding fathers meant to preclude by the adoption of the contracts clause. Using Mr. Curtis' techniques, will he tell us what attention, if any, he will pay to the intent and practice of the eighteenth century with regard to each?

CURTIS: I think the first one is a very neat example of why I should discard original intention entirely. It is cruel as of the present, and it is unusual. There is no basis for restriction to what was unusual at that time. I should certainly hold whipping unconstitutional, looking for guidance to the present meaning of the word "unusual."

Take your second one, freedom of speech. I should ignore any restrictions put on it by the common law or the practices of the eighteenth century and look rather to what We believe now—I am using "We," as the Constitution does, with a capital W—and I should expect the Supreme Court to pick out the best views and try to give us their version of modern freedom of speech.

Answering your third question, I should ignore the contemporary practice. I would ignore any common law or eighteenth-century notions with respect to mortgage moratoriums.

CAHN: You would not feel a duty to consult what Madison said on the subject?

CURTIS: I should be exceedingly interested in reading it in exactly the same way that I should be interested to read his biography or any other relevant history; but I was asked whether that bound the Supreme Court. To that I say no.

FREUND: If I may revert to something that John Frank said earlier about the role of history, let me say that I have been pondering his question and, like him, am groping for an answer. He suggested tentatively, you remember, that perhaps the guarantees in the Bill of Rights are minimal guarantees. They represent a floor beneath which we must not fall but above which we are free to rise. Let me just put a couple of cases to test that.

The notion is rather seductive but it troubles me. Take the guarantee of due process of law. Suppose it is shown that at the time the clause was introduced due process of law required before the beginning of a lawsuit the arrest of the person, or at least the physical presence of the person within the jurisdiction. Let us assume one of these was essential to due process of law. Now, subsequent to that time we have enlarged our notions of personal jurisdiction so that absentees can be reached by process on various bases, such as doing acts and so forth. If the due process clause represents a minimal guarantee, are we bound to say no, our citizens had that minimal protection procedurally in .1787 and we cannot enlarge legislative power consistently with due process of law today?

The other type of question raises the problem of the double standard, about which we have circled cautiously. If we take this idea of a minimal guarantee as applicable, say, to freedom of speech and freedom of press, what about the guarantee against impairing the obligation of a contract? Suppose it is shown that historically that meant simply impairment of executory agreements? Should the Court be as free to increase the protection there by bringing in executed acts as it is free to increase the protection in the realm of free speech, for example?

You may say this is just what has been done, and I would not disagree. But, on principle, are we prepared to say that the guarantee is expansible in the area of what we like to call civil liberties but not expansible in other areas?

HURST: I think some of this discussion is unduly abstract because it seems to ignore the fact that when you are talking about constitutional law, you are talking about the balance of power in the community and that the question of how you find meaning boils down concretely here to who finds the meaning.

I say that because I suspect in concrete cases Mr. Curtis and I would not find ourselves far apart, but I think a large part of the difference in formulation boils down to the fact that he is a greater friend of the Court than I am.

It seems to me that his approach is a way of practically reading Article V out of the Federal Constitution. The men who wrote the Constitution, after all, included that Article as being as important a part as anything else. They provided a defined, regular procedure for changing or adapting it.

Many times what we are talking about here boils down to the question: Do you want your community policy choices to be made by judges, by legislators, by presidents, or by the electorate? And I stick to my basic distinction that you are dealing with language that sets up a standard. We have set up a way of doing business, which means we are willing to delegate adaptations and adjustments in certain realms to those who hold official power when the adjustment happens to become necessary. Nevertheless, a very basic principle of our constitutionalism is a distrust of official power. Hence I am not anxious to see the category of standards expanded.

We may not like everything to which the men of 1787 commit us. Of course, the world has changed. Nobody wants to run a twentieth century society according to the eighteenth century. The real issue is who makes the policy choices in the twentieth century: judges or the combination of legislature and electorate that makes constitutional amendments. If you are dealing in an area (like the due process clause) which involves the matter of standards, there we have, for better or worse, committed our fortunes to the current holders of official power at the time the problem arises. So be it! If we are dealing with a question which is not in the realm of standards, we have a different way of dealing with it. Personally I am satisfied with the difference.

CAHN: There is one more illustrative item to call to your attention. It seems to link Mr. Curtis' treatment of the constitutional text to Professor Freund's treatment of federalism [in Chapter IV of this book], so I shall solicit their respective comments. In a word, what do you think of the Court's struggle with the full faith and credit clause * in matters of marriage and divorce?

CURTIS: I should comment only that when Congress is not interested in a subject or is amused with other affairs and when things have to be done, somehow the Supreme Court finds itself doing them. We run into the same problem in connection with the application of the Sherman Act. There you have a complex economic, commercial, and financial policy which Congress has largely neglected, enacting only some

---

* Article IV, Section 1 of the Constitution provides: "Full Faith and Credit shall be given in each State to the public Acts, Records, and judicial Proceedings of every other State. And the Congress may by general Laws prescribe the Manner in which such Acts, Records and Proceedings shall be proved, and the Effect thereof."—EDITOR.

vague generalities and leaving it to the courts to give them meaning. If no one else is interested enough to do it, I suppose the courts must.

FREUND: *Although Congress has the power to implement the full faith and credit clause, I think we will wait a long time before it enters that politically forbidding field. Meanwhile the Court struggles along as best it can. The handicap under which the Court struggles is the supposedly compulsory requirement of domicile. I would follow Justice Rutledge's lead and suggest that something more workable than domicile be adopted as a requirement. As long as we insist on domicile, I think the impasse we are in will continue. Recognizing that, the Court has helped the situation somewhat by using a liberal view of res judicata.*

CURTIS: *If commercial law can progressively take title out of sales, why can't we take domicile out of divorce jurisdiction?*

3. by Ralph F. Bischoff THE ROLE OF OFFICIAL PRECEDENTS

MOST DISCUSSIONS of the role of precedents in American public law begin with the observation that they exert substantially less binding force than in private law. For how can a written constitution be a living one unless judges have the power to change old meanings for new and to reverse past decisions which are no longer consonant with a present established way of life? Opinions concerning the degree to which previous decisions should be controlling in public law vary however, and it is my thesis that the Supreme Court has departed too far from the respect for precedent which has been a working maxim of the common law. The Court has the opportunity, in a measure self-created, to return to the proper judicial role implicit in *Marbury v. Madison.*[17]

Possibly I may be forgiven if, instead of Aristotle, I quote from Bentham and in place of Holmes I remind you of an almost forgotten commentary of Mr. Justice McReynolds. The Bencher of Lincoln's Inn regarded the common law as a chaotic and unpredictable arrangement produced by an alliance between the sinister interest of judges and the equally sinister interest of professional lawyers. In his *Rationale of Judicial Evidence* he had the following to say:

> It was and is the interest of the partnership that the law be throughout as irrational as possible. Why? That it may be as unconjecturable as possible. . . . From this unconjecturability, two intimately connected but perfectly distinct advantages accrue to the partnership, and, pro interesse suo, to the judge: 1. In proportion as the law really is unconjecturable, the failures made by the suitor in his attempts to find it out are frequent. . . . and 2. the obligation he feels himself under of having recourse to the professional lawyer.

Again, talking of the matchless excellence of English laws, he wrote:

> What there is good in the system, will be found to exist in a much larger proportion in the form of statute law, than in the form of jurisprudential law: in other words, to have been in a greater degree the work of king, lords, and commons, the legitimate legislators.[18]

For Mr. Justice McReynolds, on the other hand, the common law was a protector because it was certain, and precedent was not to be lightly overruled. His dissenting opinion in the Gold Clause cases does not include some extemporaneous remarks:

> The Constitution, as we have known it, is gone. This is Nero at his worst.
>
> It seems impossible to overestimate the result of what has been done here today. . . . The guarantees to which men and women heretofore have looked to protect their interests have been swept away. This is not a thing I like to talk about. God knows, I wish I didn't have to. But there are some responsibilities attaching to a man on this bench to reveal to the bar, in all its nakedness, just what has been done. . . . Loss of reputation for honorable dealing will bring us unending humiliation; the impending legal and moral chaos is appalling.[19]

I am certain that if a layman had spread in front of him at one time all the decisions of the Supreme Court since *Marbury v. Madison* he would not only lose some of the traditional American reverence for the Court but would also be convinced that his welfare and liberty were ultimately at the mercy of a self-conceived super-legislature instead of a court of law. Losing sight of the fact that for the first hundred or more years the Court had occasion to overrule itself rarely, he would be over-impressed with the years since 1936 in which so many earlier decisions have been discarded or refined away and in which one faction or another of the Court has accused the other of playing Nero. In a span of one hundred and fifty years of history, even gradual change in a doctrine or the slow evolution into an opposite may appear as an arbitrary and sudden reversal. To mention but a few: *Erie Railroad v. Tompkins* replaced *Swift v. Tyson* and its progeny;[20] *Graves v. New York* discarded most of *McCulloch v. Maryland* and its disciples;[21] *United States v. Darby Lumber Company* outlawed *Hammer v. Dagenhart;*[22] and *United States v. South Eastern Underwriters Association* killed the principle if not the decision of *Paul v. Virginia.*[23] Consequently, in diversity of citizenship cases the federal courts must follow the common law of the states; the federal government may include in its taxes the income of a state official, may regulate child labor or the insurance business; and yet, a short while before, all this was untrue. Illegal though it was for a state to regulate minimum wages in 1936, the shift of one judicial vote in 1937 decreed otherwise; the action of the Democratic state convention in Texas confining party membership and voting privileges to white citizens was not forbidden state action in 1935 but became so in 1944. In this last decision, *Smith v. Allwright*, Mr. Justice Roberts, who had not too long before changed his mind in the minimum wage cases, said:

> It is regrettable that in an era marked by doubt and confusion, an era whose greatest need is steadfastness of thought and purpose, this court, which has been looked to as exhibiting consistency in adjudication, and a steadiness which would hold the balance even in the face of temporary ebbs and flows of opinion, should now itself become the breeder of fresh doubt and confusion in the public mind as to the stability of our institutions.[24]

The process of synthesizing the dynamic role of the Court which resulted from the decision of 1803 with the more static nature of the common law and the binding force of precedent is not made easier by the failure of liberals and conservatives to differentiate between the "transient results" and the "enduring consequences." As Mr. Justice Jackson put it in the Steel Seizure case,[25] we must not confuse "the issue of a power's validity with the cause it is invoked to promote." Mr. Roosevelt's attempt to pack the Court was as anti-constitutional as the effort of the "Four Horsemen" who sat on the Court in the early thirties to use *stare decisis,* or respect for precedent, as a weapon against any change.

If laymen, and often the scholars, are confused by the revolutionary decade in which precedents fell to the left and to the right, they are hardly enlightened by the recent emphasis on prolixity, the frequent concurring opinions, and the mass of dissents. Are our chances of an enduring democracy enhanced by five opinions in the case of the Communist leaders and seven in the decision on the Steel Seizure? Very recently, the Court rendered a six to three decision affirming North Carolina's right to use property and poll-tax lists for the selection of juries, but it required nearly 40,000 words and six different opinions to "settle" the hardly novel issue of the "white jury." [26] One of the dissenting opinions was written by Mr. Justice Frankfurter, but he also issued a 16,000-word statement commenting on various aspects of the three cases involved. Has the Court succumbed to the flexible logic of the pragmatist, using legal concepts and precedent only as support for desired ends? Do the members of the Court have any common conception of its function in our democratic way of life?

To return to our original premise: *stare decisis* is not an absolute with the identical role to play in public and in private law, nor for that matter even in the various branches of constitutional or private law. It would be unduly emphasizing minutiae to dwell on the historical contribution of *stare decisis* to our common law or on the relative importance of the concept in the sundry philosophic explanations of the law as a method of control. History, social needs, the personality of a judge, philosophical attitudes, deductive logic, linguistics—all of these may be forces in the formation of a particular judicial decision in the public law. But in the words of Mr. Justice Cardozo, what is most important to remember is that *stare decisis* is the "everyday working rule of our law." [27] The Supreme Court would do well to remember this.

My quarrel with the Court is one of emphasis. I believe that the Court has overstressed its own role as the overseer of our democracy and the judge of social need and that therefore *stare decisis* and the processes of adjudication have too often played a secondary role or have been a mere means to an end. As a result of *Marbury v. Madison* the Court's relation to Congress is, to be sure, far different from that of the British courts to Parliament. If the Supreme Court declares minimum wage laws unconstitutional, only the Court or a possible amendment can change the decision as an omnipotent Parliament can. It is in the very nature of our government that some decisions will have to be overruled or refined away when they become too far removed from the norms of the period. In the nineteenth century, for example, the needs of government were not great; dual federalism was of the essence and the Court produced the doctrine that one government cannot tax the instrumentalities of the other. But by the time of the New Deal this doctrine had to be overruled to a great extent. Segregation was once more accepted than now and I dare say it will soon be declared illegal. But much of this overruling of precedents or of previously established concepts has only been necessary because the Court has transposed the policy of an era into constitutional dogma. Because laissez faire was constitutionalized it had to be deconstitutionalized.

The difficulty is that in the post-laissez-faire period the Court has continued to act as an overseer and has only too often added to the problems which the future will be forced to face by turning the decision of a particular case into a broad generalization "good for all time." Some of these decisions are in the realm of statutory interpretation, an area in which *stare decisis* should reign since Congress can reinterpret through additional legislation. For example, the Court, rightly or wrongly, had interpreted the oath in the Naturalization Act of 1906 as requiring of an alien about to become a citizen that he promise to take up arms in defense of the country. Yet, when the same oath was repeated in the statute of 1940, after three similar interpretations, the Court decided to the contrary.[28] In effect, the

Court was saying to Congress that if the latter did not have sense enough to overrule the previous decisions, it would. Even granting that *Paul v. Virginia* did not necessarily decide the *South Eastern Underwriters* case, the Court suddenly after fifty-four years included insurance within the Sherman Act and thus informed Congress that it was constitutional to do what Congress had not yet done. One is reminded of the instance not involving statutory interpretation but the constitutionality of the required salute to the flag in public schools. The Court declared this requirement constitutional in the *Gobitis* case [29] of 1940, practically suggested in its *Opelika* opinion [30] of 1942 that the issue be revived, and reversed the earlier decision in the *Barnette* case [31] of 1943.

That the attempt to settle a problem has an unhappy way of back-firing when different circumstances arise is well illustrated by the famous trilogy of cases on the issue of church and state. In the *Everson* case [32] Mr. Justice Black's opinion for the majority created a high wall between church and state, although the Court then found that reimbursement of bus fares to parochial school children did not violate this separation. The released-time program of the *McCollum* decision [33] was readily subsumed to the major premise because there religious instruction was conducted in public-school buildings; but the New York released-time program involved in *Zorach v. Clauson* [34] was upheld by a majority of the Court because this element was missing. The attempt to create an all-encompassing concept in the first case engendered doubt rather than certainty.

Properly used, a common law system of *stare decisis* contains within itself an adjustment between the static and the dynamic elements which will solve most problems in constitutional law. Uniformity, symmetry, predictability, and certainty are its products. Yet a case may be different on its facts, or one analogy better than another, or a void exist which allows a judge to legislate "interstitially," particularly when the phrase to be interpreted is as broad as interstate commerce or due process of law.

The Court has itself in recent years abdicated enough of its power in certain areas so that *stare decisis* should be more easily the rule. A summary of the Supreme Court decisions in the calendar year 1952 reveals the following:

cases interpreting federal statutes	51
unanimous opinions	16
cases on federal civil rights	18
unanimous opinions	2
cases on state civil rights	14
unanimous opinions	4
cases on federalism	8
unanimous opinions	1
cases on separation of powers	1
unanimous opinions	0

Where constitutional issues involving a definition of interstate commerce once dominated, now statutory interpretation and civil rights lead the field. With the large number of cases on the meaning of federal laws, the function of the Court should be similar to that of a British court interpreting the will of Parliament and of the common law courts in matters remediable through legislation. The question is, for example, what power Congress gave the Federal Power Commission or the National Labor Relations Board, not whether the grant interferes with states' rights. Many of the decisions on civil rights also come within the orbit of the state or national legislature's power to change. A statute which is too vague may be made more concrete; the broad power of the police chief to issue permits may be curtailed; the generalities of breach of the peace may be made more specific. The areas of free speech and of free religious worship must be gradually defined, case by case. Occasionally, to be sure, old decisions must be overruled. But above all the Court must be made aware that its function in our tripartite system, partly because of the judicial review of *Marbury v. Madison*, is primarily one of adjudication. To quote Mr. Justice Frankfurter:

> The pole-star for constitutional adjudication is John Marshall's greatest judicial utterance that "it is a constitution we are expounding." . . . That requires both a spacious view in applying an instrument of government "made for an undefined and expanding future," . . . and as narrow a delimitation of the constitutional issues as the circumstances permit. Not the least characteristic of great statesmanship which the Framers manifested was the extent to

which they did not attempt to bind the future. It is no less incumbent upon this Court to avoid putting fetters upon the future by needless pronouncements today.[35]

DISCUSSION

HURST: *I think a good deal of criticism of the overruling of decisions or the recasting of doctrine reflects poor workmanship back along the line, largely the poor workmanship of lawyers who did not render their full service as officers of the court in the presentation of the cases.*

Dean Bischoff's comments on the spawning of opinions might be annotated with a reference to one consideration which he does not emphasize so much, and that is the Court's role as a maker of the symbols of political communication. I have a hunch that the Supreme Court has probably had a greater impact on our society by its contributions to the language of our politics—I don't mean just the words, but the meanings by which Americans talk politics to one another—than by any actual imposition of power on its part.

If that is a sound judgment, I think it gives a criterion by which to look with regret upon dissent or separate expressions of opinion except in the most soberly considered instances, because the force of the Court as symbol-maker is weakened by division. I think one of Marshall's most statesmanlike strokes was his inauguration of the practice of an opinion of the Court speaking through one voice.

CAHN: *Do you want to append some comments on the subject of official but non-judicial precedents?*

HURST: *This topic is relevant to my earlier remarks on the role of history. In the practical working history of American constitutionalism, a living part of the Constitution has been shaped and hammered out by legislative and executive practices.*

The Court itself has recognized that part to a considerable degree. One instance, of course, is the Court's characteristic treatment of things done by the first Congress of the United States, which the Court has treated virtually as if it were an adjourned session of the Philadelphia Convention, and I think with good practical reason.

As another example of the same thing, I think that the doctrine of political questions has been considerably enriched and in some aspects to its betterment by the Court's use of the answers given in instances of legislative practice over a number of years.

FREUND: I have a good deal of sympathy with Dean Bischoff's complaining about the spawning of opinions. I suspect that the unfortunate defendants in the North Carolina case had scarcely enough time to read the 40,000 words before the date of their execution arrived and they may never have understood what the distinctions were.

I think there is a tendency in the Court, an unfortunate one from my point of view, to write for the anthologies too much and for the litigants too little.

It seems to me if the Justices would make a more concerted effort to narrow the issues, they might find grounds of accommodation. That would make their opinions less interesting to the law reviews but I think might enhance the prestige, and particularly the utility of the opinions for the profession. Furthermore, it would be an intellectual accomplishment to demonstrate areas of agreement rather than to intensify areas of disagreement. I have a feeling that some of this proliferation is due to psychological reasons. I have the feeling there is less respect for problems and more disrespect for persons than one would like.

FRANK: On the matter of stare decisis in the application of statutes I strongly agree with Dean Bischoff. He said it so well that I will not attempt to say anything more. But at the point of his criticism of stare decisis as to the constitutional decisions, I don't know which ones he is against and I would like to know that. Of the great overrulings in the last fifteen years, which ones do you object to? Take the West Coast Hotel case [West Coast Hotel Co. v. Parrish, 300 U.S. 379 (1937)] and all the other overrulings on social and economic issues in the late thirties and through the forties. Do you have any objections to those overrulings or does your objection go to the fact that the Court had to overrule the earlier decisions?

BISCHOFF: It is the latter completely. If laissez faire had not been put into the Constitution by the Court, then laissez faire would not have to be removed from the Constitution.

CURTIS: I think with respect to these rulings or overrulings, we always forget the people who suffer the most. I don't object to them. I think the people who do suffer from them are the judges in the lower courts. It is a little difficult for the lower court to have to follow the Supreme Court of the next succeeding year.

IV.
REVIEW AND FEDERALISM

by Paul A. Freund

THE LATE Robert Benchley is said to have written a thesis at college on The Alaskan Fisheries Dispute as Viewed through the Eyes of a Fish. Something of the sort should be undertaken for American federalism. We know a good deal about the statecraft of federalism, the jurisdictional conflicts at the governmental level, and the legal devices by which the conflicts may be resolved. We know too little of the impact of the system on the individuals for whom, with considerable effort, the complex mechanism is maintained. What we do know has been gleaned largely from the records of lawsuits in which investors or producers or distributors or consumers or passengers have sought to be relieved from some burden of tax or regulation challenged as improper under our federal division of powers.

In one aspect this circumstance merely confirms Dicey's celebrated dictum that federal government is legalistic government.[1] But there are legalisms and legalisms. It may be assumed that some form of arbitrament is necessary in a federation to settle questions of jurisdiction, and that a court is the most appropriate arbiter in the final resort. At all events each of the modern federations relies on judicial settlement of such controversies, and subjects the laws of the constituent states to judicial review for this purpose. Moreover, aside from Switzerland, where popular referendum is employed, each federation similarly subjects national legislation to such review.

But legalism in the United States has two sources of strength—not equally available elsewhere—which give a useful quality of realism to judicial review at its best. One is the calculated generality of the principal constitutional provisions on which the framework of the federal structure depends: the power vested in Congress to regulate commerce among the several states, together with the necessary-and-proper clause; the requirement that full faith and credit be given in each state to the public acts, records, and judicial proceedings of other states; the declaration in the Tenth Amendment that powers not given to the national government are reserved to the several states and to the people; and, after 1868, the injunction in the Fourteenth Amendment against deprivation by any state of life, liberty, or property without due process of law—an injunction capable of fixing a territorial limitation on state powers. These provisions stand in contrast with the attempt made in the Canadian constitution (the British North America Act of 1867) to catalogue the powers of government into those vested exclusively in the provinces, those vested exclusively in the Dominion, and those vested concurrently in both. While our system, after periods of fumbling and relapses into abstractions, has enabled the courts to classify powers in terms of their consequences, the Canadian system has promoted a quest for labels based on intrinsic attributes, the "pith and substance" of a law. Is, for example, a Dominion law regulating monopolies and combinations in restraint of trade, under penal sanctions, a criminal law, confided to the exclusive competence of the Dominion, or a law dealing with property and civil rights within a province, confided to the exclusive competence of the provinces? [2] Our own system facilitates, though it by no means guarantees, pragmatic as against nominalistic judgments; this comports with the classic admonition of law teachers that their students think things, not words.

A second and related source of strength in the legalism of our system is the avoidance of judicial decisions on abstract or merely textual questions. Judgments from experience are preferred to judgments from speculation. In more technical terms, advisory opinions are not within the province of the federal courts, and declaratory judgments on constitutional issues are approached with caution.[3] Constitutional issues are decided only as and when it becomes necessary to do so in the course of a controversy between parties whose interests are within the conventional protection of the courts. Again a contrast is patent with Canada, where advisory opinions on proposed legislation are available to the governor general and to the lieutenant governors in the provinces, and with Australia, where decisions on constitutional validity may be procured by public officials promptly after the enactment of a law.[4] No one, I think, can read the opinions of the Canadian and Australian courts and of the Privy Council on questions of federalism without being struck by the relatively formal approach which is taken to the problem. Nor is this a prejudiced American view. A recent writer in the *Canadian Bar Review,* himself an Australian, has referred to a current decision of the Supreme Court of Canada as "another example of the purely mechanical judicial approach to the important subject, in a federal system of government, of the areas of national and state action in the field of commerce." [5] Doubtless this judicial bent may be traced to a number of sources: legal education and the recruitment of judges, the statutory form of the Australian and Canadian constitutions, and the relatively specific language used in those instruments. But part of the source is surely the practice of rendering opinions before the law has been tested in its application, and without the benefit of a factual record.

Something of the same cast of mind regarding the process of judicial review in a federal system is exhibited in recent European constitutions which set up a separate and distinct constitutional court. In Western Germany, for example, constitutional questions arising in the course of litigation are referable at once to the constitutional court, which also sits to hear original applications for opinions at the behest of public authorities. The isolation of constitutional questions from the other issues in a controversy carries with it the danger of accentuating the abstractness of the process of decision. A supreme court which, like our own, is able to avoid constitutional questions or to narrow them in the light of the particular facts or the particular framework of the litigation, and which at the same time exercises the function of interpreting and applying statutes in nonconstitutional cases, enjoys a resourcefulness and an immersion in the actualities of the legal order that are denied to judges whose function is solely to pronounce on constitutional questions. It is of interest to recall that the Italian constitution makes provision for a separate constitutional court, apart from the ordinary supreme court or court of cassation, but that for political reasons having to do with the division of authority in the selection of judges the constitutional court has not in fact been established. It will be worth watching to see whether the constitutional court will in fact be missed, in view of the existence of the supreme court, which in the decision of ordinary controversies could very well determine constitutional questions as the need arises.

Thus Dicey's dictum that federal government is legalistic government, while true enough, may mean different things under the procedures and traditions of judicial review in different federal systems.

It was also part of Dicey's exposition that federal government is weak and conservative. This view has been echoed by many voices, and particularly in latter years. The argument of Harold Laski, writing of American federalism in 1939, is worth reproducing in his own words: [6]

No one can travel the length and breadth of the United States without the conviction of its inexpugnable variety. East and West, South and North, its regions are real and different, and each has problems real and different, too. The temptation is profound to insist that here, if ever, is the classic place for a federal experiment. . . . The large unit, as in Lamennais' phrase, would result in apoplexy at the center and anemia at the extremities. Imposed solutions from a distant Washington, blind, as it must be blind, to the subtle minutiae of local realities, cannot solve the ultimate problems that are in dispute. A creative America must be a federal America. The wider the powers exercised from Washington, the more ineffective will be the capacity for creative administration. Regional wisdom is the clue to the American future. The power to govern must go where that regional wisdom resides. So restrained, men learn by the exercise of responsibility the art of progress. They convince themselves by experiment from below. To fasten a uniformity that is not in nature upon an America destined to variety is to destroy the prospect of an ultimate salvation.

This kind of argument is familiar in a hundred forms. I believe that, more than any other philosophic pattern, it is responsible for the malaise of American democracy. My plea here is for the recognition that the federal form of state is unsuitable to the stage of economic and social development that America has reached. I infer from this postulate two conclusions: first, that the present division of powers, however liberal be the Supreme Court in its technique of interpretation, is inadequate to the needs America confronts; and, second, that any revision of those powers is one which must place in Washington, and Washington only, the power to amend that revision as circumstances change. I infer, in a word, that the epoch of federalism is over, and that only a decentralized system can effec-. tively confront the problems of a new time. . . .

I do not think this argument is invalidated by the rise of coöpera-tion between the federal government and the states, or between groups of states. That use has been carefully investigated in detail by Professor Jane Clark in an admirable and exhaustive monograph ("The Rise of a New Federalism," 1938). When all is made that can be made of the pattern she there reveals, I think it is true to say that, compared to the dimension of the problem, it amounts to very little. And set in the background of the urgent problems of time, it is, I think, clear from her account that in no fundamental matters will the pressure of political interests (behind which can be seen at every turn the hand of giant capitalism) permit the necessary uni-formities to be attained by consent within the next fifty years. Not even the resiliency of American democracy can afford to wait so long. . . .

Very recently Professor Karl Loewenstein has sung a requiem over the body of federalism in an age of economic planning: [7]

Federalism is on the decline, and this in spite of various institu-tionalizations in the West and the East. Experience in the oldest and best integrated federal states, the United States and Switzer-land, demonstrates that, whatever strength of tradition and emo-tional values of political theory federalism is still imbued with, the economic imperatives of the technological state require unified if not uniform economic policies throughout the entire territory and do not brook that kind of economic fragmentation which goes with effective member-state sovereignties. To point it up sententiously: A state with a federal income tax is no longer a genuinely federal state. On the other hand, the realization is equally general that, even in relatively small areas, decentralization enhances administrative efficiency. Federalism as an organizational device cannot be divorced from the general political philosophy of the age. Federalism is a product of liberal thinking. It applied the (relative) freedom of the individual to the (relative) freedom of organization of territorial entities. It thrives as long as a free economy thrives. Speaking again sententiously: Economic planning is the DDT of federalism. Constitutions, therefore, that take their federal premises too seriously can hardly escape becoming anachronistic.

Perhaps the short answer is to be found in a single sentence by Dean Pound: "No domain of continental extent has been ruled otherwise than as an autocracy or as a federal state." [8] Like the report of Mark Twain's death, the demise of federalism may be exaggerated. It remains to assess the role of the Supreme Court in furthering or hampering the operation of a serviceable federal system. Our successes and failures are no longer of interest to ourselves alone; they are the subject of anxious study by the newer federations of the world and those which may yet be called into existence.

II

We turn first to the power of a national government to govern a domain of continental extent. Fortunately, the bare words of the Constitution were called into life by Marshall, who recognized that it was a Constitution "intended to endure for ages to come and consequently, to be adapted to the various crises of human affairs." [9] To be sure, in his day this vision was reflected only in part by upholding of national power, as in the case of the United States Bank, and in part by denying to the states powers over ". . . that commerce which affects more states than one" [10] and thus leaving private enterprise to its own devices in the absence of control by the national government.

A series of dramatic decisions threatened from time to time the power of the national government to cope with problems of national concern. But for the most part these decisions did not have a radiating or enduring effect. The Dred Scott decision—one of the Court's self-inflicted wounds, in Chief Justice Hughes' phrase [11]—was perhaps the most spectacular, but the issue of civil war or peaceful solution of the slavery problem hardly turned on that case, though it stands as a grim reminder that the Court cannot by a rash employment of the judicial veto shape the political and social destiny of the nation.[12]

The *Civil Rights Cases*,[13] holding to a minimum the scope of the Reconstruction legislation, reflected a view of the majority of the Court that the road to reunion was through conciliation. Here as elsewhere the attitude of the Court is revealed not simply in the constitutional doctrine laid down but in the treatment of narrower questions such as the inseparability of the invalid provisions of the statute from those which could be sustained independently.[14] If federal enforcement of the rights guaranteed by the Fourteenth Amendment was laggard for many years, the blame cannot be placed on the decision in the *Civil Rights Cases*. The Civil Rights Unit of the Department of Justice has shown in the last decade that much can be done under the remnants of the Reconstruction legislation, and the difficulties have arisen more from the inept and patchwork character of the legislation than from barriers raised by the *Civil Rights Cases*.[15] Not judicial review but legislative inaction has stood in the way of more thoroughgoing congressional enforcement of the civil rights guaranteed by the Amendment.

In the area of economic regulation the impediments to national power thrown up by the Court proved to be more pervasive. The Income Tax Cases [16]—another of the self-inflicted wounds—rested on a special economic theory regarding the meaning of the direct taxation clause in Article I of the Constitution. Hence the decision did not have ramifying effects, but it was serious enough in its direct application to the fiscal needs of the Government and the establishment of a soundly-based revenue system. The early anti-trust cases, with their formal separation of production from commerce, portended a rocky road for the enforcement of the Sherman Act.[17] Nevertheless, the realities of trade soon came to prevail in the thinking of the Court, and decisions applying the anti-trust laws to combinations of labor carried with them consequences for business combinations as well. A striking portrait of the advocate for big business moving into an era when economic change had filtered into the thinking of the judges is given in a biography of that redoubtable Philadelphia lawyer John G. Johnson, who had successfully argued the *E. C. Knight* case and was by many regarded as "The King of the American Bar." [18] Chief Justice White is reported to have said this about Johnson: "When I first became a member of the Court Johnson was constantly before us, and we all thought of him as by far the most powerful advocate of his day. But when later Johnson argued the great anti-trust cases, which in fact gave him his national reputation, all the Justices felt that he was not at his best because he had lived into an economic era which he could not understand." [19]

The Child Labor Case [20] decided in 1918 was probably, in its implications, the most severe obstacle raised by the Court to the national power over economic abuses national in their impact. Thereafter the Court had available to it two starting points leading in opposite directions: the decisions of the Marshall era and the later anti-trust cases on the one hand, and on the other hand the Child Labor Case along with dicta differentiating production from commerce in cases sustaining state control but not directly involving the problem of national control. The early New Deal constitutional crisis was precipitated when the majority of the Court chose the latter line. This is not the place to explore all the issues of statecraft involved in the President's plan for reorganization of the Court. It is worth recalling, however, that in all the vigorous denunciation of the President's plan there were few voices indeed which ventured to defend the decisions of the Court on their merits. As in the Reconstruction era, there was telling evidence of a state of mind in the treatment of the issue of separability of the provisions in the Bituminous Coal Act. The Court majority held the Act's price provisions inseparable from its wage provisions in the teeth of a statutory declaration of separability and over the protests of Chief Justice Hughes and Justices Cardozo, Brandeis, and Stone.[21] Perhaps the best commentary on that span of the Court's life was the observation reported to have been made by Mr. Justice Cardozo: "We have ceased to be a court."

How the change came about in 1937 which launched the Court into the present era of validation of national power is thus far known to us only by its manifestations and not its wellsprings. The cynics observed that a switch in time saved nine. A distinguished, if inferior, federal judge reverted to a passage in Fielding's *Jonathan Wild*: ". . . he . . . would have ravished her, if she had not, by a timely compliance, prevented him." But the discussion produced by the Court Plan was an educational experience which, quite apart from the pressure involved, may have had its effect inside as well as outside the Court.

Today national power over the economy is scarcely challenged. It is unnecessary to recount the development from the National Labor Relations Act to the revised agricultural programs, social security, wage and hour legislation, and the extended application of the anti-trust laws.[22] Mr. Justice Jackson has summed it up with characteristic wit: "If it is interstate commerce that feels the pinch, it does not matter how local the operation which applies the squeeze." [23] This contemporary development in the area of national power suggests two questions. First, is there any limit which the Court will impose in the name of a federal system? My own judgment is that we have not actually reached the point where Congress could do whatever might be done in a unitary system. The Child Labor Case has been overruled, to be sure, so that the channels of interstate commerce can be closed where they would be used to spread and perpetuate an evil. Perhaps, although marriage and divorce are the most local of concerns in our federalism, Congress could penalize the movement of persons from one state to another to obtain a divorce *ex parte* on less than, say, six months' residence. But could Congress deny the channels of interstate movement to anyone who may hereafter obtain such a divorce? In the first case there is a functional relation between interstate movement and the abuse; in the second there is not. But present doctrines, if adhered to, seem adequate for all practical purposes.

The second question is whether we can depend on present doctrines to be observed or whether the gains which have been achieved for national power are at the hazard of shifts in the personnel of the Court. Some hazard there undoubtedly is, for if our constitutional history teaches anything, it is that it matters enormously what the outlook of the members of the Court may be. But it would be a great mistake to ignore the institutional quality of the Court and its effect on the members. It is frequently asserted that our development as a nation would have been markedly different had Spencer Roane of Virginia been appointed by Jefferson as Chief Justice in lieu of the appointment of Marshall by Adams. Still one wonders whether Justice Roane of Washington would have been precisely Judge Roane of Virginia. The Federalist Kent surely stood in contrast to the Federalist Marshall on the subject of state power over commerce, as is reflected in the reversal of the New York court by the Supreme Court in *Gibbons v. Ogden.* Indeed, the member of Marshall's Court who outdid even the great Chief Justice in the assertion of an exclusive national power in that case was Justice William Johnson, a Madisonian appointee from South Carolina. It required courage in those days of circuit riding to face one's local community with nationalistic doctrine. It was that courage which Johnson displayed when, even before the decision in *Gibbons v. Ogden,* he ruled on the federal bench in South Carolina that the law of that state requiring the detention of Negro seamen from vessels putting in at South Carolina ports was unconstitutional under the commerce clause.[24] This episode suggests, incidentally, that the commerce clause was relevant in the view of a great judge no less for the protection of what we have come to term civil rights than for the protection of commercial interests.[25] The institutional effect of membership on the Court seems to have been exhibited likewise during the Reconstruction period, when, as Mr. Justice Jackson has reminded us, the decisions drawing some of the teeth from the Civil Rights Acts were reached ". . . by a Court, every member of which had been appointed by President Lincoln, Grant, Hayes, Garfield or Arthur—all indoctrinated in the cause which produced the Fourteenth Amendment, but convinced that it was not to be used to centralize power so as to upset the federal system." [26] More recent examples, drawn from the elevation of attorneys general to the Court, are too familiar to require designation. It is often observed by law students that the effect of legal education is accordion-like, forcing extreme partisanship of the left or right closer to the center, when it is seen that polar views thrive on fragmentary understanding of complexities. Something of the kind may operate on the level of the Supreme Court, which in a real sense is our greatest legal educational institution.

To put the whole matter of judicial review in the field of national power summarily, its contribution has been most serviceable when it has been of a passive sort. Perhaps "passive" is not the most apt description, for although the decisions themselves are in the form of *nil obstat*, the fact of their pronouncement is important in itself as an authentication of the powers claimed. If we had to strike a balance on the historical record between the hazards of judicial review to adequate national power and its value as an authenticator of legitimate national power, the tally would probably have to be unfavorable. But the institution of judicial review is not designed primarily to check national power; there the inner check of representation of local interests and the clash and compromise of factions serves as an independent safeguard. The institution performs its most useful task in repressing the parochialism of local interests at the local level, and to that subject we must now advert.

III

"It is easy," Mr. Justice Frankfurter remarked fairly recently, "to mock or minimize the significance of 'free·trade among the states,' . . . which is the significance given to the Commerce Clause by a century and a half of adjudication in this Court. With all doubts as to what lessons history teaches, few seem clearer than the beneficial consequences which have flowed from this conception of the Commerce Clause." [27]

In assessing the claims of local welfare as against the national commercial interest the Court has been more successful in its pragmatic adjustments than in its explications. The task presents questions of fact and questions of judgment. When we speak of judgment, it should be possible to formulate intelligible standards against which to weigh the facts. Too often the Court has contented itself with such meaningless standards as "direct burden" and "undue burden" on interstate commerce. Those who find futility in the effort to formulate standards in this area will draw comfort from Professor Powell's proposed Restatement of the subject. *Black letter text*: Congress has power to regulate interstate commerce. *Comment*: The states may also regulate interstate commerce, but not too much.

Caveat: How much is too much is beyond the scope of this Restatement.

Mechanical standards have proved unworkable. Of such a kind was the original-package doctrine, which sought to draw a line between national and state power at the point where the original package was broken or the first sale was made after arrival of the goods in the state. We now know that the doctrine is both too restrictive and too generous concerning state power. A state can exclude diseased or falsely labeled products whatever their package, and yet it cannot prohibit the resale of goods even after the original package is broken, where that prohibition depends on the price which had been paid to out-of-state producers.[28]

The standard most easily discernible in the decisions is the one that precludes discrimination against out-of-state merchants or goods in the interest of local competitors. But the state legislatures are rarely so ingenuous in their draftsmanship as to avow discrimination. Usually a local interest other than the competitive commercial one is brought forward—the interest of public health, for example, or conservation of resources. The local interest may be asserted by the state of origin or the state of destination; the law may resemble either an export embargo or a non-importation act. The first type is illustrated by the Louisiana statute which forbade the shipment out of the state of shrimp in an unshucked condition, on the ground that the shucks and shells must be removed and conserved for use in fertilizer or in chicken feed, which could themselves be shipped out of the state.[29] In view of the proximity of a canning enterprise in the neighboring state of Mississippi, the operation of the statute was not very difficult to uncover. It was a case of local commercial preference masking under what Holmes once called "the convenient apologetics of the police power."[30]

Local protection in the state of destination is illustrated by the recent case involving the milk ordinance of Madison, Wisconsin, which made it unlawful to sell any milk as pasteurized unless it was processed and bottled at any approved plant within five miles from the center of the city.[31] The ordinance was held invalid despite its plausible claim to be a health measure, a claim which was accepted by Justices Black, Douglas, and Minton, who dissented. They pointed out that since it was not impossible for milk dealers in Illinois to send their milk for pasteurization in Madison, no monopoly of the milk supply was created by the local ordinance. But there was a monopoly of the business of pasteurization. The treatment of the problem by the majority is revealing of the whole process of judicial review of local legislation in our federal system. The Court considered what it called reasonable and adequate alternatives available to the city. The first was to rely upon its own officials for inspection at distant milk sources, charging the cost to the importing producers and processors. The second alternative was to exclude from the city milk not pasteurized according to standards as high as those enforced by the city itself. The latter possibility suggests the more general question of the extent to which a state or locality may attempt to equalize the conditions of production without infringing the constitutional postulate of a national market.

In the realm of employment, equality of conditions of production might be achieved if the state of destination could exclude goods made under labor conditions below the standard it applies to domestic goods. If this power had existed, the no man's land which for many years prevailed with respect to goods produced by child labor would have been eliminated; but it is quite plain that no such power on the part of the states was recognized. Equality was also sought with respect to prices paid to out-of-state producers prior to the shipment of the goods into the state for resale, but this effort at what was in essence a flexible tariff was struck down.[32]

Still another field in which the idea of equalization has been tried is that of taxation. Can the competitive advantage of lower taxes in the state of origin be offset by a tax in the state of destination? On the assumption that direct sales by out-of-state sellers could not be taxed by the state of destination, a substantial competitive advantage was enjoyed by sellers operating outside the state, either because they were not constitutionally subject to a sales tax in the state of origin on such sales or because the state of origin had not adopted a sales tax or had adopted one at a relatively low rate. Eventually, the resourcefulness of legislators having asserted itself, the complementary use tax was put into effect. By this device, the purchaser was taxed (the seller being made liable for collection) but with a credit allowed for any sales tax paid on the same transaction. The purchaser from a local merchant was relieved by the credit; the purchaser from an out-of-state merchant was taxed; and the tax burden on the two kinds of transaction, taking the sales tax and the use tax together, was equalized. This device was sustained.[33] And so the principle of equalization, approved conditionally in the case of sanitary standards for milk, and disapproved in the case of price and labor differentials, has been given a limited application in the case of fiscal burdens.

The upshot is that Professor Powell's "not too much" covers not a formula but a process, a process which weighs many elements but cannot escape the need for an ultimate judgment in terms of a social balance. The process places a large responsibility on lawyers to discover and present the relevant facts. It is not hard to find cases which would probably have been decided otherwise on the basis of a fuller record. New York, for example, was permitted to enforce against Wisconsin cattle raisers a requirement that each shipment of cattle be accompanied by a certificate that the herd from which they came was free of Bang's disease.[34] There was evidence which could have been adduced that at the same time Bang's disease was widespread in New York State and no steps were being taken to see that the incoming cattle were placed in clean herds.[35] But the Court did not have the benefit of a disclosure of that information.

Counsel's task regarding facts is overshadowed by the Court's responsibility in reaching a judgment. Although there is no formula, there are pertinent questions whose answers go to make up the judgment. Is the state giving a preference to its own commercial interests, or merely equalizing their competitive relation? How severe is the handicap to out-of-state interests: does the law prohibit, or add to the cost of doing business, or simply inconvenience by requiring reports? What is the nature of the local interest and how exigent is it: is it protection against pestilence or against cheap goods? What less severe means of protection could be utilized? On the whole, the Court has asked the right questions and has evolved answers which—if "right" is not an appropriate description—are at all events serviceable accommodations from the standpoint of a working federalism.

If this achievement is thought too easy to warrant praise, a comparative view may produce some satisfaction. In 1937 the Privy Coun-

cil, a tribunal of large experience in resolving the problems of confederated peoples, was called upon to consider a statute of Northern Ireland which restricted the selling of milk in that territory to persons whose premises had been inspected and approved by certain licensing officials. The complainant, who operated a dairy just outside of Northern Ireland, was refused a license because it was impracticable to apply the act to producers outside the territory. The Government of Ireland Act excluded from the authority of Northern Ireland, with certain exceptions not relevant, the power to make laws "in respect of . . . trade with any place out of the part of Ireland within their jurisdiction." In this setting, the Privy Council quite summarily sustained the legislation, stating: "The true nature and character of the Act, its pith and substance, is that it is an Act to protect the health of the inhabitants of Northern Ireland; and in those circumstances, though it may incidentally affect trade with County Donegal, it is not passed 'in respect of' trade, and is therefore not subject to attack on that ground." [36] Contrast with the case of the Madison milk ordinance could hardly be more marked.

In all that we have said it has been assumed that it is for the Court, and not simply for Congress, to safeguard ·the national commercial interest against local barriers. This assumption has not gone unchallenged. Mr. Justice Black, reviving a position which had not been taken since Taney's day, has insisted that the Court oversteps its authority when it, rather than Congress, "regulates" interstate commerce. Mr. Justice Black himself has not been entirely true to his point of view.[37] One may suppose that the opportunity was not unwelcome to him to join in overturning the segregation law of Virginia as it applied to interstate bus transportation [38]—or at least that the opportunity was more welcome to him than it would have been to Taney. The acquiescence by Congress through all the years is sufficient indication that its silence amounts to assent to the responsibility undertaken by the Court. It is doubtful, moreover, that as a practical matter Congress could effectively deal with the myriad problems of state impediments to national trade. At best Congress could set up a special tribunal to which might be delegated not merely adjudicating functions but rule-making functions as well. Even this appears hardly feasible in view of the difficulty of formulat-

ing standards much more general than those the Court has employed
or implied in its judgments.

In the field of state taxation of interstate enterprise, the case for a
special tribunal with rule-making powers is stronger. The possibility
of framing standards and of working out their application through
more continuous supervision than the Court can furnish might well
justify the establishment of a federal commission comparable to the
Interstate Commerce Commission.[39]

The work of the Court in the field of state taxation has shown the
pulls and counter-pulls of formalism and pragmatism.[40] At times the
Court has been concerned with the formal subject of the tax—whether
it is "on" interstate business (hence forbidden) or "on" some local
activity, such as the maintenance of local facilities, and "measured by"
receipts from interstate business. The emphasis on the formal subject
of the tax is unrealistic and unfortunate, with two qualifications. First,
the subject of the tax deserves scrutiny where it is an especially selec-
tive one, such as a tax on the business of railroads, lest in the guise
of a non-discriminatory exaction the state take more toll from interstate enterprise than from comparable domestic business. Second,
the subject of the tax may be important to the extent that non-
payment of the tax may result in a denial of the privilege which is
taxed; if the sanction for the tax is related to the formal subject the
enforcement penalties may themselves be too drastic an interference
with the conduct of interstate activity. But this latter difficulty should
not be anticipated when the question is simply the liability of the
taxpayer and when the further question of sanctions has not arisen.[41]

Even if the Court professes a more pragmatic test it is by no means
clear just how the object of the immunity is to be defined. We are
told that interstate commerce is to be unfettered by state taxation but
that interstate commerce must pay its way. The early cases invalidating taxes on gross receipts derived from interstate business were
probably based on the premise that interstate commerce deserved to
be free of toll even though it was thereby given an advantage over
purely local competition. At any rate, the idea seems to have taken
hold that gross receipts from the business of transporting goods in
interstate commerce should be free of local taxation, as a means to
promote the national market envisaged under the commerce clause.

With the advent of net income taxes, a line was drawn between gross receipts and net profits; the latter were taxable by the state, for the double reason that the enterprise was by hypothesis profitable and that the tax did not vary dollar for dollar with the volume or value of the interstate business.[42] There was at work here the kind of practical compromise which underlay the original-package doctrine. More recently the countervailing principle that interstate commerce must pay its way has challenged even the immunity of gross receipts, provided they are allocated fairly to the taxing state.[43] What is meant by "paying its way"? The idea seems to be that the interstate transaction should not be saddled with an aggregate tax burden higher than it would bear if it had taken place in the same volume and over the same distance within a single one of the pertinent states.

Thus put, the ideal of paying its way appears to be only very roughly attainable, at least as administered through judicial review. No means lies at hand by which a Court can control the rate of tax as between one state and another, so that even the most meticulous allocation formula is imperfect when the rates are different. Moreover, the allocation itself has been controlled only to a very limited extent through judicial review.[44] The problem is more legislative than judicial in character. How, for example, shall the value of aircraft be apportioned among the states with which the aircraft has contact? One has only to examine the various formulas proposed to note the advantages that accrue to one or another group of states depending on the factors selected and the way they are weighted.[45] What weight shall be given to originating and terminating traffic, and to departures and arrivals? What weight, if any, shall be given to the miles flown above the land —a factor of special advantage to the so-called bridge states? The more multi-factored the formula, the more likely that it will not take an undue share for the state which enacts it. But unless there is authority to prescribe a uniform formula for the several states, immunity from excessive multiple taxation will not be secured.

In fact it can be said with some assurance that, despite the Court's valiant efforts, interstate business is both under-protected and over-protected on the score of local taxation. The business is under-protected when, because of differences in allocation formulas, each being designed to favor the enacting state, more than one hundred per cent of the property or receipts of an enterprise becomes the aggregate tax base. The business is over-protected when a tax valid in its measure is struck down because it is imposed on an improper formal subject, such as the privilege of engaging in a business which happens in fact to be wholly interstate.[46] There is over-protection, too, to the extent that gross receipts may still be regarded as wholly immune from state taxing claims.[47] In addition, interstate business has been protected against merely contingent multiple taxation, as where a state is forbidden to tax one end of a transaction because another state might seek to tax the other end.[48] This kind of protection against hypothetical burdens is at odds with the Court's practice in other fields, where actual and not merely speculative injury must be established as the foundation of a constitutional claim.

A federal commission, then, having both adjudicating and rule-making powers would find no lack of problems pressing for solution. Such a commission would have to address itself to the device of equitable and uniform allocation formulas. The commission would have to concern itself with the double taxation that results when the corporate domicile taxes the entire value of the "corporate excess" although this amount includes the values of corporate property allocated among the states in which the corporate system is situated.[49] It would also have to consider the sales tax and use tax issue, with a view to selecting the state of destination or the state of origin as the favored taxing jurisdiction. In that connection it would consider Mr. Justice Rutledge's preference for the state of destination, as the market state where competitive tax burdens are sought to be equalized, as well as Professor Abel's objection that the state of origin has the greater claim by reason of its larger contribution to the value of the product. This debate recalls Professor Powell's inquiry whether the taxable value of articles in the state of destination should be ascribed to the goodness of the goods or to the gullibility of the customers. Professor Abel has pointedly expressed his differences with Mr. Justice Rutledge:[50]

> In discussing *Freeman v. Hewit* with him, I questioned the preference for the state of market and suggested the superior interests of the state of origin, on the various grounds that its resources of

materials and labor were incorporated in the commodity and often depleted to the extent of the transfer, that the tendency of the preference was to a further colonialization of producing regions of the country for the benefit of those already favored historically by previous accumulation of capital (to an appreciable extent as a result of the Court's own prior decisions), and that the tax resources of the producing states were on balance apt to be more limited in quantity and variety than those of states of market. His answer was that the problem merited further consideration but that the preference expressed did not represent a holding and that the Court had not had the benefit of argument as to which state should be given the green light, a matter which could be definitely decided when it should be presented for decision.

The commission would have to reflect on the greater protection which has been accorded to business enterprise coming within the ambit of the commerce clause than has been given to the ordinary taxpayer. The latter is subject to multiple taxation on his intangible property, and so is his estate at death. After a period in which the Court endeavored to apply the "one thing, one tax" rule to intangibles, fixing on the taxpayer's domicile as the favored state, the Court beat a retreat and left the field open to multiple tax claims.[51] The practical situation is not as horrendous as the theoretical claims would suggest, in view of reciprocal statutes containing self-limitations, doubtless prompted by the fable of the golden egg.

Why should intangible property held by an ordinary taxpayer be treated differently for constitutional tax purposes than tangible property? Why should the Court's solicitude for interstate commercial enterprise not carry over to the individual who scatters his time and assets in a number of states? Is the difference to be inferred from the presence of the commerce clause? Does it reflect a judgment that interstate commercial enterprise is more to be fostered than multistate property-holding? Or does it indicate that the inner checks on the state are less dependable in the case of an interstate business enterprise than in the case of an individual who plans to establish his residence or to set up a trust fund there? Because of the doctrinal divisions between the so-called commerce clause cases and the so-called due process cases, these comparative issues of state taxation have been given less attention than they deserve.

Whether or not a federal commission is a politically feasible idea, and even without the rule-making power, the Court might well take occasion to reflect on the mass of particulars and essay a more philosophic treatment of these problems. There is strength in particularism, as the Court's work in this field has strongly demonstrated. But there is added strength to be found in a periodic larger view, restating objectives and assessing in a broad way the goals achieved.

IV

Thus far we have spoken of judicial review largely as a governor in clashes between local and national interests. Somewhat less dramatic, but perhaps even more pervasive in their importance for the ordinary citizen, are conflicts in the application of state laws to the transactions of daily life. The problem is familiar enough to the man on the street in the form of migratory divorce and Gretna Green marriages. But it lurks in most other events of life, from problems of family support when the members of the household have scattered, to issues of inheritance at death. Perhaps the chief formal instrument in the Constitution for the resolution of these conflicts of laws is the full faith and credit clause. Mr. Justice Jackson has said: "It was placed foremost among those measures which would guard the new political and economic union against the disintegrating influence of provincialism in jurisprudence, but without aggrandizement of federal power at the expense of the states." He went on to reproach the Court for the feeble way in which this ideal has been pursued: "Indeed, I think it difficult to point to any field in which the Court has more completely demonstrated or more candidly confessed the lack of guiding standards of a legal character than in trying to determine what choice of law is required by the Constitution." [52]

No one was more concerned than Mr. Justice Brandeis to maintain an efficient federal system, avoiding the duplication, friction, and uncertainty of unchecked state jurisdiction and also the nationalization of power and administration which is often regarded as the only alternative. Mr. Justice Brandeis saw in the full faith and credit clause a device for achieving the middle way. In a series of opinions he undertook to apply the clause as a limitation on the choice of governing law by state courts. In one case, he wrote the Court's opinion holding that the State of Georgia could not permit a widow to introduce in evidence the fact that a misstatement in her husband's insurance application had been inserted with the knowledge of the insurance agent, inasmuch as under the law of New York, where the contract had been taken out and the marital home had been situated, nothing outside the application and the policy could be considered.[53] In a second case, writing for the Court, he invoked the full faith and credit clause to preclude recovery by an injured workman under the law of the place of injury, where the workman had been hired in another state which made its law exclusively applicable.[54] In a third case, also writing for the Court, he denied the claim of a minor child to additional support after she had moved to a new state, where a decree of support rendered against her father at her former home purported to fix an unmodifiable obligation.[55]

It will be observed that in these cases Mr. Justice Brandeis rejected, almost literally, the claims of a widow, a laboring man, and an orphan. He was following implicitly the Biblical injunction addressed to judges: "Neither shalt thou countenance a poor man in his cause." [56] What is more relevant to our own subject, he placed the requirements of an efficient federal system above the humanitarian appeal of the specific case. Is there not reflected here the faith of a judge that humanitarian ends can best be furthered in the work of a constitutional court by attending to the structures and processes through which a democracy reaches for those ends?

Despite the efforts of Mr. Justice Brandeis, the Court has become relatively passive in meeting problems of choice of law by the states. Once more the impulse to criticize is tempered by the doubt whether the subject can be treated in any systematic and satisfying way short of legislative standards. Aside from interstate compacts, reciprocal legislation, and the like, there is legislative power vested in Congress to implement the full faith and credit clause. It would be a service if Congress would undertake a study of a few areas in the conflict of laws, as for example those relating to custody of children, divorce, life insurance, and corporate dividends.

In the meantime, the Court could do more than it has been doing to resolve some of these problems. To a large extent the choice of law by a state court is now free of constitutional review, unless the law applied bears no relation to the transaction except that it happens to be the law of the forum.[57] In most instances the controversy will at least be settled by a judgment, however questionable the judgment may be, and there will have been an opportunity to present the choice of law problem to the state court for its decision. But in some instances, because all the interested parties cannot be brought before a single court, the freedom of the states to choose the applicable law may result in multiple liability in successive lawsuits. This has been true in the case of controverted domicile as a basis for state inheritance taxes,[58] and it may well be true in the case of state escheat of unclaimed securities, dividends, and life insurance proceeds.[59] It seems also to be true that a state in which a corporation does some of its business is allowed to fix the standards for the entire financial structure of the enterprise as a condition of doing local business, or to apply its own law of dividends, thus in effect subjecting the corporation in its total activity to the highest standard set by any of the states in which it conducts business.[60] This is a kind of inverted Reno. There are obvious reasons why the technical domicile of a tramp corporation should not be allowed to set the standard for transactions affecting creditors elsewhere; but the protections which a state may claim in respect of the business conducted locally should not be unlimited in their out-of-state effects.[61]

When we turn to devices whereby the states and the national government have arrived at an accommodation of interests, nothing but praise can be given to the Court for the hospitable way in which these measures have been received. Federal statutes implementing state laws by allowing the latter to operate on goods brought into the state under interstate sales could have been viewed with hostility on a number of grounds: that the federal statutes unlawfully delegate power to the states, that the statutes were not a uniform regulation of commerce, or that since the Constitution expressly provided for congressional consent in certain matters such as state taxation of imports and exports, the maxim *expressio unius* precludes consent under the commerce clause. Fortunately, these theoretical objections have not prevailed.[62] Nor have barriers been erected to other co-operative devices such as the federal tax and credit, a most useful mechanism for assuring certain minimum standards on the part of the states while allowing marginal and experimental differences and local administration.[63] The device of the tax and credit has surely not been exhausted in its application to the problems of federalism.

There are those who maintain that federalism is a mystic concept which misses the real problems of man and the state, the problems of who gets what and how, and how quickly. But no man was less mystic in these matters than Mr. Justice Brandeis, whose concern for federalism was a governing passion in his work as a judge. In order to accept the complexities and face the perplexities raised by a federal system one must have a certain faith in the rightness and efficacy of means as well as ends. One must be aware of the importance of process and structure in developing disciplined thinking, manageable responsibility, and accountability for public power brought to bear on one's fellows. Within that structure and through those processes the great ends of government are to be sought. A constitution cannot guarantee happiness but only some of the conditions for the pursuit of happiness. Federalism, whether in the institutions of government, of business, or of education, is mystic only if procedures for the release and discipline of human power are mystic.

The close of this discussion must revert to its beginning, to Robert Benchley and the fish-eye view of maritime affairs. This discussion, all too regrettably, has been conducted on the juridical rather than the piscatorial level. Some years ago Oscar Wilde wrote a study entitled "The Soul of Man under Socialism." We still await a study on The Soul of Man under Federalism.

V.
REVIEW AND BASIC LIBERTIES

by John P. Frank

I. INTRODUCTION

A JUDICIAL OPINION interpreting a constitution or a statute may be appraised in terms of its faithfulness to the purposes of those who drafted the document, or in terms of its logic, or in terms of its consequences. One hundred and fifty years ago, John Marshall for the Supreme Court declared the American doctrine of judicial review of the validity of acts of Congress. While his logic has been exposed to much scholarly criticism, his faithfulness to the historic design of the Constitution seems so well established as to be no longer a fruitful subject of discussion. That Marshall's result was in accord with the Constitution's plan makes his detailed steps unimportant.

Marbury v. Madison, in this view, was inevitable. It did not create, it recognized the American plan of review of congressional acts. The real task of scholarly thought at this late date is to appraise not the history or the logic of Marshall's opinion, but the consequences of this judicial function in American life. We have lived under the system for a century and a half, and we may fairly examine whether we like it, and whether it needs any improvements, basic or slight.

In this discussion, I will cling closely to certain partially self-imposed jurisdictional limitations in my own subject matter in the belief that one precise problem needs close attention. That precise problem is the relation of judicial review to civil liberty, to the rights of free speech, press, religion, assembly and to the great procedural rights of the Constitution. For this purpose, the term judicial review is to be given the narrowest of several available constructions. To emphasize this narrow construction, the term "pure judicial review" will occasionally be used. It will mean here no more and no less than what was involved in the *Marbury* case, that is, review by the Supreme Court of the validity of acts of Congress. This excludes several matters commonly included as within the meaning of the term. Specifically excluded are (a) review of acts of Congress by tribunals other than the Supreme Court, which is put aside as quantitatively insignificant; (b) review by the Supreme Court of state legislation, which is based on the Constitution's supremacy clause quite apart from *Marbury v. Madison*; and (c) review by the Supreme Court of executive action. The excluded matters will be discussed only where they bear on review of the validity of federal legislation.

II. USES OF THE POWER

A. *Invalidations*

The most obvious measure of judicial review is in the instances where it has been used. Here, so far as civil liberties are concerned, the balance is if anything against judicial review.

Using Mr. Warren's list [1] brought up to date, there have been 78 instances of invalidations. Of these, the overwhelming bulk had no direct bearing on basic liberties. They dealt, as *Marbury v. Madison* did, with distribution of the powers of government or, as for example in *Adkins v. Children's Hospital*,[2] with economic matters. A numerical breakdown will make the point:

Distribution of All Invalidations

Cases unrelated to basic liberties		59
Holdings aiding liberty	3	
Holdings limiting liberty	8	
Holdings peripheral to civil liberties	8	
Total cases bearing on basic liberties		19
		78

The eight peripheral cases are those which involve civil liberties either of a minor sort or in a minor way, and are decisions which could fairly well have gone either way without greatly affecting the course of the republic. Three involve minor points of criminal administration in the District of Columbia,[3] and a fourth relates to the type of jury required in Alaska.[4]

The other four of these peripheral cases are somewhat more substantial. *Tot v. United States* [5] involved a point as to permissible presumptions in criminal statutes, and the *Cohen Grocery* [6] case made a contribution to the requirement of definiteness in statutes. *Boyd v. United States* [7] and *Counselman v. Hitchcock*,[8] the remaining two of this group, have helped shape the law of searches and seizures and of self-incrimination. Some sense of the long-term significance of these eight cases may be suggested by the fact that in Professor Dowling's excellent casebook, which cites or quotes some 1,200 cases, only two of them are mentioned at all, and those two only in passing. Consideration of the same eight cases in my own book is equally casual. Emerson and Haber, whose book deals exclusively with civil rights, index 1,300 cases, but quote only one of the eight cases alluded to in this discussion.

However, testing constitutional significance by what seems in our own generation worth calling to the attention of law students may be too brutal a standard; by that test there is not a single case of real consequence in which, in 160 years, judicial review has buttressed liberty. This includes the three cases listed above as "holdings aiding liberty," for none of the three is identified, except in a minimal way, either by Professor Dowling or by me.

Here is that group: *Ex parte Garland*,[9] a distinctly benign holding invalidating the test oath for lawyers after the Civil War. One of its largest practical results was to retain for the country the services of Mr. Garland, an outstanding lawyer and, later, Attorney General. A second case was that of *Wong Wing*,[10] a holding giving some procedural rights to aliens; specifically the holding prohibits imprisonment of aliens at hard labor without judicial process. (It should be noted in passing that a subsequent decision permits their imprisonment, without bail, for protracted periods pending hearing, largely on the say-so of the Department of Justice.[11]) A third case, the most recent, is that of Messrs. Watson, Dodd, and Lovett,[12] whom Congress attempted to strike from all present and future government employ-

ment by name. The Court, going back to the *Garland* case as a
precedent, held the congressional effort a bill of attainder. The holding was undoubtedly of substantial importance, for Congress regarded
the naming of the three as a test case, and would undoubtedly have
followed with further proscriptions had the door been left open by
the Court.

Against these blows in behalf of basic liberties, specialized as they
are, must be balanced prodigious counterblows. In eight cases the
Court's holdings, putting aside any issue of how good their constitutional law may have been, had the effect of limiting liberty. Concededly, this is a matter of interpretation. What one reader thinks limits
liberty, another may think extends it. Let me put it this way: Most
students north of the Mason-Dixon line and many students south of
it will think that the decisions now under discussion limited, rather
than extended, basic liberties.

This group begins with Dred Scott's case,[13] declaring that Congress
could not preclude slavery in the territories. The other seven cases are
all invalidations of legislation passed primarily for the protection of
Negroes under the Civil War Amendments. The leading three of
these cases include, first, *United States v. Reese*,[14] holding invalid
under the Fifteenth Amendment a statute forbidding state election
officials from keeping "any citizen" from voting. The second was
United States v. Harris,[15] holding the punishment of a lynch mob
beyond the federal power. The third is the *Civil Rights Cases*,[16] which
held that Congress could not use Fourteenth Amendment powers to
prevent private acts of racial discrimination.

On the basis of this brief enumeration, this much seems inescapable: If the test of the value of judicial review to the preservation of
basic liberties were to be rested solely on consideration of actual
invalidations, the balance is against judicial review. On the benefit
side lie abolition of the test oaths after the Civil War, the benefit to
aliens from Wong Wing's case, and the repudiation of congressional
proscription lists. On the loss side, still using benefit to liberty as the
sole test, is the destruction of what was intended to be comprehensive
legislation to give some measure of equality to the vast number of
Negroes in our midst.

This conclusion by no means requires the further conclusion that judicial review is valueless to basic liberties. What it does mean is that the case for judicial review must be made, if any can be made, on some basis other than consideration of the Court's direct use of its power.

B. *The Court in the flow of history*

The same result is reached if the Court is studied in terms of the general trends of American history. Neither the spirit of liberty nor the spirit of repression is ever totally absent from the American scene. From time to time, one or the other achieves sufficient dominance to provide the basis for a cyclical interpretation of the history of liberty in America. If I may repeat here a theory often advanced before, the cycle of liberty and repression is, in some superficial respects at least, similar to the more familiar economic cycle of prosperity and depression. To accentuate the similarity of form, we may use as a parallel to the economic term, depression, the term "repression" to symbolize the downsweeps in this cycle. It may be noted in passing that repressions usually occur at the opposite end of an economic cycle from a depression—our repressions are frequently concomitants of prosperity.

The term "repression" may be defined thus: It is an intense spasm of social fury in which a commonly latent impulse to destroy opposition without regard to the norms of democratic behavior becomes a dominantly conspicuous element in the American scene. It normally results in some destruction of opposition, and, to date, has always been followed by a period of renewed affection for democratic values.

The most striking fact in the relation of the history of repressions to the history of judicial review in particular or to the Supreme Court in general is that no direct action by the Court has ever had any significant bearing in either *stopping* or *slowing* a repression. I am not speaking here of the effects of the Court's decisions in moments of calm upon our conduct in moments of frenzy, nor of the effects of individual expressions by particular Justices, but solely of the effect of the Court at the storm center during the storm. This may be illustrated tabularly, including for this purpose every kind of judicial review no matter how broadly considered:

Supreme Court Response to Repressions

EPISODE	JUDICIAL RESPONSE
Alien and sedition scare, 1795–1801	None called for
Anti-Masonry, ca. 1830	None called for
Climax of nativism, ca. 1850	None called for
Anti-anarchism 1880s–90s	No restraint
Espionage and Bolshevik flurries, 1917–27	No restraint
Contemporary repression, at pinnacle 1946—	No restraint [17]

If the foregoing is true as to the action of the Court in all fields, including review of state laws, review of the executive, and interpretation of statutes, it is *a fortiori* true of the more narrow judicial review. The bald fact is that, except for the very narrow points involved in the *Garland* and *Lovett* cases, Congress has never yet passed a statute in a fit of repression which the Supreme Court has invalidated. On the contrary, except for the very special and unusual reaction after the Civil War (excluded from this Table because of its unique circumstances), the Court has stamped the repressionist acts as "Approved." The dominant lesson of our history in the relation of the judiciary to repressions is that courts love liberty most when it is under pressure least.

One is compelled to conclude again that if judicial review has had any wholesome effect on the basic liberties of Americans, that effect must be found elsewhere than on the occasions of the direct exercise of the power.

III. THE INTERACTION OF JUDICIAL REVIEW AND NON-CONGRESSIONAL INTERFERENCES WITH LIBERTY

In a familiar passage, Mr. Justice Holmes said, "I do not think the United States would come to an end if we lost our power to declare an Act of Congress void. I do think the Union would be imperiled if we could not make that declaration as to the laws of the several states." [18]

This statement, as it seems to me, is sound in both its halves. It does, however, suggest a completeness of disjunction between these two types of judicial review which could be misleading. At the beginning of this chapter I excluded from consideration the Supreme

Court's review of executive action and of state legislation, except insofar as they *must* be commingled with discussion of "pure" judicial review; but there is an area in which they cannot be separated.

There is in fact a dual interaction between pure judicial review, or review of acts of Congress, and review of state action. This dual quality can be discussed separately, in terms of (a) the effect of judicial review on the states (or on the executive) and (b) the effect of review of state action on pure judicial review.

A. *Effect of judicial review on state (or executive) review*

The principal consequences of pure judicial review on review of state action are wholly psychological, rather than tangible, but they are immensely important. The very existence of the power of judicial review is the greatest single source of the Supreme Court's prestige. That prestige in turn gives the Court's decisions on state laws far more effect than they otherwise would have, and also greatly increases the self-confidence of the Court.

Prestige is not necessarily based on rational considerations. Veneration of the Supreme Court because it has the power of judicial review sometimes approaches religious ecstasy. There is a spirit which shines even through the oddity of the figure of speech used in the *New York Sun's* memorable declaration after the Income Tax Cases, "Five to four, the Court stands like a rock!"

The great, the almost mystical admiration for this feature of our governmental system is unending; it is old and new. In the nineteenth century, Bryce described judicial review as one of the most admirable features of our system. More recently a Supreme Court Justice quoted *Marbury v. Madison*, and said, "Upon this rock the nation has been built." [19] And still more recently one of the leaders of American legal education described the case as "one of the most significant and dramatic developments in the history of our country" and Marshall's opinion as one which could "inject fiber and character into the irresolute nation." [20]

Whether these enthusiasms are warranted or not is outside the scope of this chapter, which deals with only one fragment of the whole of judicial review. What is important is that these attitudes exist and are generally shared, whether warranted or not, and their very existence has the broadest of consequences on basic liberties. The Court may be timid, it may be (as I think) unduly timid in standing up to Congress; but it has not been nearly as timid in standing up to the states or to the President. In these battles, the aura of prestige stemming from the power of judicial review undoubtedly aids its effectiveness.

It is not accident that the episodes of state or of executive defiance of the judiciary antedate the establishment of judicial review as a common practice. Today the President and the states largely accept the Court's mandates. Such episodes as the states' and oil companies' uproar over the tidelands decisions or the current attempt of South Carolina to frustrate an anticipated decision prohibiting racial segregation in its schools are so rare as to be almost freakish. The current acquiescence in judicial decisions is very different from the response of the sovereign state of Virginia to the cases of *Hunter's Lessee* or of *Cohens* [21] 125 years ago; or the response of Ohio to the decisions on its attempted abolition of certain bank tax exemptions; [22] or President Jackson's famous "John Marshall has made his decision . . ."; or Abraham Lincoln's defiance of Chief Justice Taney over the matter of Merryman. In those days, judicial review was not a workaday practice.

This is to say that the mere possession of the power of judicial review gives the opinions of the Supreme Court an extra prestige in wholly unrelated matters. The Court is a little like the multimillionaire whose opinion is asked on Paris art or the affairs of the world when he returns from Europe—perhaps his possessions should not give these extraneous opinions any added weight, but nonetheless they do. There is no way of knowing how much of the Court's prestige comes from its possession of the power of judicial review, but undoubtedly some of it does.

That prestige is directly useful to basic liberties. The libertarian decisions of the Hughes Court in the 1930s in such cases as *Near v. Minnesota, Herndon v. Lowry, Lovell v. Griffin,* [23] and a dozen other decisions were accepted by the states which received them in remarkably good grace. The invalidation of many forms of racial discrimination in the last several years, such as white primaries, restrictive covenants, segregated transportation and law schools, and restrictions on alien land use have none of them directly involved judicial review. Nonetheless each of them flew in the teeth of strong local sentiment, and the consequences of the decisions for good have ranged from at least a little to a great deal in the various areas mentioned. The acceptance of each of the decisions mentioned is, to some unknown but real extent, aided by the fact that the Court which made them had in addition the power of judicial review. One may suspect, though he cannot know, that the self-confidence with which the Court sailed into those tough problems was also increased by its possession of the larger power.

To a lesser extent this is also true of the relations of the judiciary and the executive. Whether the Steel Seizure case [24] involved a "basic liberty" as that term is being used here is arguable; but at least the instant acquiescence of the President may have been conditioned by his acceptance of the Court's power over acts of Congress. From *Ex parte Milligan* [25] to *Ex parte Quirin*,[26] in which the Court overrode without discussion executive interference with habeas corpus, to the Hawaiian martial law cases,[27] the Court has approached the problem of occasionally rampaging executives with a sense of power nurtured in part by its possession of the power of judicial review. In this indirect, but important, sense, the existence of the power of judicial review has contributed to the maintenance of basic liberty in the United States.

B. *Effect of state review on judicial review*

This effect is doctrinal. Since some parts of the Bill of Rights are equated to the "liberty" of the Fourteenth Amendment (or to the "privileges and immunities" of that Amendment), and since equal protection concepts can be read back into the Fifth Amendment's due process clause, there is no necessary doctrinal difference between review of some state conduct and some federal conduct. The clear and present danger concept, for example, originated in interpretation of the First Amendment, languished for a time in interpretation of the Fourteenth, was developed to some glory in the thirties and early forties as an interpretation of both, and then collapsed to its present toothless state in the fifties as a matter of interpretation of both.

Because of the interacting quality of the substantive doctrines used in judicial review and in state review, judicial review has these two additional indirect consequences to basic liberty. (1) Historically, it has somewhat raised the standard to which state laws relating to liberty, particularly to free speech, are held. Before the *Gitlow* case [28] there was no federal review of state free speech infractions, and but for the judicial review cases clustered around World War I, it is extremely doubtful that jurisdiction would ever have been asserted in *Gitlow*. That some good to liberty has come from the assumption of jurisdiction in that case is too obvious to warrant elaboration. (2) The existence of a reservoir of cases on state law enlarges the body of civil liberties law. To the extent that Fourteenth Amendment law and First Amendment law are the same, the mere existence of these state cases operates to give the Congress a few more hazards to circumvent when it would restrict basic liberties.

Let me enlarge briefly on this last thought by way of preface to the next section of this chapter. It has been seen that so far as direct consequences to basic liberties are concerned, judicial review has in fact operated as more of a drag than a protection to freedom. But the indirect consequences may alter the total picture. As one indirect consequence, the sheer existence of judicial review makes the Court more effective in protecting basic liberties outside the scope of judicial review. As another, judicial review has had the effect of fostering review of state intrusions upon liberty and of giving a doctrinal base for the inspection of intrusions.

But the greatest indirect consequence of judicial review, at least theoretically, might be its restraining effect upon the Congress. Whether Congress in fact is more moderate in its laws than it would otherwise be because of respect for judicial review is the subject next to be considered. But certainly the interacting quality of the two types of review materially increases the education of Congress. Before the *Lovett* case, if Congress was to pass a bill in the nature of a bill of attainder, it had to consider *Cummings v. Missouri* [29] (state review) as much as *Ex parte Garland* (pure judicial review). When it was passing the Smith and McCarran Acts, *Herndon v. Lowry* (state review) was as relevant as *Abrams v. United States* [30] (pure judicial review). One important indirect effect of judicial review, therefore, is that it contributes to the development of a related body of doctrine which may have the effect of restraining Congress in passing laws restrictive of liberty.

IV. CONSEQUENCES IN CONGRESS

Judicial review, even though it resulted in negligible invalidations or indeed in no invalidations at all, might have a very substantial effect on the legislative process, whether for good or for evil. Some of these consequences could be:

1. Congress might abstain from passing repressive legislation because of a fear that it would be invalidated—or, at a minimum, might eliminate some of the more repressive features of legislation for that reason.

2. On the other hand, the fact that judicial review is in the offing might cause Congress to abandon any serious constitutional consideration, passing the responsibility to the Court.

3. Judicial review might at least have the effect of slowing and sobering congressional action while constitutional issues are considered.

4. Judicial review might furnish the rhetoric of legislative discussion, providing useful symbols for debate as well as furnishing concrete information to legislators.

A. *Review and rhetoric*

The latter two of these possibilities, while important, are subordinate to the first two and will be discussed briefly. In this connection I have considered the legislative history of a series of bills which might be considered test cases, the Smith Act of 1940; the legislation of 1940 aimed at deporting Harry Bridges; the oath provisions of the Taft-Hartley Act of 1947; and the McCarran Internal Security Act of 1950.[31]

As to rhetoric, there is no doubt that judicial review has furnished much of the verbalization for our discussion of constitutional issues. For this result, however, judicial review was unnecessary. While judicial review was contemplated from the beginning, the power went almost unexercised until the Civil War [32] and yet, for the first seventy years of national experience, almost all issues of moment were debated in constitutional terms. A listing would only enumerate the obvious; indeed, the level of constitutional argument in Madison's Remonstrance on the Alien and Sedition Acts, or Lincoln's address at Cooper Union, or Binney's pamphlets on habeas corpus is, qualitatively, far superior to any recent debate by public figures on constitutional questions. There is a very serious possibility that by enmeshing great principles in the minute details of the case system, judicial review has rendered serious public discussion of constitutional questions less instead of more valuable; there is in any case no evidence that the quality of discussion has been improved greatly by judicial review. The great dissents are rhetorically helpful, but *quaere* whether on balance they are worth the cost.

Insofar as judicial review has increased the stock of constitutional rhetoric, it may be a misfortune. There are two angles to be considered: (a) the consequence of excessive attention to constitutionalism and lack of attention to the merits; (b) the related equating of constitutionality with merit.

As to the first, Chafee has pointed out the vice of discussion which concentrates excessively on constitutional factors. "What you are really saying then is that [a legislature] ought not to pass the measure even though they are not persuaded that it is undesirable. Whatever they think about it, the Supreme Court will annul it and so it will be useless. But this argument will fail unless you can convince your hearers that the Court will in fact be against the measure. In order to do this, you have to turn aside from the reasons about desirability which are part of everybody's thinking and *stick to the kind of language which lawyers use* [emphasis added]. You have to be absolutely sure of your ground, for if other lawyers (on the legislative committee or elsewhere) can raise plausible doubts about the validity of your constitutional position, you will get nowhere." [33]

For the reasons already stated, judicial review cannot be blamed for the American habit of debating issues in constitutional terms, with too little regard for the merits. That habit was ingrained long before judicial review became routine. But Chafee does raise serious doubt as to whether the lawyers' talk into which judicial review has pushed these debates has been an improvement.

The second branch of the subject is more serious; the practice of judicial review has tended to equate constitutionality with merit. No matter how loudly the Supreme Court proclaims that it is not passing upon the wisdom of legislation, validation is treated as an imprimatur. An extreme instance is the outbreak of anti-Jehovah's Witness riots which followed the Court's approval of the enforced flag salute.[34] The act of upholding a statute has a way, not always but very frequently, of ending debate on the merits; the syndicalism acts, once upheld, not only stay on the books permanently but become models for future statutes.

Without judicial review, we would experience the constitutional discussion, but there never would be a final resolution of the issue by a single dramatic act. Hence the debate on the merits would not so brusquely end. There are of course exceptions to what is being said here, but it is at least a reasonable hypothesis that frequently, as judicial review has worked in fact in relation to basic liberties, it has depressed the status of those liberties toward the lowest common level of constitutional acceptance.

As to whether the case law flowing from judicial review has slowed and sobered congressional discussion, a fuller discussion follows immediately below. Suffice it to say here that there have been few instances of a substantial sobering effect. In most, but not all, cases of serious constitutional doubt, the constitutional element of the discussion is ritualistic. Proponents of the bill under discussion arm themselves with legal opinions upholding constitutionality of the bill. These memoranda, written by leading members of the American Bar Association, may be introduced as a first point of business in committee hearings.[35] For most Congressmen, the stately opinions end all need for further intellectual ferment. When opponents of the bill arrive with legal memoranda on the other side, their statements will ordinarily be received into the record with politeness but without even a modicum of discussion.[36] Some witnesses may be questioned at length on non-constitutional matters; if they persist on a constitutional line, they may be assured that the Committee has a memorandum that clears everything up.[37] When debate reaches the floor, the prepared opinions may again be cited,[38] and only a minute fragment of debate time is usually consumed in a spontaneous discussion of constitutional principles. The serious consequences of judicial re-view, if any, lie elsewhere.

B. *Judicial review: legislative restraint or excuse?*

The precise problem here is whether judicial review operates on the one hand to restrain the Congress or on the other to give it a sense of irresponsibility.

This discussion is exclusively in the context of legislation restrictive of civil liberties. Everyone knows that judicial review may have a major role in some fields. For example, *Willing v. Chicago Auditorium Ass'n*,[39] by casting doubt on the validity of the declaratory judgment, slowed that procedural reform for years; and the Brandeis opinion [40] invalidating one Frazier-Lemke Act became a model for design of the next.[41] But there is no strong impulse to repress basic liberties except when emotion is hot, hotter than it becomes over procedural reform, or over bankruptcy or production control. In this respect, basic liber-ties might be in a special class.

The discussion must begin with the concession that there can be no assured conclusions. It must proceed into legislative history as its only available source, there to discover a pattern of words and acts. But no matter how much talk on constitutional points is found, not even the fiercest proponent of content analysis will claim that social science techniques can determine the motives underlying an utterance or the precise effect these symbols have upon the attitudes of others.[42] Systematic content analysis rejected, the analyst is cast back upon judgments via impression. His impressions may be based in part on (a) quantity and quality of constitutional discussion; and (b) osten-sible response to constitutional discussion.

(1) *Quantity and quality of constitutional discussion.* The legisla-tive history of the Taft-Hartley Act reveals only a single occasion upon which the constitutionality of the non-Communist affidavit require-ment for union officers was even perfunctorily drawn into question,[43] and this though Justices Murphy and Rutledge still sat on the Court. Nor was this paucity of consideration attributable to unawareness of the affidavit clause; the measure was fully considered, with a lengthy discussion of alternative proposals to reach past as well as present Communist Party members.[44] Yet constitutional power to enact the

provision was either assumed or regarded as an improper matter for legislative concern.

The famous advocacy-of-overthrow section of the Smith Act,[45] as another example, received only slightly more constitutional consideration in Congress. Direct references to constitutionality were made twice in the House [46] and once in the Senate,[47] and in all instances the debate was casual. One discussion ended with a disclaimer of opinion as to the constitutionality of his own bill by Representative Smith. ("I cannot tell . . . anymore when anything is constitutional or unconstitutional." [48]) In the hearings, discussion was equally negligible; one witness received a polite request for the citation of the *Gitlow* case from which he had earlier quoted.

On the other hand, the McCarran Act was accompanied by considerable legal discussion, although the arguments were not brought squarely in relation one to another, the two sides simply passing each other by. Concrete examples are discussed immediately below. The only legislative debate studied in which constitutional discussion took foremost consideration was in the abortive congressional attempt in 1940 to deport Harry Bridges by name. Here Congress was squarely confronted with *Ex parte Garland* and the related state review decision of *Cummings v. Missouri,* and there was abundant discussion of the relation of these cases to the bill.

When constitutional discussion does appear, its quality is extremely variable. Many Congressmen are not lawyers, and of those who are, many have only a remote acquaintance with the Constitution. Hence discussion may be ornamented with a good deal that is irrelevant, and some that is absurd. For example, the Senate managers of Taft-Hartley felt compelled to read to their colleagues a lengthy and citation-laden memorandum supporting the proposition that the union shop provisions of the bill were valid under the commerce clause—a matter not open to much dispute.[49] Helen Gahagan Douglas, a non-lawyer, solemnly predicted to the House that the whole act would be invalidated because in two Labor Board cases, the Court had said that collective bargaining was a good thing.[50] In a hearing on the Taft-Hartley Act, Representative MacKinnon took the unusual step of precipitating a free speech discussion with a witness, from which the following excerpts will give the flavor:

REP. MACKINNON: *You said there was a Supreme Court decision on Communists.*

WITNESS: *There have been several.*

MACK.: *Free speech.*

W.: *I think the most noteworthy one is the one defended by Wendell Willkie.*

MACK.: *I have read that. . . .*

W.: *. . . There is one I think that is interesting, the case of Whitney versus California, statement by Brandeis. He says: [quotation].*

MACK.: *What is the man talking about? Is that a majority or minority decision? . . .*

W.: *Well, a Communist was brought before the Court.*

MACK.: *The Whitney case is not a Communist case, is it?*

W.: *Yes, . . .*

MACK.: *That man was not an alien, was he? . . .*

W.: *No, I do not think so. . . .*

MACK.: *[Triumphantly, no doubt] The case that you were talking about that Wendell Willkie defended was the case of a former alien.*

W.: *The cases are not comparable.*

MACK.: *Exactly.*

W.: *But I think they are both relevant.*

MACK.: *[Goes on to a wholly unrelated subject.]* [51]

The point is that no amount of that kind of constitutional discussion could illuminate anything.

On the other hand, some constitutional debate in Congress is thoroughly cogent. Some of the best of it, for logic, reasoning, and authority, appears in leisurely filibusters on civil rights legislation. In the bills under discussion here, there was much sensible constitutional talk, particularly on the Bridges bill.

This much may be concluded as to quantity and quality: The quantity of constitutional consideration of legislation is irrationally unpredictable, and even where discussion occurs it may pass by the hard points to center on the obvious. Much of it is ritualistic, taking the form of statements put in the record simply as part of the routine, like the first and second readings of a bill. On the other hand, some of it is squarely to the point, as will be seen in the next section. Quality is uneven, varying from the silly to the acute. Insofar as the words reflect what is actually felt, one must conclude that for many a Congressman, the practical effect of judicial review is to create a mass of cases too large and complex to be digested.

(2) *Responses to constitutional discussion.* Responses of individual legislators to constitutional arguments are of three types, typified in the discussion of the Bridges bill:

1. The legislative buck-passer, *e.g.*, Representative Case: "This bill may be unconstitutional; the lawyers here seem divided on that question; the balance of us can only register the heart and mind of America on the broad question involved." [52]

2. The stickler for constitutional regularity as he sees it, *e.g.*, Representative O'Connor: "We have got something at stake here today much bigger than Harry Bridges. Of course, I will agree with my friend; I think he ought to rot. The gentleman is right. But . . . do you want your Constitution to become punctured with holes like this, by reason of which it will gradually be broken down. . . . The precedent we are establishing this afternoon will rise up to plague us in the future." [53]

3. The conscientious compromiser, *e.g.*, Senator Danaher, on a different phase of the Bridges bill, after a proposal of his own had been included: "I believe most, if not all, of my objection has been met, chiefly for the reason that if there be any question as to the constitutionality of someone undertaking to organize a society to overthrow the Government of the United States by force or violence, I would much rather err in favor of the public policy of sustaining the Government's right to protect itself than I would to protect the rights of an individual" of criminal intent.[54]

While the separate types may be identified, the insoluble problem remains as to how many of each type may be expected to be found in a Congress. The Bridges bill is a good test: How many men could be found who would vote *against* their convictions on the merits, because of constitutional persuasion? The excellence of the bill for purposes of this test is that a large number of legislators might reasonably have been expected to entertain constitutional doubts here if ever they would.

There were a few. Representative Dickstein rested on the constitutional point alone.[55] Representative Leavy, who had ten years of experience as a trial judge, pledged himself to vote for the bill if it could be revised into constitutional form, but not otherwise.[56] Representative Hobbs, remembered equally for his legal integrity and his passionate attacks on Communism, applauded the deportation of Bridges as a goal, but said, "I deplore, strongly, the proposed means." [57] And so with a few others, each relying on *Garland* and *Cummings*.

The bill passed the House 330 to 42, but its attainder characteristics were removed in Senate committee, and it was eventually enacted without them. The Senate committee's report makes clear that its action was heavily, though not exclusively, influenced by the cases.[58]

Here is an instance, then, in which well-defined Supreme Court decisions prevented a congressional relapse into the precise activity previously proscribed. But even here, 330 members of the House of Representatives withstood the clearest of Court holdings and the most lucid floor discussion.

As has been noted, in the Smith and Taft-Hartley Acts, the Constitution had not even rhetorical significance. Not so for the McCarran Act, which was appreciably affected by constitutional discussion. The effect, however, was of a sort quite different from that of the Bridges bill. In the McCarran Act the constitutional discussion went to perfecting details, so that the decisions became one vast map showing how the legislation could be brought safely to its designed end.

Some basic decisions may have been influenced by fears of invalidation. The House Committee report on the McCarran Act shows that serious consideration was given to proposals to outlaw the Communist Party outright, which were rejected because of "risk of [its] being held unconstitutional." [59] Provisions in the Smith Act concerning the outlawing of civilian military organizations were stricken because of "questionable constitutionality." [60] Apart from these examples, possibly important, there was little serious constitutional impact. For example, a provision that the Attorney General should determine an organization's Communist tinge read, "having regard to some or all of the following considerations," followed by a series of criteria. This was attacked as unconstitutionally vague, and was therefore redrafted to read: "The Board shall take into consideration the extent to which" the same criteria are present.[61]

The big constitutional debate in connection with the McCarran Act went to the so-called "concentration camp" provisions. As the bill was approaching final action in the Senate, it contained provisions for registration of Communists and for dealing with alien Communists. The following legislative history is exceedingly confusing, but appears to be this: The liberal bloc in the Senate, foreseeing the passage of the act, offered the Kilgore substitute, a provision which would have permitted the ruthless incarceration of "subversives" in time of actual war, but would have eliminated most of the other provisions of the act. Their move seems to have been intended as a tactic to defeat the peacetime provisions of the measure.

Foreseeing this result, Senators McCarran and Ferguson immediately opposed the "concentration camp" provision on a number of constitutional grounds. Senator McCarran pointed out that the substitute would amount to a total elimination of the provisions of his own bill, and that it would replace his bill with a thoroughly unconstitutional measure because (a) detention would be without warrant; (b) would prevent a speedy public trial; (c) would deny trial by jury; (d) would not provide for confrontation of witnesses and cross-examination; (e) would deny the right to process for obtaining witnesses in the detainee's behalf; and (f) might result in involuntary servitude.

The Senate thus observed the unusual phenomenon of Senators Kilgore and Douglas defending a bill against the charge that it invaded personal liberty, and Senators McCarran, Ferguson, and Mundt attacking the same measure on the ground that it violated the Bill of Rights. But once the Kilgore measure was defeated, Senator McCarran added a detention camp provision to his own bill.[62] On September 12, 1950, one day after he attacked the Kilgore measure as unconstitutional, he defended his own version as curing the defects of the Kilgore proposal.

The intriguing fact about the McCarran measure is that, while it cures some of the Kilgore defects, it denies several of the identical rights which Senator McCarran had found wanting in the Kilgore measure. He complained of want of trial by jury;[63] his own bill has an administrative procedure and no jury.[64] He complained of want of a speedy public trial;[65] again, his own measure is administrative and some of the evidence may be kept secret.[66] He complained of want of confrontation;[67] his own measure permits the Attorney General to withhold from the detainee the "identity or evidence" of witnesses and to put in "confidential evidence" when security requires.[68]

There is scarcely a blunter exposure of the Constitution as rhetoric rather than as substance than this McCarran Act history. For reasons of strategy, the liberals pushed a bill of most doubtful constitutionality; the conservatives opposed the bill on constitutional grounds and then within twenty-four hours were sponsoring legislation with many of the very vices they had just decried. In such a situation, surely the prospect of judicial review is having no effective bearing on the affairs of the Capitol.

C. Conclusion as to review and legislation

Measures restrictive of basic liberties usually spring from a strong legislative demand. With a preponderant number of legislators, the existence of judicial review has negligible effect on the demand except where outstanding cases are so directly in point that they are inescapable; even then, doubtful legislation may pass, as the Bridges bill swept through the House. Individual legislators will stick for constitutional principle, just as Representative Bingham, leading House radical, voted against the Civil Rights Act of 1866 because he thought it would be unconstitutional without the Fourteenth Amendment. But for a variety of reasons including simple want of understanding of legal refinements, the Binghams and the Hobbses are the colorful exceptions.

If we had not become a "judicial democracy," we might have become, in a sense, a "parliamentary democracy," with exclusive authority in Congress to interpret the Constitution. Whether, from the standpoint of liberty, this would have been for the best is arguable; there is no way of knowing whether greater responsibility might have gone with greater power. Before the Civil War, when judicial review was largely theoretical, constitutional debate in Congress was of a higher order than we now know,[69] but whether it was more objective and responsible is not demonstrated. In the great debate of the 1830s and 1840s over the right of abolitionists to petition Congress, the discussion was constitutional, but the final vote was sectional.[70] Perhaps most Americans from the beginning have subordinated their constitutional judgments to their substantive wishes—the point is not proved either way.

It is distinctly possible that judicial review has encouraged a tendency to congressional irresponsibility (a) by proliferating the law through so many decisions that Congress cannot be expected to cope with it; and (b) by giving an appearance of a judicial veto in the field of liberty when in fact there is almost none. The average Congressman would be surprised to know how little actual restraint the Court puts upon him. The repeated episodes of buck-passing exemplify Congress' refusal to trouble itself about legal issues in a comfortable, if mistaken, assurance that the judiciary will correct the worst errors.

V. APPRAISAL AND PROPOSALS

Have the civil liberties of the American people been safeguarded by the principle of *Marbury v. Madison?* Would our liberties throughout this century and a half have been more secure if the case had been decided the opposite way?

It would be better, for the sake of drama, if we had a clear answer to those basic questions, if we could say categorically that the great case had been either a blessing or a curse. We cannot, for a categorical reply requires too much speculation as to what might have been. As scholars and not as dramatists, we may reach no larger conclusions than these:

First, the actual overt exercise of judicial review of acts of Congress has been of almost negligible good to civil liberties, and has probably harmed those liberties more than it has helped them. The great inescapable fact is that in a century and a half no substantial restriction on liberty has yet been invalidated.

Second, the institution of judicial review has had the indirect consequence of increasing the Court's prestige and thus rendering it more effective in protecting basic liberties in instances which do not involve judicial review of acts of Congress.

Third, judicial review has been a vital and useful link in fostering helpful review of state actions.

Fourth, as a consequence of the third development, judicial review of acts of Congress has helped to create a larger, auxiliary body of law for the information of Congress.

Fifth, judicial review as an overhanging threat may have had the consequence of putting some restraint upon repressionist impulses of some Congressmen, and it has undoubtedly furnished a rhetoric for public discussion by those who oppose repressive measures. Whether, however, these values are overshadowed by the buck-passing irresponsibility which judicial review may have fostered in Congress, and by the unfortunate practice of debating public issues in terms of constitutionality rather than in terms of their merits, is not clear.

One need not conclude with assurance whether, so far as civil liberties are concerned, *Marbury v. Madison* is a social asset or a social liability to be able to reach a sixth conclusion: Any benefit to basic liberties from judicial review has been slight. The system of judicial review, as contemplated by the fathers and as expounded in *Marbury v. Madison*, has at the very best been a near failure.

For all of their prophetic wisdom, the founding fathers made some profound mistakes as to how the government they were establishing would work. The electoral college is a classic example. Judicial review in its relation to basic liberty must be regarded as a failure of prediction almost as great as the electoral college.

The founding fathers expected so much more of this institution than the event has realized. To use another list by Mr. Warren,[71] Sam Adams finally abandoned his opposition to the Constitution on the assurance that judicial review would prove a bulwark to the Bill of Rights. Jefferson saw judicial review as a most significant protection of liberty. Even that deadly critic of the Constitution, Patrick Henry, saw the judiciary as a shelter against tyranny. In a passage which must be regarded in retrospect as equally noble in intent and pathetic as prophecy, James Madison advocated the Bill of Rights in the First Congress with the words:

> . . . [I]ndependent tribunals of justice will consider themselves in a peculiar manner the guardians of those rights; they will be an impenetrable bulwark against every assumption of power in the Legislative or Executive; they will be naturally led to resist every

encroachment upon rights stipulated for in the Constitution by the declaration of rights. [72]

Clearly the event shows that Mr. Madison was seeing a mirage. Indeed, the mists cleared almost overnight and sober second sight set in. Within a few years, Jefferson was to realize that in the last analysis the ultimate protection of freedom can only be the people themselves, that institutions and even constitutions are at most rallying points. After the Alien and Sedition Acts were dead, Jefferson said:

> . . . [I]t is still certain that tho' written constitutions may be violated in moments of passion or delusion, yet they furnish a text to which those who are watchful may again rally and recall the people: they fix too for the people principles for their political creed.[73]

From the standpoint of historical analysis, it may be interesting and worthwhile to evaluate the worth of the institution of judicial review of acts of Congress, and to speculate a little as to the course of history if *Marbury v. Madison* had been decided the other way. But there is a larger, a more forward-looking question to be considered. At best, I repeat, judicial review is, so far as civil liberty is concerned, a near failure. Are there ways of improving it? Is it within the power of our generation, at this late date, to make of review of acts of Congress at least a little more of what Madison contemplated when his hopes were so high for freedom in America?

Let me state my conclusion first, and then develop it: I believe that Madison predicted the impossible when he dreamed of a judiciary which would be "an impenetrable bulwark" against the foes of liberty. We may expect something of judicial review, but not that much. At the same time, it is within the realm of possibility for the judiciary to come much closer to Madison's dream than, as yet, it ever has.

These are some of the basic limitations on the judiciary:

First, experience shows that there is not enough power in any five or nine appointive officials long to resist the overwhelming demands of democracy. When public opinion reaches the proportions of a tidal wave, no merely intellectual appeal can stop it. The fates of the Dred Scott decision, of the Income Tax Cases,[74] of *Lochner v. New York*,[75] of the decisions of 1935 and 1936 are proof enough. The judges have power, but not all power. In a democracy this is fitting and proper. The judges are not the pilot of the ship, they are its gyroscope; and their function is done if they keep us in some kind of balance. But for all this great limitation, the judges can slow the speed and soften the force of repressions. This is within their power, though they have never done it.

Second, the judges are human. They partake of the spirit of the majority, they are appointed by the representatives of the majority, and they may experience some of the same fears as the majority. The switch from the repression of the twenties to the liberalism of the thirties and back to the repression of today is, judicially, the switch from Chief Justice Taft and Justice Sanford to Chief Justice Hughes and Justice Roberts in the thirties, and the switch away from them again in the forties. By the time repressive legislation reaches the Supreme Court, we may expect that almost always some appointees of the repression period will be there too. If the judges have not a will to resist repression, then no mechanical or doctrinal changes can matter.

And yet one always hopes. Each of the concrete proposals about to be offered is a change that lawyers could make. There are doubtless others. If they were made, judicial review would still not be attempting the impossible. The mere re-assessment of these issues might do good, for they involve only legal accretions rather than fundamental, meditated social decisions. I suggest that the following proposals would bring us a little closer to the plan of the fathers:

First, a severe contraction of the area of non-justiciability. The doctrine of political questions ought to be fundamentally reconsidered and slashed to the minimum. When we find, as we did recently, that the political-question doctrine serves to limit review of the power of Congress to deport a particular alien under a retroactive statute making offenses out of acts which were licit when they were performed,[76] we need to take another look at the doctrine. Similarly we should re-examine the doctrine of the virtual unreviewability of executive power in wartime, especially when it is applied as it was to treatment of the Japanese-Americans in the late war.[77]

Second, there should be a complete revision of the doctrine of standing to raise constitutional questions where basic liberties are concerned. Particularly when the First Amendment is involved, there should be no necessity to show the kind of immediate interest hitherto required. Examples of what seem to me to be the wrong approach are *United Public Workers v. Mitchell*,[78] the test case challenging the Hatch Act, in which eleven of the twelve employees involved were held not to have standing to sue; and those dissenting opinions in *Joint Anti-Fascist Refugee Committee v. McGrath* which, similarly, found want of standing to challenge the subversive organization list. In sum as to this point, the whole law of procedure for raising constitutional questions should be reconsidered so that the Court, instead of avoiding the Madisonian responsibility of becoming an "impenetrable bulwark" against invasions of First Amendment rights, may welcome the opportunity to do its most magnificent duty.

Third, the doctrine of presumption of constitutionality should be completely eradicated in cases involving basic liberties. In that area, a presumption of unconstitutionality should prevail. In free speech cases, in particular, the Supreme Court has no business paying "great deference," or indeed any deference to the judgment of the legislature. It should do the exact opposite.

Utilization of the presumption of constitutionality reduces all constitutional issues to a question of "reasonableness" and then upholds the law if the legislature is found to have had any "rational basis" for its action. It would surely have surprised Madison to have learned, when he designed an institution to resist "every encroachment" on the Bill of Rights, that he had done no more than set up a psychiatric institute for an occasional grand inquest into the mental stability of the Congress. A presumption of unconstitutionality by which the Court puts under most rigorous scrutiny all laws restrictive of the democratic process is not in itself incompatible with democracy, but instead serves to further it. This was the position which Mr. Justice Stone suggested [79] and which he and other liberals on the Court have developed in detail.[80]

Some of the earlier restrictions of free speech were upheld by application of the presumption of constitutionality; the *Gitlow* case is an example. For a time, however, the theory of a counter presumption seemed on its way to establishment, but with the death of Stone and subsequent shifts of view, it slides farther and farther away. Recent decisions such as the *Douds*, *Dennis* and *Beauharnais* cases,[81] show that in matters involving free speech the Court is applying either the presumption of constitutionality or something very close to it. We thus have the legal phenomenon of the circular pass: Some Congressmen vote for a law in the happy reliance that the Court will give it close inspection, and some judges then uphold the law because, by presumption, Congress gave close thought to what it was doing. The result is that the primary responsibility for the protection of our liberties lies with none of our institutions. As I see it, if judicial review is to be anything more than an empty ceremonial, the judges should uphold a law restrictive of First Amendment rights only when they have been personally convinced on the facts that the law is imperative to the national welfare.

Fourth, the definition of criminal punishment should be thoroughly revised to keep the Bill of Rights abreast of the times. The Bill of Rights was aimed at the kinds of limitations on freedom which the eighteenth century knew. As a result, the procedural restrictions apply primarily to courts levying punishments in the form of fine or imprisonment. In 160 years, our society has devised numerous new methods, brought to a high polish in the past fifteen years, for punishing without the use of criminal sanctions. As Professor Carr says in his work on the House Committee on Un-American Activities, "There can be little doubt that certain witnesses before the Un-American Activities Committee have suffered and been punished in just as realistic a sense as though they had been placed on trial in a criminal court and traditional criminal sanctions had been invoked against them." [82] He cites as a good example the Hollywood hearings as a result of which ten witnesses lost their jobs.[83]

Another common example is the government loyalty program, in which a man can be, and many have been, ruined for life on the basis of proceedings which totally ignore the procedural guarantees of the Fourth, Fifth, and Sixth Amendments. And in the baldest fantasy of all, we are continually reminded that denaturalization and deportation are not "criminal offenses" and therefore criminal standards do not apply. An *ex post facto* law under which a pickpocket got a ten day sentence would be clearly unconstitutional; yet very recently the

Supreme Court has told us that this defense cannot be raised by an alien faced with deportation against a statute punishing him for an offense which he had committed more than ten years before the Act was passed, because deportation "has been consistently classified as a civil rather than a criminal procedure." [84]

This is not an argument that the Court should set itself up as a roving commission against evil, even in the field of liberty. Perhaps even if it recognized the reality of the "punishment" in the Un-American Activities investigation or in the loyalty program, the Court would still have some sound reason to stay the judicial hand. But these questions should be faced on their merits, and should not be sheltered from inspection by a hypertechnical insistence that constitutional safeguards apply only to devices used a half-dozen repressions ago. Just as the Constitution keeps pace with the counter movements necessary to meet each new economic depression, it should keep pace with each new period of repression. Seventy-five years ago in the *Boyd* case the Court had no difficulty in deciding that a particular administrative inquiry was within the protective scope of the Fourth Amendment because the potential financial loss to be borne by the businessmen involved was in the nature of a criminal punishment. The most famous line in Magna Charta pledges due process of law not only for him who is imprisoned or outlawed or exiled, but also for him who is in any other way destroyed.[85]

A fifth suggestion is offered more tentatively. It may be that we need a whole new legal doctrine on the constitutional permissibility of interference with speech and press. For thirty-five years the Court has been experimenting with the clear-and-present-danger concept. That concept, as expounded by Mr. Justice Brandeis in the *Whitney* case [86] and by Mr. Justice Douglas in dissent in the *Dennis* case seems to me wholly adequate. But it is possible that a formula that permits both the majority and the minority opinion in the *Dennis* case to be presented as sound applications of the same principle is too general.

The basic object of the clear-and-present-danger test is to allow great protection to free speech without allowing excessive protection. As it actually operates, we find that whenever it is applied by the Supreme Court in a period of repression, it never in fact allows any protection. Professor Chafee, the outstanding academic exponent of the clear-and-present-danger rule, alludes at one point in his writings to the "scores of men" who have been kept out of jail by the formula; [87] but he appends the names and addresses of none of them, and I confess that I cannot imagine who more than a few of them may be. While I would be wholly content if the doctrine as expounded by Holmes, Brandeis, Douglas, and Chafee might be applied, it is possible that, in the luxury of dissent, a few Justices might develop some new, more nearly absolute and hence less malleable theory. Since clear and present danger has been cheapened to a catchword by the *Dennis* majority, now may be the time for experimenting, for example, with something like the theory offered by Professor Meiklejohn; [88] and some of the opinions of Mr. Justice Black [89] may point in that direction.

Let me conclude by turning back to the role of analyst of facts and trends. I conclude as a fact that *Marbury v. Madison,* and the system of review of acts of Congress which it represents, has not been of any great significance to the civil liberties of the American people. Whether it has in fact encouraged or discouraged those liberties is a sufficiently close question so that no assured answer can be given; but certainly any good it has done in the field has been slight. Judicial review has fallen far short of what was contemplated for it by those responsible for the Bill of Rights. If the present trend continues, the institution 150 years from now may well, so far as civil liberty is concerned, have only a ceremonial significance in American life.

No system of judicial review can bring the millennium for liberty. Sober reflection compels the conclusion that Madison's generation expected too much of the institution they devised. But if the bar and the bench had a will to do so, they could lead America a little closer to James Madison's dream. The potential use of *Marbury v. Madison* is not yet wholly lost; it could still become a cornerstone of American liberty.

SUPPLEMENTAL STATEMENT AT THE CONFERENCE

FRANK: *In what has been said above, I have defined "pure judicial review" as review of acts of Congress and nothing else. My appraisal* has largely excluded all the other sectors of judicial review, such as review of the executive department, review of state action in any of its forms, and enforcement of procedural guarantees in the federal courts where the issue does not involve legislation.

Professor Cahn has suggested that it would be well to add a word as to the operation of judicial review in these remaining areas. The suggestion is surely a good one, not only for the sake of rounding out the discussion but also for putting the so-called "pure judicial review" in a better perspective. Judicial review has been far more effective and has made far more of a contribution to American life in these other areas than it has with respect to acts of Congress. In these areas, what has judicial review accomplished? Why has it been more successful than where acts of Congress are concerned?

The major area of success has been in connection with federal criminal procedure. Specifically, the guarantee of the right to counsel has been effectively applied. It may even have been broadened a little beyond the original purpose of the Sixth Amendment. It now happily includes the right not merely to appear with counsel but the right to have counsel appointed if this is necessary. The right to be free of self-incrimination has also been given substantial effect. The right to a jury trial, though occasionally circumvented in details which seem to me important, has on the whole been well maintained.

Less successful, but still not insignificant, has been the enforcement of the provisions against unreasonable searches and seizures. For a moment, in the case of Trupiano,[90] the Court held what seems to be the sound position, namely that search warrants must be obtained at least when there is a reasonable opportunity to get them. Unfortunately, this opinion was soon overruled. The Court has of late been far too generous in permitting the ransacking of a man's entire house in connection with an arrest. I should be astonished if any of my colleagues had a good word to say for the Harris case,[91] in which the Court upheld the police in going into a man's bureau drawers and tearing open his personal papers without any search warrant at all. On the other hand in the best of the Court's decisions in this area, the Weeks case,[92] it gave effective enforcement to the Fourth Amendment by refusing to allow illegally obtained papers to be admitted in evidence in a federal criminal trial. Without this disqualification, the

Fourth Amendment would be an empty letter. It would put scarcely any restraint on the police if they could make as much use of ill-gotten as of legitimate gains.

As it seems to me, the Court's largest failure in connection with searches and seizures has been its failure to respect the right of privacy. Its constitutional decisions on wire tapping, on dictaphones or detectaphones, and on the other devices by which the police in this technological age can surreptitiously invade the home, have lamentably failed to agree with Justice Holmes' view as to what is "dirty business." [93] The On Lee decision [94] is the latest in a long line of misfortunes. In that case, Dick Tracy came to the Supreme Court with a vengeance. You will all remember that great detective's wrist-watch radio which permits him to overhear the plotting of scoundrels at a distance. In the On Lee case a Narcotics Bureau stool pigeon wearing one of Tracy's little devices went to the defendant's laundry, engaged him in an incriminating conversation, and as a result the defendant's words were recorded by a distant agent and he was prosecuted on the strength of them.

It would be better if the police had read more constitutional history and less Dick Tracy. As Judge Jerome Frank pointed out [95] objecting vainly to this device, it smacks of the setting in Orwell's 1984, where Big Brother watches the individual's every move and reads his every thought via a "telescreen." I predict that as a result of this unfortunate decision, someone within the next five years will be charged with an offense in which the evidence will be a conversation at his own dinner table picked up by a guest wired for sound.

Such success as there has been in the field of federal criminal procedure is, I believe, due basically to two factors: First, the sense of power which the Court feels over subordinate instrumentalities; and second, the superb police work of the FBI. In part the yielding to unconstitutional practices, when this occurs, is due to a sense of necessity—a belief that there is no other way to protect society from the criminal. The FBI, with its well trained, highly paid staff, does not need to rely on forced confessions; hence there is very little pressure to permit it to do so. On the other hand, the federal police apparently do believe that they have a great need to go sneaking about with electrical gadgets, and so they are often permitted to get away with it.

The record on the state side is not very impressive. The right to counsel is clear in capital cases only; in the remaining situations, there is a serious absence of a good rule of thumb as to when lawyers are required and when they are not. As for forced confessions, the cases go off on tenuous factual distinctions at the very point when they ought to be most clear. This is the level of the law of the policeman's billy club. If the judiciary is to be effective in setting norms for the police, they must be norms so clear that the police can remember them when no one is present but the defendant, the officers, and the rubber hose. A sound solution would have been the extension of a rigorous rule against detention incommunicado, so that there would be little opportunity for police brutality. But this is clearly not in the cards.

Judicial review of state criminal procedure has been at its lamest in connection with searches and seizures. The case of Wolf v. Colorado [96] represents, I believe, the outstanding triumph of form over substance in constitutional law. The issues were: first, whether the prohibition of unreasonable searches and seizures was applicable against a state, and second, if so, whether the Weeks rule (which forbids federal courts to admit illegally seized evidence) should be used likewise in a state court to enforce the prohibition. The Court, after holding that the state was prohibited from engaging in unreasonable searches and seizures, declined to hold that the state court must exclude the illegally seized evidence. Since, as I believe, this leaves no effective enforcement at all, the decision is an empty gesture, announcing a requirement which does not have to be respected.

In respect to other civil rights, judicial review of state action has had some appreciable consequences. In most of the large matters, the states have been permitted to do about as they please—thus, the state loyalty programs have been upheld, with only technical limitations. On the other hand, the making of invidious racial distinctions by the states has been sharply limited; and this alone may offset many defects in the system of judicial review. But for the most part, the civil rights limitations on the states have been a collection of magnificent trifles. Handbills can be distributed, picketing is upheld (sometimes), there must be fair distribution of privileges of the parks, and sound trucks can be used (sometimes). By rulings like these, public tolerance of dissident minorities has been increased to a noticeable extent.

VI.
REVIEW AND THE DISTRIBUTION
OF NATIONAL POWERS

by Willard Hurst

To APPRAISE judicial review in any of its aspects is an elusive business. So many diverse factors enter in—formal legal doctrine, the technique of law men, political tradition and practice, and above all else public opinion. These factors make it desirable to look at the institution, as we do in this book, from a variety of points of view.

The practical influence of judicial review has been much exaggerated and importance has often been attributed to it for the wrong reasons. In particular, exaggerated attention has been given to overt clashes of power between the Court and the Executive or between the Court and the Congress, and too little attention to the background effect of the Court as a contributor to the symbols and ideas with which we conduct our politics.

We can get a more realistic view of the institution if we look at it from four different viewpoints. First, the process of defining certain essential terms will suggest important characteristics of judicial review. Second, if we look skeptically on the evidence offered to prove the importance of the institution, we will see better its field of operation. Third, an examination of the structure of judicial review, especially when matched against the demands of the times, suggests inherent limitations on its practical effect. Finally, if we ask ourselves what main shifts have in fact occurred in the relations between the major agencies of government in the United States during the past 150 years, we can then usefully ask what has been the role of judicial review in this evolution.[1]

II

What are we talking about, when we speak of judicial review with reference to the separation of powers in the national government? Who does what? To whom? How?

Judicial review, with reference particularly to the separation of powers, means judicial review in the Supreme Court of the United States. Since John Marshall set the tradition that the Court should speak through a single spokesman, the Court itself has emphasized its peculiar role as the authoritative voice of the Constitution. The famous "Judges' Bill," which produced the Judiciary Act of 1925, expressed the Court's own sense that it must win time so that it might adequately treat the important issues of policy brought to it. For this purpose, the act conferred very broad discretion on the Court to accept or reject cases it might be asked to consider. In recent years, by its own practice in handling "appeals," the Court has further contributed to saving its time for the significant policy cases.

In legislation protecting the Court's time against business of limited significance, Congress has recognized the Supreme Court as the unique agency of judicial review; it has endowed the Court with full discretionary control of its docket; and it has expedited review of lower federal court decisions of a constitutional character. From an early time, appointments to the Supreme Court, as compared with those to the lower bench, have been made with prime reference to the policy views of prospective nominees as well as to their supposed representation of sections and interests.

Most important, within the last seventy-five years public opinion has identified the Supreme Court peculiarly with the function of judicial review. This was reflected when opinion rallied to the Court in the 1937 "Court packing" fight. Plainly, a considerable opinion viewed the Court's independence as essential to a desirable balance of power within the federal government.

Of course, the lower federal courts have practical importance in the operation of judicial review. On the level of tactics, the middle

1930s showed how federal policy and administration could be brought to a standstill by a flood of injunctions in lower federal courts pending review by the Supreme Court. Timing is often of the essence in law and in politics; the practical power of lower federal courts to suspend the operation of a policy for months pending Supreme Court review can be of great impact. But this is tactics rather than strategy. Later we shall see how in this generation the lower federal courts move to a position of new influence in the operation of judicial review.

What is done in the name of judicial review? Formal theory is clear: It is the Court's job to declare the meaning of the Constitution from within the four corners of the Constitution; the task of judicial review is not the announcement of judge-made principle. True, of course, in *Fletcher v. Peck* [2] Marshall more than hinted that judges were entitled to enforce certain equitable principles as superior to legislative power. Mr. Justice Miller, for the Court, echoed this suggestion in *Loan Association v. Topeka*. [3] However, in *New York Central R.R. v. White* [4] the Court made plain that judge-made doctrine (even the most permanently established elements of the common law) in no respect limited legislative power; the mere fact that legislation departed from common law doctrine did not show that the legislature had acted unreasonably.

But of course we cannot rest with a purely formal definition which derives judicial review solely from "the Constitution." With a generation of the well-won battles of realist jurisprudence behind us, it labors the obvious to point to the breadth of policy discretion enjoyed by the Court within the broad constitutional terms which it applies. Less obvious, perhaps, is the extent to which policy of "constitutional" significance has often been made in the name of statutory interpretation. Measured by the intent of their framers, many statutes have in practical effect been ruled unconstitutional when the Court "interpreted" the words of the act in such manner as "to avoid a serious constitutional question." Interpretation, guided by principles of justice or fairness, has often amounted in effect to the application of policies of constitutional aspect. In functional reality, such rulings have been as much a part of judicial review as the decisions which the digests list under the formal heading of constitutional law.

What is the reach of what is done in the name of judicial review? The formal theory is that all that the Court does in the name of judicial review is to declare a rule of law applicable to the disposition of a particular law suit before it. This has been official dogma since Marshall. But it is perfectly plain that the substantial impact of judicial review, the reason why it has weighed in practical politics and in the working relations of official agencies, has been not only because of the immediate ruling in the immediate case. What has also counted has been the general expectation that doctrine announced by the Court will be followed by other agencies of government in other situations. There is ample evidence of this, for example, in the concern expressed by Mr. Justice Stone, in his dissent in the AAA case, for the effect of the decision upon the general authority of Congress.[5]

Only in the light of this general reach of judicial review do key aspects of the institution take on their full meaning. Herein is the importance of the assignment of opinion-writing to one Justice or another, and the tactics and timing of constitutional litigation. Hence it is that the Court has had such influence in shaping the concepts and symbols by which we measure the legitimacy of power in our politics. Rather than the overt clash of power, or the surveillance of the exercise of power, this symbol-making contains the deepest political reality of judicial review.

To say that judicial review has grown to include an expectation that other government agencies will heed the Court's reading of the Constitution, is to say that part of the history of judicial review is the behavior of agencies other than the Court. This behavior has not always been consistent. When he vetoed the Webb-Kenyon Act, President Taft declared that the President and the Congress ought to refrain from action the constitutionality of which they deemed questionable in the light of Supreme Court decisions.[6] On the other hand, President Franklin Roosevelt urged that Congress' job was to decide whether in fact legislation was needed in the public interest, and then with good conscience to leave to the Court whether the legislative action squared with the logic of previous Court decisions.[7] This is a colorful clash of attitudes as to the working respect which the other agencies should show the Court. But colorful instances need to be put into the perspective of the general run of things. Legislative draftsmen have sometimes shaped their work with an eye to the logic or the presumed temper of the Court; Congress has reshaped laws and put into statutes terms which it otherwise might not have used, in deference to its understanding of previous Court decisions.[8] For a full judgment of the practical impact of judicial review, we need to put such instances into perspective with the total flow of legislative business.

In what areas of policy does this institution of judicial review operate? First, it affects the workings of each of the major branches of government, the judiciary not the least. Of the last point, we have *Marbury v. Madison* itself to remind us.[9] Second, the Court has left itself freedom to define the aspects of government it will pass on in appropriate cases, and those on which it will not pass, however appropriate the formal shaping of the issue. This presents the vaguely defined area known as "political questions." This policy is one of the earliest, and it has been one of the most persistent, aspects of judicial review. It testifies to the strong practicality which has generally marked the institution.

It is not the task of this chapter to summarize the doctrine of political questions. The decisions under this heading have been of secondary significance for the division of powers in regard to domestic policy; they have been of prime importance in emphasizing the President's leadership in foreign relations.

It is appropriate to our subject to note that the doctrine of political questions has been shaped by regard to the most effective division of labor among agencies, and to the conditions of mutual forbearance and good will needed for a working minimum of government co-ordination. Doctrine has not often been formulated in these terms. But the cases suggest the Court's concern to avoid high-level conflict where the Court would find it difficult if not impossible to enforce its orders; the judges have recognized the limited facilities of courts to investigate and resolve issues of fact inextricably caught up in issues of policy regarding foreign governments; other cases reflect the practical importance of not upsetting public reliance on executive and legislative action which bears on its face the marks of legitimacy.[10]

The frontier of judicial review is in the area of its impact on non-official agencies of public policy-making, notably political parties, pressure groups, and the mass media of communication. There is no need to underline the extent to which the operation of these non-official agencies enters into the very fabric of modern government. In form, two familiar doctrines would seem to bar any connection between judicial review and these non-official institutions. The Court tells us that judicial review has to do only with the law found in the Constitution, and here we are speaking of agencies unknown to the words of the Constitution. Further, the Court tells us that constitutional limits are on official action only.[11]

But certain practical aspects of the policy-making history of the Supreme Court do not fit readily with this formal doctrine. The oldest of these trends concerns pressure groups, or "special interests." Sometimes the Court has spoken as if it were the guardian of some equity of the general welfare against special pressures which it has in effect judicially noticed as lying behind an act of legislation. In the name of statutory interpretation, Taney announced that statutes granting particular privileges, franchises, or exemptions should be construed strictly against the grantees. This, said Taney with a bluntness not often seen in the reports, was because the Court knew that usually the public was ill-represented in the framing of such grants; it was proper for the Court to supply the representation of the general interest which was probably not present in the framing of the legislation.[12] Doctrine developed under the equal protection clause of the Fourteenth Amendment has in some measure put judicial curbs on the influence of modern pressure groups. In effect the Court here offers the legislature protection against forces to which legislators may be especially vulnerable, and against which judges enjoy greater insulation.[13]

The mass media of communication are an important element in the modern balance of power. The Court has rejected their claim to a special status exempt from regulation. On the other hand, there is the continuing controversy of recent years, whether civil liberties, including guarantees of free speech and press, do or do not enjoy a preferred status of judicial protection.[14] Apparently it is too early to know the outcome of this latest dispute. But it is pertinent to note that this issue presents an aspect of the influence of judicial review on the division of powers within the national government. Finally, there is the matter of the political parties. The *Classic* and *Allwright* cases recognized the realities of party conflict as fundamental to the functioning of our form of government.[15] The Court's intervention there, to affect the conduct of party primaries in one-party states, extended its concern with the separation of powers to take account of a political phenomenon which the framers could not have known.

How does judicial review operate? The trial of a constitutional issue is not the same as the trial of other issues in our system. Elsewhere in this book consideration is given to the special techniques of the trial of constitutional questions, and I shall not go into the subject here. However, it is relevant to this chapter to note that no phase of the special techniques of the trial of constitutional issues can be separated from the problems and policies involved in the relations between the branches of government. The evolution of a peculiar technique for the trial of constitutional issues, which has become one of the most marked characteristics of judicial review, is itself an important aspect of the relation of judicial review to the separation of powers. It involves a body of self-limiting doctrine on the part of the Supreme Court.[16]

III

How can we prove how far judicial review has in fact affected the working distribution of power within the national government? For reasons natural to the institution, it is hard to prove its actual impact. If a government is at all a success—and our national government is— major collisions of power among its several parts are apt to be the exception rather than the rule. One can spin logical patterns of doctrine from handfuls of cases well spiced with dicta. But in proportion as the actual instances of decision are few, one can be the less sure that his doctrinal patterns describe or predict any firm pattern of behavior possessing continuity and substance. Take the instances in which the Court has held acts of Congress unconstitutional. As one looks at the table of scarcely four score instances in which this has happened, the main thing that strikes the eye is how few the instances are in relation to the great volume of congressional legislation, and secondly what a rag bag of miscellaneous items they are, the bulk of them obviously of secondary importance.[17]

The more significant the collisions of power, the more likely—if only because top-level conflicts spell unusually complex policy issues —that the circumstances will be highly individual. Perhaps this is especially true where action of the Chief Executive comes into question. How far may the recent Steel Seizure decision [18] have important limiting effects in the future, and how far may its very importance in its day limit its practical compulsion on events of another day? How significant for the future was the Dred Scott case [19] except with regard to slavery?

The more significant the collision of power, the more likely that many variables are involved in the situation. How measure their comparative weight? Take the *Schechter* case.[20] Surely NIRA did not drop out of the national political picture because of the Court's decision. It disappeared because it had already lost public support and the backing of important interests.

The aspect of judicial review in which the Court has had the clearest effect on the division of powers in the national government has been in the definition of judicial power itself. Here is an area immediately within the control of the Court. Perhaps if the Court had asserted certain kinds of power, the other agencies would have contested its pretensions, and the Court might have lost. In fact, however, by declaring in the name of the Constitution that it would not claim certain prerogatives, the Court has shaped this aspect of the division of powers.

The Court's self-denying doctrines have touched all the main branches of government. From the outset the Supreme Court has maintained stoutly that the Constitution limits the judicial function to the decision of "cases" or "controversies." It has held to this doctrine against the blandishments of both the Executive and the Congress. Here is an area where fact and doctrine have coincided. An analogous item in the record is the Court's regard to limits on the enforceability and the propriety of judicial action against officials of co-ordinate authority, expressed, for example, in its refusal to enjoin action by the President.[21]

Regarding the substantive power of Congress, the Court's most categorical limit on judicial review was *Luther v. Borden*.[22] There it declared that the question whether a state possesses a republican form of government according to the Constitution's guaranty is a matter for Congress to decide when it admits the senators and representatives elected by the state. The history of the special techniques under which constitutional issues are tried enters also at this point. The "presumption of constitutionality" expresses the doctrine that debatable policy choice is entirely the business of Congress, and not at all the business of the bench. While the Court has many times in fact refused to give this measure of autonomy to the Congress, it has generally paid lip service to the doctrine. It came closest to expressing a contrary theory in 1923 when it accorded a preferred position to freedom of contract in the *Adkins* case.[23] But that is now ancient history. Of course, the current dispute concerning the preferred position of civil liberties presents a new chapter of this story.[24]

Both in doctrine and in practice, the Court has resigned to Congress the question of conformity to constitutional proprieties in the procedure of legislating. For example, it is not a justiciable issue whether the legislative branch gave adequate consideration to a measure before enacting it. The Court has ruled that there are no judicially enforceable requirements of notice or hearing prior to the enactment of legislation. And the Court has refused to go back of a duly enrolled bill to take evidence of even the most fundamental defects in the procedure by which the act was passed.[25]

Judicial self-limitation has also marked important aspects of review of executive and administrative action. *Luther v. Borden* [26] bears on executive as well as on legislative power; the Court's decision there indicated that it would be within the non-reviewable discretion of the President to decide on the use of federal troops to enforce the Constitution's requirement that a state have a republican form of government. On executive action of more general character, the Court has announced that the presumption of constitutionality applies to administrative legislation.[27] And where the Constitution singles out the executive for some special responsibility, the Court has shown great reluctance to intervene. This policy has resulted in defining as a political question the judgment of the executive in various matters of the conduct of foreign affairs, and has accorded the strongest presumption of regularity to the executive decision to use the troops.[28]

The Court has left legislative procedure to the legislature; it has not been willing in the same measure to leave executive procedure to the executive. True, the Court has now apparently finally barred judicial review of the state of mind with which executive or administrative officers do their work; the extent of consideration given to decision by an executive or administrative officer is probably now as much a non-justiciable question as it is in the case of a legislature.[29] But, on the other hand, due process of law presents an important range of judicially enforceable limits on executive proceedings. Significantly, the Court has shown here none of its usual readiness to mark out non-reviewable issues.

Cases concerning the division of powers within the national government fall into two obvious categories—where the Court has denied the existence of power, and where it has affirmed the existence of power. As to both categories, it can only be said that we have no sufficient histories of the other branches of government to tell us accurately what the net influence of judicial review has been.

There are the cases where in the name of the Constitution the Court has affirmed the existence of rightful authority—its own as well as the other agencies'. Would such authority not have been claimed or not have become operative but for the Court's pronouncement? Would it not have remained operative but for the Court's benediction? The "case or controversy" concept itself recalls us to the fact that the Court cannot properly initiate policy action. That an issue of power is brought before the Court means that someone else has already acted. Moreover, in this connection it is relevant to recall President Jackson's veto message on the bill to recharter the second Bank of the United States; though the Court's opinions indicate the existence of power, said Jackson, this does not relieve the Congress or the President of their responsibility to refrain from action which they deem unconstitutional.[30]

History shows instances where the Court's language in upsetting a piece of legislation has in effect invited a further exercise of legislative power. But the initiative does not rest with the Court. It lacks the power of the purse and the power of investigation, which are the essentials of rational affirmative action. These as well as the doctrinal considerations remind us that the Court, in the nature of the case, can have little effect in shaping the positive development of authority.

How much effect on the growth of positive powers have the Court's approving decisions had? Where the record is one of authority generally undenied or regularly affirmed, the influence of the Court seems to be merged with the general history of the times. Consider the delegation of powers doctrine, and the development of the administrative arm in the federal government. For nearly a hundred years, dicta warned that conceivably the Congress could overstep its bounds by making an invalid delegation of power to an executive agency. But over this whole period until 1935,[31] there were only affirmative rulings, sustaining congressional delegations of power. How much does that fact account for the growth of the administrative process, and particularly of delegated legislation? It is impossible to believe that the Court's permissive attitude was as important as the practical pressure of events. On the other hand, where power is affirmed after court opinions or dicta have long denied that the power existed, one might expect more obvious signs that the new judicial attitude encouraged action in other agencies. Consider the authority of Congress to regulate matters that "affect" interstate commerce, e.g., its authority to regulate "production." How far has the expanded use of the commerce power since the 1930s been due to the reversal of position shown in the decisions upholding the National Labor Relations Act? How far has the new reach of federal law been determined by the urgent need for national action to deal with problems of nationwide or sectionwide markets, and with the swings of the business cycle? [32] When one matches the permissive doctrine against the compelling facts, it is hard to assign priority of influence to the doctrine.

How does the evidence stand in those cases where the Court has denied the existence of authority in Congress, or in the President or in some executive agency? One test of practical judicial influence might be the public policy importance of measures which the Court has upset. So far as substantive policy is concerned, the record as to Congress is spotty. A few measures of prime importance in the life of the nation may be found in the list of the powers denied; one thinks of the Dred Scott case,[33] the Income Tax Cases,[34] the upset of the early New Deal laws.[35] But most of the few-score congressional statutes which the Court has set aside have obviously been of minor importance, the cases have been most heterogeneous in subject matter, and have in no sense presented an important across-the-board review of congressional activity. Denials of substantive executive power have been so few in number as to give little evidence of the Court's actual impact. One thinks of *Humphrey's Executor v. United States*,[36] but chiefly because it stands out by its novelty. Most of the Court's actions prior to the Steel Seizure decision upheld substantive executive authority; the detailed examination of precedents in the Steel Seizure opinion was devoted mainly to explaining why executive claims had previously been sustained. There was little in them to explain why in the instant case those claims must be upset.[37]

I have already noted that legislative procedure has been characterized by the Court as presenting non-justiciable issues. The absence of strong judicial guidance is particularly marked in the area of legislative investigations. On the other hand, executive procedure has been much affected by the Justices' case-by-case definition of permissible limits. The judicial influence is apparent in recent legislative definitions and regulations of administrative procedure, built on judge-made concepts. When one touches the history of judicially enforced limits on executive procedure, he finds the area where the evidence most convincingly suggests that the Court has had great restraining and shaping influence.

Another test of the significance of judicial restrictions upon other agencies of government might be in terms of duration. When the Court has denied claims of power by other branches, how long has the denial held? If one catalogues important judicial barriers that have stood for more than ten or fifteen years, the list is very small. Shall we cite the Child Labor case? But the Lottery cases and the decisions sustaining the Webb-Kenyon Act in effect denied much of the apparent scope of the Child Labor decision.[38] Shall we cite the Income Tax decision? [39] But that was overruled by constitutional amendment within twenty years of its announcement. The outstanding instance would seem to be the decisions restricting the scope of the Civil War Amendments' grants of substantive power to Congress.[40] The drama of the Court's dealings with the Civil War Amendments immediately suggests a modern analogy—the conflict over New Deal legislation in the years 1934–1936. In limiting the Fourteenth Amendment to regulation of official action, the Court squarely vetoed the intention of the framers of the Amendment, yet the bold judicial action has stood for seventy-five years. Then how explain that in the 1930s the Court's veto on using national power against the downswing of the business cycle lasted barely two terms? The contrast surely turns on timing. What the Court did to the Fourteenth Amendment did not accord with the earlier intentions of Thaddeus Stevens, but it did accord with the dominant policy of the generation in which the action was taken. Men were tired of refighting the Civil War; the new leaders of the Republican Party wanted reconciliation with the South, which would allow them to get ahead with their main interest, the industrial and financial development of the country. In contrast, the Court's decisions of the middle 1930s ran counter to very deep shifts in popular values. The contrast points up the quite limited scope of the Court's practical influence in denying large and urgent demands of policy.

But, it may be argued, one could make an impressive catalogue of legislative and executive action withheld out of fear of, or deference to, the Court's rulings. One could instance again the veto of the Webb-Kenyon Act, in which President Taft announced the duty of withholding action which seemed to run against the logic of Court opinions.[41] However, isolated incidents like the Taft message tell nothing of the whole picture. As one looks at the responses of legislation to public pressures of the past seventy-five years, it is hard to list examples of any strongly desired action which was not taken because of barriers assumed to exist in judicial doctrine.

Implicit in any weighing of the importance of judicial review is a comparison with other modes of judicial influence. Two aspects of the Court's work are particularly germane to the comparison. First, the Court's influence on the working procedures of the executive branch has undoubtedly been exerted in part through its supervisory power over the lower federal courts, particularly in matters of admitting or excluding evidence in criminal trials. For example, the Court has passed on the admissibility of illegally obtained evidence and has established the so-called *McNabb* rule excluding confessions obtained during an excessive detention prior to arraignment.[42]

Secondly, the Court has influenced the development of public policy through statutory interpretation. As one looks at the lasting effects of judges' interpretation of legislation in fixing lines of public policy, one wonders why judicial review should be considered the pre-eminent realm of judicial influence. Statutory interpretation has been the channel for substantive policy decisions which, in character and weight, cannot be distinguished from pronouncements made in the name of the Constitution. For example, take the *Louisville & Nashville Railroad* case [43] with its declaration that trade unions enjoying the support of federal law must accord equal rights regardless of race to claims by all labor falling within their fields. If one measures judicial impact by how long it lasts, consider *Caminetti v. United States.*[44] The Supreme Court there interpreted the Mann Act to cover conduct (transporting a woman across state lines for the purpose of concubinage, not of prostitution) which its framers clearly had not intended it to reach. Yet, once the decision was made, as a matter of practical politics it became as fixed as any doctrine of constitutional law that one can name. No organized pressure group exists to press for correction of the interpretation; no congressman will put himself in the ambiguous position of urging amendment of the Mann Act to withdraw federal enforcement from the enlarged area to which the *Caminetti* case committed it. Such examples suggest that more convincing evidence can be marshalled to show significant judicial impact on policy through statutory interpretation than through judicial review.

IV

We can learn other things about judicial review by reminding ourselves that we are talking of action by a court. I am not now speaking of features peculiar to the trial of constitutional issues, such as the presumption of constitutionality, but rather of the ways in which the very function and structure of a court affect the force of judicial review.

By nature, courts are passive agencies; they do not go out looking for trouble, but sit tight and wait for parties to bring trouble to them. Second, their job limits their consideration of issues to the matters crystallized before them in the shape of "parties," and to those issues which parties present to them. Not only do the parties define the issues, but they largely determine the evidence on which the issues will be considered. Finally, tradition sharply limits the means by which courts may deal with issues; their tradition limits them chiefly to negative sanctions, and this is markedly true of judicial review.

These working characteristics of courts must be weighed in the light of the demands which events have made on the institutions of government, particularly in the last seventy-five years. So weighed, these working characteristics do not seem to fit the times in such a way as to have offered the Court much opportunity to influence the division of power through judicial review.

Change has pressed hard on us, and with accelerating tempo since 1850. When change is so much to the fore, influence naturally goes to agencies that can take the initiative and go out to meet events. In contrast to the limits of the judicial tradition, the legislative branch has possessed incomparable assets in the powers of the purse and of investigation. Though lacking ultimate control of the purse, the executive has possessed wide and rich sources of information out of which to detect the existence of trouble, to define issues, and to shape means of dealing with them. Tradition gives it a legitimate initiative in public affairs.

In a time of overshadowing change one can predict that judicial review will have little effect on many great emerging issues. Take, as one example, the problem of civil control of the military, which bids fair to assume unique significance in our generation. The President's recall of General MacArthur was a more potent precedent for the assertion of civil control of the military than any likely to come from the Court in our time. The Court's opportunity in this field is mainly to create and enrich the symbols of legitimate power. This it did in *Ex parte Milligan* [45]—though, it must be noted, after events had abated their urgency. It is impossible not to contrast the example of the *Milligan* case with the lost opportunity of the suits [46] that came out of the "relocation" of Japanese-American citizens on the West Coast in World War II.

The control of the flow of information seems likely to be a crucial issue in the evolution of civil-military relations in our time. This will be partly a tug-of-war between legislative control of purse and policy, and executive power derived from the intricacy of data and claims of the need of secrecy in the interest of security. The outcome will be shaped mainly by the pull and haul of these conflicting claims of power as worked out in appropriation legislation and congressional investigations on the one hand, and on the other in the operations of government contracting and security officers and the day-to-day policy conferences in the Department of Defense. It is hard to see how courts can play a significant role here, unless in an occasional criminal prosecution arising out of mishandling of official secrets; in the nature of the case this would be likely to present not only a limited, but also a very belated, opportunity to affect the situation.

Beside the range and tempo of change, another mark of our times is the intricacy of the cause-and-effect networks in the human relations problems with which we deal. Perhaps cause and effect work no more intricately now than in the nineteenth or the eighteenth century; perhaps it only seems so, because we feel pressed to make more conscious efforts to order events and, hence, are more conscious of their intricacy. But whatever the comparison in time, the complex interdependence of events stands out as a prime factor in the matters with which government must deal. Against this, we must match the limitation of judicial proceedings to issues definable by the interests of parties engaged in a formal law suit, and to data those parties bring into the record. Here again, there is no greater testimony to the inherent limitations of judicial process than the self-limiting doctrines and techniques which the Court has emphasized in the last generation.

Herein is the significance of the narrow range of judicial scrutiny of legislative investigation. It is a reasonable summary of the scant judicial doctrine and the predominant body of legislative precedent, to say that there appear to be no judicially enforceable limits on the subject matter of legislative investigation; that, barring some Bill of Rights limitations (of which only the guarantees against self-incrimination and unreasonable search and seizure have been substantially tested), there are no judicially enforceable limits on the taking of evidence in legislative investigation; and, finally, that there are no judicially enforceable limitations on the order of procedure or the

dignity with which legislative investigations are conducted. Undoubtedly it would be unwise to have any large measure of judicial surveillance of these processes; there is imperative need for the investigating
power in its full scope and flexibility. But in any case, this is not an
area in which judicial review has played a shaping part; nor do recent
decisions indicate that the Court will attempt a materially larger
role.[47]

In the past, the "presumption of constitutionality" often appeared
in the decisions more as a ritual formula than as a working reality.
But during the past fifteen years the presumption of constitutionality
has expressed the realities of judicial review insofar as it affects legislative regulation of the economy. This dramatic change further reflects
a new judicial sensitivity to the pressures of events, which have
reminded the judges that fact-finding and policy-choice are primarily
the business of legislators, and that courts have only limited means to
match legislative performance.[48]

Twentieth century America is marked not only by the tempo and
complexity of change, but also by the high premium—indeed the
survival value—which events put upon our capacity for social invention. We confront not only great but also novel troubles. There is
more felt need for positive response and for efforts to channel, if not
to direct, the forces that play on society. Negatives, we feel, are not
enough; acquiescence is not enough. Yet, in its nature, judicial review
offers the Court only the opportunity to say "yea" or "nay" to what
others attempt to do.

Evidence that this is a real consideration of our times may be found
in the sincere and deeply felt support of many law men for the
"Court packing" plan of 1937. Why did so many men of good will
support this measure, with obvious distress that they felt it necessary
to do so? When one considers the policy objections to the proposal
and the strength of the symbols invoked against it, the puzzle is not
that the measure lost, but that it so nearly won. Back of the striking
support which the "packing" bill attracted was conviction that, because the times so urgently called for creative and affirmative policy-
making, there was a new responsibility put on the Court. The judicial
negative must clearly justify itself. Obviously, many felt that a majority of the Court had not measured up to their new responsibility—

indeed that they had fallen short to a degree that imperiled national safety, that the negativism expressed by a majority in key decisions of 1934–36 was, in the face of the depth and pace of events, an irresponsible use of power. Conversely, the general approval of the Steel Seizure decision of 1952 expressed a different judgment of the balance between the need for action and the desirability of restraint.

The issues over the social value of positive policy-making as against restraint of power are more sharply drawn in the twentieth than they were in the nineteenth century. Nineteenth century America seemed better able to be indifferent to social invention, and to ride with the current in the hope that all would be well.

After these rather negative views, realism requires noting also that the characteristics of the judicial process I have stressed give it a highly important job and a very real relevance in another area. Just because judicial review is designed to provide a forum for the initiative of aggrieved persons whose interests, defined in lawsuits, give them standing as parties, and whose grievances against the impact of law can be most often relieved by interposing a restraining hand upon the power of the law—just for these reasons, the judicial forum is the natural place to protect the individual in the fair application of law in an increasingly administered society. I have noted before that the case for judicial influence seems clearest in the limitation of executive application of the law to individual cases. So, here, it must be noted that those attributes of the judicial process which sharply restrict its effectiveness in the realm of general policy-making do not limit its capacity to safeguard decency in the application of law. To our age, newly sensitive to the possibilities of oppressive legal administration, this should not seem a lesser function.

In another aspect, the very existence of courts contributes materially to the balance of power. Inertia, a major factor in society, may defeat just claims of individuals or minorities; against a background of general indifference or helplessness, it may allow the majority or an aggressive minority to wrong individuals or other minorities. To get Congress or a state legislature to act, one must typically organize a pressure group or induce an existing pressure group to espouse the cause. But to get the courts to act—within the limits of their resources —one needs only a proper party with the means to sue. Though lawsuits do cost money, one may set the judicial machinery in motion with far less means and effort than are usually required to move a legislature. Within the framework of the judicial process, the litigant constitutes his own pressure group. Here is one branch of government whose resources he can at least bring into motion by his own unaided action.

V

Division of power is a matter more of practice than of doctrine. What may we learn about the role of judicial review with reference to the separation of powers if we measure it against the behavior of the major agencies of government over the past 150 years? What have been some of the main shifts in the powers and functions of the respective branches of government, and how far has judicial review figured in these shifts?

As concerns judicial review, there has been little important formal change in the definition of the relative roles of the agencies of the Federal Government. Only two items in the history of constitutional amendment have first-rate importance in this connection.

The framers of the Fourteenth Amendment aimed at a revolutionary extension of the substantive lawmaking authority of Congress. If the result had been as Thaddeus Stevens wished, it would not only have destroyed the federal balance but would also have enormously enlarged the importance of Congress compared to either the executive or the judiciary. The Court decisions which so radically reduced the effective scope of the Fourteenth Amendment form a unique chapter in the story of judicial influence on the separation of powers within the national government. Whatever the general economic, social, and political factors behind the North's turn away from the fervor of Reconstruction, it was the Court's decisions which crystallized the end of Radical Republican policy. Of course, since the Court had no practical resources to back up its decisions against stout opposition, its unique success derived from the timing of the effort rather than from any inherent force in judicial review.

The Sixteenth Amendment likewise aimed at a great extension of congressional authority. Indeed, in the light of later events it worked an extension as important in its way as that attempted by the Fourteenth. As we know, the need to have a Sixteenth Amendment testified to the blocking power of the Court; it was the decision in *Pollock v. Farmers' Loan & Trust Co.*[49] that made the Amendment necessary. On the other hand, the fact that the Constitution was amended within twenty years underlines the point that the negative force of judicial review is apt to be felt in delay, not in a final veto. If the *Pollock* case had fallen in a season when the Federal Government faced the imperative need of revenue that depression and war years were to bring, it is reasonable to suppose that the Amendment would have come more promptly.

The Sixteenth Amendment has in fact operated to give Congress the wider scope of authority which was intended. The draftsmen of the Sixteenth phrased it in the classic generic terms which have marked the great grants of constitutional power, like that under the commerce clause. The Court has played its part by recognizing the implications of this generic grant and giving them full scope. Certainly, however, the success of the Amendment is not unrelated to the fact of timing. Since the Sixteenth Amendment, two great wars and a depression have created demands for federal revenue on a scale undreamed of when the federal income tax was contested in the 1890s. These facts go far to explain the Amendment's success in increasing congressional power.

Among changes in the division of power within the national government outside of formal constitutional amendment, three categories stand out: (1) expansion of the general regulatory and service activities of the federal government; (2) fixing of central government responsibility for the over-all functioning of the economy; and (3) a relatively enlarged responsibility to provide for the national security against outside enemies.

One of the results of these shifts has clearly been an absolute increase in the policy-making function of Congress. With little exception the Court's role has been to approve the trend and to declare it legitimate. One thinks of the Child Labor Cases [50] as exceptions in the field of general regulation. But, except for the important humane aspects of these decisions, they seem on the periphery of policy. So far as concerns government's responsibility for the state of the economy, of course there are the great judicial vetoes of 1934–36.[51] But surely the historic point of these decisions is that their force lasted scarcely two terms of Court. And in the field of national security, judicial review has put no curb on the expansion of the power of Congress.

How weigh the creative force of judicial review in legitimizing this expansion of congressional authority? The question brings us back to ambiguities of proof already noted. Plainly the common note in all of these expansions of the functions of the Federal Government and its agencies is a response to deep-running currents of social change which proceed from far outside the formal law. Physical and social technology—affecting transport, industry, and distribution, and giving rise to broad, interdependent, sectional, national, and international markets—have provided one main base of change. Of course, in this connection, one recalls that Marshall laid the doctrinal basis for our single free-trade area, and in so doing asserted a great power both in the Supreme Court and in Congress to protect domestic free trade. But the initiative of change lay in the movement of science and technology.

Shifts in federal functions have also responded to shifts in men's conceptions of their world and their place in it—shifts in the relative emphasis upon adventure as against security, upon individual as compared with collectivity, upon the realities of class and nation and interest group as uniting and divisive ideas. Again, in such social forces outside the law one senses the deep initiative which has produced major shifts in agency functions and authority.

Another, more dramatic product of the growth in federal government functions has been the development of the policy-making as well as the policy-applying power of the executive. This has been accompanied by the rise of what—in terms of its practical degree of independence—is a fourth arm of government, the administrative. So far as concerns substantive power, the Court's role has been almost wholly to give legitimacy to this growth through a broad tolerance of congressional delegations of power. Here the Court's role as symbol-maker and validator has been especially prominent through the development of doctrine; we have seen a marked shift over the past fifty years in readiness to recognize the legitimacy of delegation, especially broad in the case of executive powers in foreign affairs. Of course, on the other side, there are the two negative decisions of the NIRA period—the "hot oil" and *Schechter* cases.[52] But the practical point of these decisions is that they stand out so prominently as exceptions to the record of 160 years. And in terms of what was in fact at stake, as distinguished from points of doctrine, one may question whether the future will not read these cases as reactions to pressure-group legislation, rather than as curbs on official agencies. The environment of the decisions suggests considerable suspicion of the role of special interest groups in the abortive cartel movement that was NIRA.

Procedurally, the story is very different. Here is a realm in which the Court has, in fact as well as in doctrine, taken an important role in shaping the division of powers. It is significant for appraisal of the future usefulness of judicial review to note again that when one touches judicial review of the law's application, as distinguished from judicial review of general policy-making, one has a surer sense of real judicial influence and contribution.

Has the shift in government functions affected the relative status of judicial policy-making? There is only one main area where judicial policy-making received impetus and grew as a consequence of the expanded functions of the federal government. This is in the field of anti-trust law, the substance of which has been made more by the Supreme Court than by Congress. The Court contributed to this process by its willingness to accept, in the Sherman Act, as sweeping a delegation of rule-making power as ever Congress made to any administrative agency.[53] But the Court could only occupy the field which Congress left to it. The starting point of anti-trust history is the question why Congress defaulted on the policy-making job. The answer is partly in an aspect of policy-making which the bench shares with the executive: In hammering out policy in a very difficult field, there may be strength in a case-by-case approach, in comparison with which statute law-making is cumbersome and awkward. Of course there may be serious question of the wisdom of leaving the definition of such basic values to the accidents and chances of litigation. But it suffices here to note that the absolute and relative policy-making role of the Supreme Court was much increased by this responsibility.

Shifts in federal functions have caused shifts in emphasis among the powers employed to fulfill these functions. So far as concerns Congress, there has been great extension of the power of the purse. Plainly, here is something which in the first instance is nowise the creation of judicial review; it is a development which expresses the whole Anglo-American tradition of legislative dominance, stemming from the rise of the House of Commons. Judicial self-limitation has been nowhere more striking than in this field. One of the most important constitutional decisions of our time was that of the "conservative" 1920s in which the Supreme Court denied the standing of either a state or a federal taxpayer to challenge the validity of federal expenditure.[54] The Court also played its part in the development of the modern spending power by decisions in the 1930s which ultimately validated the spending power as an independent power of Congress.[55] As we have noted, the single outstanding example of judicial veto on the purse power was the rather short-lived Income Tax decision.[56]

Apart from the power of the purse, shifts in federal functions have expressed themselves particularly in the expanded use of the commerce power. Aside from its implications for the federal balance, the growth of the commerce power has marked a greatly extended role for the Congress and also for the President as program makers. The idea of the positive potentialities of the commerce clause certainly did not originate as a consequence of judicial review; it may be found amply indicated in the writings of Alexander Hamilton and in the speeches of Henry Clay. The Court's role in this case was one of general acquiescence in a development which responded to policy pressures originating outside constitutional law.

What of the powers employed by the executive branch in its newfound role of policy leadership? The 1952 Steel Seizure decision naturally raises the question of executive "prerogative." [57] In theory, from the outset our history denied the existence of executive prerogative. This denial did not wait upon the Court; the remarks of James Wilson document the point in the Federal Convention.[58] But though the theory has been clear and stable, likewise the fact has been steady, and the fact has been the continued growth in the practical importance of presidential initiative. The Court has seen comparatively little challenge to the growth of presidential initiative. In foreign affairs there is no question of its weight; in practice the President can almost irrevocably commit the country to major decisions. The Court recognized the necessities underlying this development when it approved the broad delegation of power by Congress in the *Curtiss-Wright* case.[59] Today the congressional powers of purse and investigation remain the principal check-reins on executive prerogative. This is a fair inference from the useful analyses of the past in the opinions of Justices Frankfurter and Jackson in the Steel Seizure case; the data there assembled emphasize the extent to which assertions of policy-making executive initiative have been exercised within the framework of delegation or ratification by the legislative.[60]

Problems of the chief executive's "prerogative" present the more colorful drama. But of more massive, because of more everyday, effect has been the growth of the administrative process as the executive reflection of expanded federal functions. Executive power in this respect has increased relatively as well as absolutely, compared with that of the legislature. In practice, the scope and intricacy of modern administrative activity have allowed administrators more and more working independence. Moreover, the growth and stability of major policies expressed in administration have created vested interests in appropriations; in practice though not in law, this trend has reduced the purse power control of Congress over these areas of executive action. The same trends have increased administrative independence even of the chief executive. So far as substantive administrative power goes, the Court's role has been almost wholly to accept and legitimize these trends; it is hard to see how the Court can be credited with much positive creative contribution in this field. On the other hand, there has been great affirmative judicial influence in the case-by-case development of canons of fair procedure in the application of law.

So far as concerns the judiciary, and especially the Supreme Court, momentous shifts in federal functions have occasionally brought weighty issues to the Court; but we have already noted the ambiguities involved in trying to assess the actual influence of what the Court did. The main influence of expanded federal functions on the types of power exercised by the Court has consisted in enlarging the opportunities for important policy-making through statutory interpretation. The number of such cases far exceeds the occasions of judicial review, and history will show this to be the area of the Court's most pervasive influence on policy.

Striking changes in working techniques have accompanied shifts in federal functions. Since the time of Henry Clay, Congress has witnessed the rise of the standing committees, their character shaped by the influence of seniority in allocating positions and chairmanships. From this development has come the working pattern of Congress as we know it today—a major shift in power as between the body as a whole and its committees, which has deep meaning to everyone in official or private life affected by legislation. This development went on wholly outside the influence of the judiciary, except as they acknowledged its legitimacy by their increased resort to committee reports and hearings in the interpretation of statutes.[61]

Another main change in congressional working technique has been the increased emphasis on the power of investigation. The primary point is the growth in the variety of purposes served by the investigatory function.

The most obvious justification for the investigating power is to help make laws. The Court's one significant negative intervention in this area—in *Kilbourn v. Thompson* [62]—might be read perhaps as an effort to restrict the investigatory power to this function. If it be so interpreted, the case has not stood the test of time; for the investigatory power has gone on to much more extensive use.

The power exists also for the scrutiny of executive performance. Of course this is linked so closely to the fundamental power of the purse that it might be deemed the classic role for the investigatory function. In recent years we have witnessed the full development of this use of investigation. But the main problem of the division of powers here does not touch judicial review. Rather, the issue has been the inadequate organization of Congress, which has in practice more and more limited the effectual and valid use of its power to ask questions about the execution of a public business. So far as the Court is concerned, *McGrain v. Daugherty* [63] in effect repudiated the narrow implications of *Kilbourn v. Thompson,* and opened the door to congressional initiative.

A third and most recent use of the investigatory power has been to build public opinion. This new function grew with the wider audience made available by mass media of communication. Investigations have been used to publicize public issues, propagandize for policies, and—most questionably—to prosecute and convict men and groups in a new forum. The Court has had little to do with all this. What it could do wisely and effectively is limited to questions of procedure; attempts at judicial review of the subject matter of investigation would inevitably plunge the Court into "political questions" of kinds it has wisely shunned. But the justices have shown no inclination to use their opportunities to enforce even minimum standards of decent procedure. On the other hand, consistently with their action in other fields, they have shown considerable readiness to curb administrative investigations, even in regard to subject matter.[64]

So far as concerns the executive branch, the main development in working techniques has been the leadership asserted, both in bringing public opinion to a focus and in shaping legislation. Because we are still so close to the drama of the Roosevelt years, we probably exaggerate the relative measure of leadership. Yet there has been an important shift here, particularly in the functions of the President. But again, the impetus has been outside the influence of judicial review. New directions have come from the growth of the country and of interest-group divisions, the persistence of localism as a prime factor in the operation of Congress, and in contrast the President's claim to represent the "general welfare." Further, the President's news value and spotlighted rostrum have given him special opportunities to exploit the mass media of communication. In all these developments there is no significant influence of judicial review.

One cannot ignore as part of the techniques of policy-making in this newly expanded Federal Government the role of the new pressure groups with their section-wide or nation-wide constituencies and their permanent organizations. Judicial review has had an indirect connection with the rise of these groups. Judicially proclaimed rights of association, free speech, and petition give scope for their organization and their work. The "presumption of constitutionality" gives a large benefit of the doubt to "public welfare" measures which may be in fact special interest measures. But all this is tangential. On the whole, the rise of pressure groups is another major division-of-powers phenomenon which has reflected little either of benefit or of hindrance from judicial review. Again I must stress the importance of what the Court has done through statutory interpretation. The Justices have affected the ultimate impact of pressure groups more by the way in which they have construed legislation than by use of their authority to review its constitutionality.

VI

The most obvious measure of the Court's role in judicial review, as affecting the division of powers in the national government, is to look at its force as a deciding agency. Power means the capacity to make decisions that count. More important than judicial review as an expression of the Court's "deciding" effect on affairs has been its implementation, distillation, and on many important occasions outright creation of public policy in the process of statutory interpretation.

Lawyers know that the greatest influence of law is felt through procedure. The Court has generally held aloof from review of the proprieties of legislative procedure. In contrast, the most positive influence of judicial review has been to develop procedural limits upon the application of law—upon executive and administrative agencies as they bring the force of public policy to bear upon the particular case and the individual person. This is not accidental. The contrast between the impact of the Court on substantive policy making and on policy execution reflects the strength and weakness inherent in the judiciary as an institution. The contrast suggests that the future of judicial review as a creative force in our public policy lies more in a jealous safeguarding of the position of the individual in the application of law, than it does in surveillance of general policy making. And because of their position on the firing line, the trial courts may in the next generation of judicial review come to overshadow the Supreme Court, as the effective force of judicial review is seen to focus on the execution of law.

On the whole this chapter has presented a rather negative estimate of the influence of judicial review—at least as regards the division of powers in the national government. Yet history books and popular print familiarly invoke the Court as a symbol of power. Is it realistic to end on a negative note regarding an institution to which power seems so generally conceded?

Reference to the Court as a symbol suggests the respect in which judicial review may have had the greatest practical effect. Plainly, it has been judicial review which has given the Court its status in the eyes of students and of a sizeable public. This suggests that judicial review may have most influenced affairs insofar as it provided politically potent concepts and language for the public debate of policy.

Making decisions and choosing lines of policy are not the sum of government. Government can go on only against the background of consent or at least of acquiescence among the citizenry. Government must be "legitimate" in the eyes of its society, or it loses all decent meaning and ultimately even its naked reality.

Constitutionalism continues to be one of the fundamental ideas by which we measure our demands for a decent way of life in society. It is an idea older with us than judicial review. But there has been no more fruitful source for the support and definition of the idea of constitutionalism than the operation of judicial review. The most influential role of this function of the Court has been to provide symbols recalling men's minds to the issue of the legitimacy of power.

But to say that judicial review has given continuing life to the idea of constitutionalism is to say something so general that it does not mean much. If we seek more particular definition, we find that the history remains to be written.

At first glance this may seem not so. The shelves are loaded with legal treatises, works on constitutional history and theory, debaters' handbooks, political pamphlets, all talking about and in terms of the symbols which judicial review has contributed to the vocabulary of public policy discussion. But whose vocabulary? Most of the printed stuff tells us only, in effect, that judicial review has counted heavily in fixing the political language of professional word-men (judges, lawyers, scholars, students, politicians, agitators). It is a fair inference—though there is little evidence as yet in the book to support it—that, through the professional word-men, judicial review has affected the public-affairs vocabulary of the more articulate minority of laymen, mainly in the upper-middle-class bracket and above. How far has judicial review affected the political ideas and behavior of the general run of people in the country, today or in the 1930s, the 1920s, the 1890s? In the past twenty years the pollsters have begun to give us a little information on this or related matters; for the period before that we have nothing except the question-begging proposition that the mass of people must have adopted the symbols used by the articulate minority.

When we learn more, probably we shall find that the symbol-making influence of judicial review has been very different in different fields of policy. In the area of this chapter, judicial review probably produced little in the way of politically potent symbols. Not the Court, but fighting presidents and congressmen have enlisted popular interest in separation-of-powers contests between the executive and legislative branches. In the 1937 battle the idea of constitutionalism— as judicial review had fostered it—rallied substantial popular support to the Court; but opinion rallied rather to maintaining the Court's independence than to a clear-cut support of the Court's role as arbiter over the other branches.

Judicial review has probably most affected popular political ideas and language with reference to the situations where the individual confronts the power of the state. The Bill of Rights comes closer home to the imagination than separation-of-powers abstractions. One of the few studies we have in this field indicates, for example, that constitutional protection of corporations as "persons" set afloat symbols which were adopted by the man in the street to the point that he would respond, as he would to his neighbor's call, to appeals to guard the "personal" rights of corporations.[65] If judicial review has affected popular political ideas most cogently in the Bill of Rights field, this would be consistent with the fact that it has affected the operations of government most notably in providing assurance of the fair application of law. But in the present unsatisfactory state of our knowledge, these propositions are little more than hypotheses.

Emphasis on the symbol-making influence of judicial review points up issues likely to be neglected or underestimated if we talk only of "great decisions." The symbol-making role of the Court puts proper stress on the intellectual quality of opinions, on the Court's dignity of conduct, and on the importance of maximum agreement and the exercise of sober responsibility in concurring or dissenting opinions.

Moreover, emphasis on the Court as symbol-maker puts in a new light the virtue of humility of judgment summed up in the "presumption of constitutionality." This appears now not just a matter of deference to co-ordinate agencies of government. Even more, it indicates the exemplary importance of subordinating self to the clearest understanding of the values which seek expression through law.

VII.
REVIEW AND MAJORITY RULE

by Charles P. Curtis

To PLAY a great role with success or to achieve something permanent —how few do both!—a man must be both bold and wary. He must act with audacity and at the same time with caution. Moderation is not enough. In great occasions it neither fails nor succeeds. John Marshall had both of these necessary qualities, and in the case of *Marbury v. Madison* he and his fellow justices displayed them both.

Marshall certainly acted boldly. He was snatching an opportunity when he held section 13 of the Judiciary Act unconstitutional. It would not be far-fetched to say that he made it—this opportunity— for surely section 13 could have been construed to mean no more than what it now says.[1] This section, which the Court held unconstitutional, passed almost scatheless through the ordeal, and it was still alive, secure, and happy in our Judicial Code as section 342 until only a few years ago—until 1948, to be precise, when the section on writs was revised.[2] Instead of construing it, the Court violated what was to become one of the cardinal rules governing the doctrine it was establishing.[3] More than this, in twenty of the twenty-seven pages of his opinion, Marshall chose to write what amounted to a decision of the case which he then, in the remaining seven pages, held that the Court had no jurisdiction to decide.[4] More than that, as Thayer has pointed out, "Marshall made a very noticeable remark in his opinion, seeming to point to the chief executive himself, and not merely to his secretary, when he said, 'It is not by the office of the person to whom the writ is directed, but the nature of the thing to be done, that the propriety or impropriety of issuing a mandamus is to be determined.' —a hint that, on an appropriate occasion, the judiciary might issue orders personally to him." [5]

Plainly Marshall was bold enough, but he was also wary enough, wise enough, not to press his point farther than the needs of the occasion. His doctrine was not novel, but it was to be newly inaugurated. Though it had been debated, it had been treated on the one hand as a matter of course, and, on the other, it had been denounced as a usurpation. This was the first time it was to be officially announced. Fairman says it was the second time, and he refers to the case of *United States v. Todd* which was decided in 1794 but was not reported until 1851, and then only in a footnote.[6] Late comers get small helpings. The next time the Court tried the doctrine out was in the Dred Scott case. We all know what a fiasco that was. The fact is, the doctrine which Marshall announced in 1803 was not only new; it was premature. It did not come into its own for a good two generations, not until after the Civil War had made us indeed a nation, which Marshall could only hope we should become.

But the trick lay in the fact that Marshall chose to announce it in a case which required the Court to renounce the exercise of the very jurisdiction it claimed to possess. The Court held that the 13th section of the Judiciary Act was inoperative so far as it attempted to grant to the Court power to issue this writ of mandamus, for it was a case of original jurisdiction not conferred by the Constitution on the Court. Marshall had chosen an occasion to assert the Court's power to declare an act of Congress unconstitutional in which the Court must deny it had any power to act. He was as cautious as he was audacious.

We are accustomed to give our ancestral heroes credit not only for what we find after mature reflection we did ourselves, but also for a more deliberate purpose and larger foresight than any hero ever had. It is hard to believe that Marshall had any idea of the magnitude of what he and his fellow justices had done. Nor does it much matter to anyone but biographers and historians, except as a measure of the achievement. You recall the old story of the lady in Philadelphia who asked Franklin if we had a republic. "Yes, madam, if you can keep it."

Marshall might equally have said that he had given us judicial supremacy, if we could take it.

We did take it. We took this function away from our Congress,
and we gave it to our Court. I don't think that even we, even now,
are any more aware of the magnitude of what we did, and much less
of the patience with which we watched and encouraged the Court's
taking what we were giving it, than Marshall was of his inaugural part.
One reason for our unawareness is our familiarity with the result, the
way we take it all for granted. And one reason why we take it all for
granted is the fact that this function is so deeply rooted in us. What
I am concerned with is the nature of these roots. Their character is
my thesis. But before I present it, let me state the paradox which I
believe it explains.

We are a democratic country. We believe in the rule of the majority. Like other happy generalizations, this is not wholly true. It is not
true of the way we elect our chief executive, nor of the way we determine our foreign relations, nor of the way we require our juries to
determine our private disputes. On many occasions we require more
than a majority to rule over us. For, it must be said, a majority
is a greedy as well as sometimes an arrogant patron. What we, with
Marshall's help, did was snatch a large portion of our government
from this idol of a majority and bestow it securely upon the most
undemocratic of all our institutions, an aristocracy of nine securely
appointed and independently acting individuals. Their individual
independence is our only safeguard. Their individual independence is
our separation of the Court's powers. It is the only mechanical restraint on their exercise of the function which we have wished on the
Court. What is this function?

My answer can best begin by recapitulating what I said a few years
ago about the interpretation of legal documents.[7] I said that vague
words in a legal document delegate authority to the person to whom
they are addressed, but within limits, the limits of their degree of
vagueness in their context and in the circumstances. This is what
vague words do, and what good draftsmen use them to do.

We look to the context. We look to the particular circumstances.
Of course we do; but too often they are the circumstances in which
the words were written or spoken. These are for the historian. I mean

the circumstances in which they were to be read or in which we indeed do read them. But the context and the circumstances of their application do no more than indicate the category into which their meaning falls, and this is not enough. They tell us only what the words are talking about. They don't tell us what they say. To give them meaning, we must look farther; and we do look farther, although, to tell the truth, we usually don't know just what we are looking for. We are like Selden's butcher, who was looking for his knife and found he was holding it in his mouth.

Our knife, what we are looking for, and what gives meaning to our vague words, is simply the patterns in our behavior, "folkways," as Sumner called them, mores. I want to make it quite clear that these patterns, folkways, mores, or whatever name we may give them, are more than what lawyers call custom. Custom is a small dense part of them. Custom must be immemorial and it must be universal. This is asking too much, and making it too easy for those whose function it is to look for these patterns and appraise them. They run the gamut from the recent, transient, and superficial to the ancient and in-eradicable.

How shall I describe these patterns? I don't think I can do it myself. I will call three expert witnesses to testify, a distinguished anthropologist and two equally distinguished jurists, for plainly the matter lies along a diagonal struck between anthropology and law.

The anthropologist is Ruth Benedict. In her book, *Patterns of Culture*, she describes these patterns like this:

> Society [she says] is only incidentally and in certain situations regulative, and law is not equivalent to the social order. In the simpler homogeneous cultures collective habit and custom may quite supersede the necessity for any development of formal legal authority. American Indians sometimes say: "In the old days, there were no fights about hunting grounds or fishing territories. There was no law then, so everybody did what was right." The phrasing makes it clear that in their old life they did not think of themselves as submitting to a social control imposed upon them from without. Even in our civilization the law is never more than a crude implement of society, and one it is often necessary to check in its arrogant

career. *It is never to be read off as if it were the equivalent of the social order.*[8]

Now a jurist, Professor Edmond Cahn. I offer the whole of his book, *The Sense of Injustice,* in evidence, but I will content myself with quoting two short extracts:

> [The free citizen] *legislates for himself by appreciating the intentional value of jural situations, as his private sense of injustice becomes more and more immanent in the public conscience. The sense of injustice that contributes to the making of law inheres in him; it has its being and its sanction in his endowment. Legal order becomes his order; the rewards of compliance and the penalties of infraction are less outside than within.*[9]
>
> *Under the American Constitution* [the citizens] *are answerable to a peculiar degree. This responsibility arises from the historical relation between the Fourteenth Amendment and the original Bill of Rights, as construed by the Supreme Court. The Court holds that it cannot interfere with the criminal procedures of a state unless they offend some fundamental principle of justice, deeply rooted in the traditions and conscience of the whole people. The public sense of injustice thus becomes a constitutional criterion. Its quality and sensitivity determine constitutional law: the basic rights of each human integer depend upon standards attained by a general mass.*[10]

My other jurist is Eugen Ehrlich. In his *Grundlegung der Soziologie des Rechts,* Ehrlich lays emphasis on associations and groups rather than on the individual:

> *Even today* [he says] *just as in the beginnings of legal development, the force of law is based on the silent, uninterrupted sway of the associations which embrace the individual. From this point of view, the law appears even today to be related, in its essential nature, to the other social norms, i.e., the norms of religion, morals, ethical custom, decorum, tact, etiquette, fashion.*[11]

Ehrlich goes on to explain why the force of these social norms is so universally traced to the coercive power of the state. "Every false doctrine must, in the nature of things, be based on a correct observation of some sort or other. All our perceptions and sensations are always true; only the conclusions we draw from them can be false." [12] There seem to be two reasons. Although that part of the law which is maintained by the coercive power of the state is neither very great nor very important, it is the part which most interests the lawyer, because he is not concerned until coercion by the state becomes necessary. And second, Ehrlich concedes that there are doubtless many norms which most people would not observe if there were no sanction in the form of penalty or compulsion. Then, later in the book, he comes to what I want to quote. It is this paragraph:

Whether the judge, therefore, arrives at his decision independently of a legal proposition or on the basis of a legal proposition, he must find a norm for decision; only, in the latter case, the judicial norm for decision is determined by the norm contained in the legal proposition, whereas in the former case it will be found quite independently. The more concrete the legal proposition, the more precisely the judicial norm of decision will be determined by the norm of the legal proposition; the more general the legal proposition, the more independently and the more freely the judicial norm will be found. But there are legal propositions which grant an unlimited discretion to the judge. Examples of this kind in private law are the legal propositions on abuse of a legal right, on grobes und leichtes Verschulden, on good faith, on unjust enrichment. In criminal law and in administrative law they also play an important part. In these cases, the legal proposition does indeed appear to contain a norm for decision; actually, however, it is merely a direction to the judge to find a norm for decision independently. It is as if the legal norm left the decision to the free discretion of the judge. These cases seem to belong to the second group. This, however, is a matter of appearance only; in reality they belong to the former, where the judge finds the decision freely. The upshot of all of this is that the difference between a decision according to a legal proposition and one not according to a legal proposition is a difference of degree merely. The judge is never delivered up to the legal proposition, bound hand and foot, without any will of his own, and the more general the legal proposition, the greater the freedom of the judge.[13]

Justice Holmes wrote Wu that he thought this book of Ehrlich's, from which I have been quoting, "about the best of modern books on legal subjects." [14] It is significant that Holmes' admiration of Ehrlich was the setting for Holmes' famous crack about hating justice. For Holmes went on, in this letter to Wu, to say, "I am tickled by the 'healthy sense of justice' business. I have said to my brethren many times that I hate justice, which means that I know if a man begins to talk about that, for one reason or another he is shirking thinking in legal terms." [15] It is significant because the setting supplements the crack. It would have been equally true, though not at all comic, to say that when a man talks only in legal terms he is shirking thinking in any other. Holmes thought in both, as we know. The same Holmes who could laugh at the sentiments of justice and admire Ehrlich, believed that the life of the law was not logic, but experience. The two lines of thought flowed together through his mind.[16]

These patterns, both those implicit in our behavior, of which we are scarcely aware, and those which we tell each other about and express in codes and regulations, loose-leaf ring-backed services, they are what give meaning to the vague words we use in our laws. When we use them, we are requiring those to whom they are addressed to conform to the expectations of the rest of us. These expectations reflect the patterns. What else does, what else can, give meaning to a vague word in the law? Nothing but the sometimes dismal and usually inadequate precedents in what still remains of the common law. When these patterns are implicit in our culture, we ask the courts to make them explicit. "There is an almost compulsive quality," Clyde Kluckhohn has said, "about the present American need for explicitness and definition of private and national norms for conduct. There is increasing dissatisfaction with rules that pretend to supernatural authority and increasing recognition of the inadequacy of those that are merely hallowed by custom." [17]

If these patterns are a discernible part of our private law, they are obvious in our constitutional law. Are they not what Cardozo had in mind when he said that "a great principle of constitutional law is not susceptible of comprehensive statement in an adjective." [18] For, as Frankfurter and Reed have said, "Great concepts like 'Commerce . . . among the several States,' 'due process of law,' 'liberty,' 'property' were purposely left to gather meaning from experience." [19]

But there is more to it, more behind it, than the deliberate vagueness of the draftsmen who were our political ancestors. They were wise in their day, and so gratuitously wise that they gave us the opportunity to prove ourselves even wiser. But we have made for ourselves even more opportunities than they provided for us. Take the phrase "due process of law." It is perhaps the prime example of a large generality in our Constitution which has gathered meaning from experience. But who made it a large generality? Not they. We did. When they put it into the Fifth Amendment, its meaning was as fixed and definite as the common law could make a phrase. It had been chiseled into the law so incisively that any lawyer, and a few others, could read and understand. It meant a procedural process, which could be easily ascertained from almost any law book. We turned the legal phrase into common speech and raised its meaning into the similitude of justice itself.[20]

We did this ourselves, and we are still busily engaged in doing the same thing to other once lapidarian phrases.[21] For one example let us take the released-time programs in our public schools, time out of school hours for religious instruction by priest, pastor, or rabbi, whomever the pupil's parents choose. The First Amendment says that "Congress shall make no law respecting an establishment of religion, or prohibiting the free exercise thereof." It is manifest that released time for religious instruction does not prohibit the free exercise of religion. On the contrary, it encourages its exercise and leaves it to the free choice of the parents. If released time runs counter to the Amendment, it must be in some sort "an establishment of religion." Now this is rather a precise phrase, "an establishment of religion." Madison, who drafted and proposed the Bill of Rights and who saw it through the first Congress, is as good a mundane source for what it meant as there is. Madison said that "he apprehended the meaning of the words to be, that Congress should not establish a religion, and enforce the legal observation of it by law, nor compel men to worship God in any manner contrary to their conscience." [22]

Look here upon this picture, and on this, of what the Court is doing; and let me at the same time say that I thoroughly agree. I offer you *McCollum v. Board of Education*,[23] in which the Court held unconstitutional one of the several versions of the released-time program in our public schools. In this case it was time out of school hours for religious instruction by your own or your parents' choice of priest, pastor, or rabbi on the school premises.

It was an exceedingly difficult decision to make, although only one Justice, Reed, dissented, and it will sharpen the point I want to make if I first say why it was so difficult. The Court was asked to separate church and state just where the two are all but inextricable, in the education of the young. Louisa Clark put it briefly and neatly in her review of Professor O'Neill's book, *Religion and Education under the Constitution:*

> Assuming that it is now unconstitutional for a state to give impartial as well as discriminatory subsidies to religion, is it likewise unconstitutional to aid religion-in-education? Any distinction seems in theory implausible, but in practice it touches the heart of the difficulty. For it is one thing to declare the mutual independence of the civil and religious spheres when thinking in terms of Locke's limited and neutral state. It is quite another to execute the principle in the disputed area of education. To do so Americans have had to divide education into two parts—the secular, entrusted to the state; and the religious, taught by church and home.[24]

Now let's see how the Justices handled it. I need quote only two sentences near the end of Black's opinion for the Court:

> For the First Amendment rests upon the premise that both religion and government can best work to achieve their lofty aims if each is left free from the other within its respective sphere. Or, as we said in the Everson case, the First Amendment has erected a wall between Church and State which must be kept high and impregnable.[25]

The Court was relying, not on the words of the First Amendment, but on its "premise," what "can best work to achieve" its aims; or, alternatively, not on the First Amendment at all, but on a metaphor, for the "wall" is nothing more. A good metaphor, one of Jefferson's, but a metaphor.

Frankfurter, Jackson, Rutledge, and Burton concurred. They said, "We are all agreed that the First and the Fourteenth Amendments have a secular reach far more penetrating in the conduct of Government than merely to forbid an 'established church.'" Then they turned to "the relevant history of religious education in America," which led them to the conclusion that "Separation in the field of education, then, was not imposed upon unwilling States by force of superior law. In this respect the Fourteenth Amendment merely reflected a principle then dominant in our national life." "Enough has been said," they went on, "to indicate that we are dealing not with a full-blown principle, nor one having the definiteness of a surveyor's metes and bounds. But by 1875 the separation of public education from Church entanglements, of the State from the teaching of religion, was firmly established in the consciousness of the nation." This was the year when President Grant made his speech to the Convention of the Army of the Tennessee on the separation of church and state, and they quoted what Grant said. "By 1894," they continue, "in urging the adoption of such a provision in the New York Constitution, Elihu Root was able to summarize a century of the nation's history: 'It is not a question of religion, or of creed, or of party; it is a question of declaring and maintaining the great American principle of eternal separation between Church and State.'" [26]

The four Justices then turned to the movement for released time. It was first proposed by a Dr. Wenner in 1905; and, parenthetically, Dr. Wenner's proposal is curiously like Jefferson's views in 1822, which Reed quotes in his dissent.[27] There follow eight pages describing the various permutations of released time. (These pages may, I think, be profitably compared with Brandeis' brief in the *Muller* case and what the Court said about it.[28]) The concurring opinion concludes with Jefferson's metaphor of the wall, Root's phrase, "The great American principle of eternal separation," and a quotation from the best of our contemporaneous poets, Robert Frost, "good fences make good neighbors." [29]

Jackson added a further concurring opinion of his own. As candid as ever, he said, "It is idle to pretend that this task is one for which we can find in the Constitution one word to help us as judges to decide where the secular ends and the sectarian begins in education. Nor can we find guidance in any other legal source. It is a matter on which we can find no law but our own prepossessions." [30]

Reed, though he dissented, approached the problem from the same direction. After a demonstration that the Court's decision was very far from what he believed was the intention of either Madison or Jefferson, Reed turned to "well-recognized and long-established practices," and concluded that "in the light of the meaning given to those words by the precedents, customs, and practices which I have detailed above, I cannot agree with the Court's conclusion. . . ." "This Court," he said, "cannot be too cautious in upsetting practices embedded in our society by many years of experience. . . . Devotion to the great principle of religious liberty should not lead us into a rigid interpretation of the constitutional guarantee that conflicts with accepted habits of our people." [31]

Thus the Court turned from the intentionally specific language of the First Amendment to the intentionally vague language of the Fourteenth, and then filled its vagueness with what they thought we thought, as expressed by Jefferson in a metaphor, by Grant in a speech following the Civil War, by the political wisdom of a Root, by the insight of a great contemporary poet, and by recent and current educational practice. Frankfurter can be as candid as Jackson. A year later, in a case where several state statutes prohibiting closed-shop contracts were sustained, Frankfurter said that ". . . these are not matters, like censorship of the press or separation of Church and State, on which history, through the Constitution, speaks so decisively as to forbid legislative experimentation." [32]

What is decisive, then, on great and critical constitutional issues is history, and the more recent the better. So the Constitution becomes, not a voice, but the trumpet through which we are constantly speaking to a listening Court. Montaigne said, "Laws take their authority from possession and usage; it is dangerous to trace them back to their birth. They increase and take on dignity as they roll on, like our rivers. Follow them upstream to their source, it is only a little jet of water scarcely discernible, which grows in pride and strength as it grows older. Consider the ancient reasons which gave the start to this famous torrent, full of dignity, honor, and reverence. You will find them so light and delicate that it's no marvel if the judgments of those people who weigh everything and reduce all to reason and who will take nothing on authority or credit are often far removed from public judgments." [33]

Three years later, in 1951, came the case of the released time system in the New York public schools.[34] The Illinois schools turned over their classrooms as well as time to religious instruction. In New York the religious instruction was given elsewhere. Only school time was released. There was no other relevant difference between the two cases. The Court felt that it had outrun us and held that the New York practice was not unconstitutional. "We follow the McCollum case. But we cannot expand it to cover the present released time program unless separation of Church and State means that public institutions can make no adjustments of their schedules to accommodate the religious needs of the people. We cannot read into the Bill of Rights such a philosophy of hostility to religion." [35] Three Justices (Black, Frankfurter, and Jackson) dissented.

For another example, let me trace what we now see was the manifest destiny of the phrase, "bills of attainder." The common law made few phrases more definite in their meaning. No one will question the Court's inclusion of a bill of pains and penalties in the phrase,[36] though it was distinct at common law. But see how much farther the Court expanded the phrase—and again I heartily agree—in the case of *United States v. Lovett*.[37]

In 1943 we were being hag-ridden by Congressman Dies, as we were later by Congressman Thomas, and still are by Senator Mc-Carthy. Dies made a speech in the House demanding that the government be purged of "irresponsible, unrepresentative, crackpot, radical bureaucrats," and he named thirty-nine government employees. He urged Congress to refuse to appropriate money for their salaries.

The matter was referred to the Appropriations Committee, and a subcommittee held hearings in secret session. Cutting the thirty-nine to three, it reported against Robert Morss Lovett, Goodwin B. Watson, and William E. Dodd, Jr.

The House took thought and tacked a rider on an Urgent Deficiency Appropriation Act, that no money from this or any other act should be used to pay salaries to these three, except for jury duty or for service in the armed forces. The Senate Appropriation Committee promptly cut this provision out, and the Senate itself voted unanimously against a conference report that left it in. The House insisted. The Senate yielded. And the President too had to yield. When Roosevelt signed the bill, he said, "The Senate yielded, as I have been forced to yield, to avoid delaying our conduct of the war. But I cannot so yield without placing on record my view that this provision is not only unwise and discriminatory, but unconstitutional." [38]

Watson and Dodd continued to serve without salary for a week or so, but Secretary Ickes persuaded Lovett to stay on for three months. Then, not to endanger future appropriations, he asked Lovett to resign.

The three brought suit in the Court of Claims for their salaries for the time they had worked without being paid. The Court of Claims found that the rider, section 304, was "notable for what it did not do, as well as for what it did do. It did not terminate plaintiffs' services." [39] No, its sponsors knew very well what they wanted and what they were doing. They were as careful as they were deliberate. So they did no more than they thought necessary. Anyone, including the Supreme Court, who wanted to block them, would have to go a long way to do it.[40]

The case was appealed to the Supreme Court. Black wrote the opinion.[41] He called the rider a bill of attainder. What is involved here, he said, is ". . . a congressional proscription of Lovett, Watson and Dodd, prohibiting their ever holding a government job." This rider ". . . clearly accomplishes the punishment of named individuals without a judicial trial." [42]

Frankfurter's and Reed's concurring opinion shows how far the Court had gone. They agreed that the three should be paid for the services they had rendered, but not that the rider was unconstitutional. "Nothing would be easier than personal condemnation" of the rider, they said, but "Not to exercise by indirection authority which the Constitution denied to this Court calls for the severest intellectual detachment and the most alert self-restraint." This is no bill of attainder, not, anyhow, as it was understood by those who wrote the Constitution. "Their meaning was so settled by history that definition was superfluous. Judicial enforcement of the Constitution must respect these historic limits." [43]

The Court had certainly gone a long way when it called the rider a bill of attainder. Having made up its mind to kill this thing for good by a blow of the Constitution, all the Court could find was the prohibition against a bill of attainder. It was an antiquated weapon, dull and rusty, but who will say that this rider was not its modern equivalent?

Its destiny is still beckoning. In the recent case of *Garner v. Board of Public Works* [44] the Court, to be sure, held that the requirement of a loyalty oath by Los Angeles of its employees was not a bill of attainder. Frankfurter said, "I think the precise Madison would have been surprised even to hear it suggested that the requirement of this affidavit was an 'Attainder' under Art. I, §10, of the Constitution." [45] But shall we say that Black and Douglas, who dissented, were not justified in following the *Lovett* case, as well as the *Cummings* and the *Garland* cases,[46] where test oaths, required at the close of the Civil War, were struck down?

The point I want to make is that the Court is still looking at the Bill of Rights as in a mirror which reflects our current political morals.[47] I shall be satisfied if I may give two more indications from recent opinions.[48]

The secret ballot did not come into our political life until 1888, when it was adopted by Massachusetts. It came to us from Australia; you will find it in the Australian Constitutional Act of 1856. I need not say that it was unknown to our forefathers, or that you will not find it in our Constitution. And yet Frankfurter, in the spring of 1950, said, "I do not suppose it is even arguable that Congress could ask for a disclosure of how union officers cast their ballots at the last presidential election even though the secret ballot is a relatively recent institution." [49] To be sure, he was not speaking for the Court. He was speaking his own thoughts on the oath required of union officers by the Taft-Hartley Act.

The other concerns the word "liberty." Once it meant no more than an absence of physical restraint. Now it is on its way to include privacy. Let us not forget that for a time it included property.

In the *Pollak* case,[50] which I want to mention later, the Court held that "music as you ride" through loudspeakers in a streetcar or bus did not violate the due process clause in the Fifth Amendment. Douglas dissented and said, "The case comes down to the meaning of 'liberty' as used in the Fifth Amendment. Liberty in the constitutional sense must mean more than freedom from governmental restraint; it must include privacy as well, if it is to be a repository of freedom. The right to be let alone is indeed the beginning of all freedom." [51]

So we are dealing with something more than our forefathers' wise and generous provision of vague generalities which they left to us to fill from our experience. We have blown up even their more definite words to serve our purpose. What is there behind our restiveness under the constraint of these definite terms? What is it that moves the Court to stretch and strain one definite and particular term after another, turning them into generalities which reflect one or another aspect of our ideals and our patterns of decency and justice?

II

I suggest that what we have persuaded the Court to do is nothing less than this: interpret for us and declare to us the immanent component in our constitutional law. We have persuaded the Court to mediate between this immanent component and the other component which is imposed upon us by the rule of a sometimes hasty, occasionally hysterical, and too often selfish majority. I rather think that I am using "immanent" with a more elaborate meaning than the dictionary permits. I take the word from Whitehead, and so I turn to him to explain it. In what I shall quote he is referring to the cosmos, but I think you will find, as I do, that what he says is specifically applicable to much of our law and to a large part of our Constitution. [52]

> By the doctrine of Law as immanent it is meant that the order of nature expresses the characters of the real things which jointly compose the existences to be found in nature. When we understand the essences of these things, we thereby know their mutual relations to each other. Thus, according as there are common elements in their various characters, there will necessarily be corresponding iden-

tities in their mutual relations. In other words, some partial identity of pattern in the various characters of natural things issues in some partial identity of pattern in the mutual relations of those things. These identities of pattern in the mutual relations are the Laws of Nature. Conversely, a Law is explanatory of some community in character pervading the things which constitute Nature. It is evident that the doctrine involves the negation of "absolute being." It presupposes the essential interdependence of things.

There are some consequences to this doctrine. In the first place, it follows that scientists are seeking for explanations and not merely for simplified descriptions of their observations. In the second place the exact conformation of nature to any law is not to be expected. If all the things concerned have the requisite common character, then the pattern of mutual relevance which expresses that character will be exactly illustrated. But in general we may expect that a large proportion of things do possess the requisite character and a minority do not possess it. In such a case, the mutual relations of these things will exhibit lapses when the law fails to obtain illustration. In so far as we are merely interested in a confused result of many instances, then the law can be said to have a statistical character. It is now the opinion of physicists that most of the laws of physics, as known in the nineteenth century, are of this character.

Thirdly, since the laws of nature depend on the individual characters of the things constituting nature, as the things change, then correspondingly the laws will change. Thus the modern evolutionary view of the physical universe should conceive of the laws of nature as evolving concurrently with the things constituting the environment. Thus the conception of the Universe as evolving subject to fixed, eternal laws regulating all behaviour should be abandoned.[53]

Now I am going to take liberties with Whitehead's language, but only just enough to show how clearly what he said applies to what we are talking about, and I will make some comments on one of the consequences of the doctrine.

Law as an immanent order expresses the characters of the individuals who compose the community in which they live. When we understand their characters, we thereby know their mutual relations to each other. Thus, according as there are common elements in their various characters, there will necessarily be corresponding identities in their mutual relations. In other words, some partial identity of pattern in the various characters of the individuals who compose society issues in some partial identity of pattern in their mutual relations. It is evident that the doctrine involves the negation of pure individualism.

One of the consequences to this doctrine is that the exact conformity of conduct to an immanent law is not to be expected. If everyone concerned has the requisite common character, then the pattern of mutual relevance which expresses that character will be exactly illustrated. Complete conformity with the immanent component in our laws and statutes is never to be expected. But in general we may expect that a large proportion do possess the requisite character and a minority do not possess it. In such a case, the mutual relations will exhibit lapses when the law fails to obtain illustration.

It follows that you cannot do anything so sensational as to violate an immanent law, or break it, or even disobey it. All you can do is not conform to it, and this will be the result of a difference in your nature, not of your willfulness or recalcitrancy. Or, perhaps more precisely, it will be the result of conforming to some other immanent law less generally or even scarcely recognized. "If a man does not keep pace with his companions, perhaps it is because he hears a different drummer." [54] Lawyers say that hard cases make bad law. What they often mean is that hard cases make new law, which more than likely is marching to a new and different drum. Knaves, on the other hand, break the law, as do the fools, sots, and clowns who, as Emerson said, make the fringes of the tapestry of life.[55] They are not part of any pattern in the tapestry itself. Tolstois, Gandhis, and Thoreaus, who recognize a duty of civil disobedience, have their place in the great design, or have at least their own pattern.

Listen to Thoreau explaining why he felt free to refuse to pay his poll tax and to choose instead a night in the Concord jail. In his essay, *Civil Disobedience*, he wrote, "The proper place to-day, the only place which Massachusetts has provided for her freer and less desponding spirits, is in her prisons, to be put out and locked out of the State by her own act, as they have already put themselves out by their principles. . . . I saw that, if there was a wall of stone between me and my townsmen, there was a still more difficult one to climb or break through before they could get to be as free as I was. I did not for a moment feel confined, and the walls seemed a great waste of stone and mortar. I felt as if I alone of all my townsmen had paid my tax." [56]

We are brought to Lord Acton's conception of freedom, which, it seems to me, can stand only on the basis of the doctrine of an immanent law:

> *Liberty is the assurance that every man shall be protected in doing what he believes his duty against the influence of authority and majorities, custom and opinion . . .*[57]
>
> *Liberty and morality. How they try to separate them—to found liberty on rights, on enjoyments, not on duties. Insist on their identity. Liberty is that condition which makes it easy for conscience to govern. Liberty is government of Conscience—Reign of Conscience.*[58]

The reign of conscience is self-government. Acton believed that "[F]reedom of conscience is the root of self-government" [59] and, though he did not use the phrase, Acton made it clear that self-government was a government of immanent law.

> *Laws are part of a thing's nature. Law is national, growing on a particular soil, suited to a particular character and wants. Legislation should grow in harmony with the people—should be based on habits as well as precepts. It should be identified with the national character and life. On this depends growth and progress. The people cannot administer a law not their own. This is the reverse of self-government, which proceeds not from a code but from custom, is learnt not from books but from practice, is administered by the people themselves. However good the code may be, if it comes from aliunde than from national life and history, it destroys self-government . . .*[60]

I grant you I am not taking conscience in as religious a sense as Acton did, but the reign of conscience need not be the kingdom of God. "Conscience really belongs to the subconscious man, to that part of the soul which is hardly distinct in different individuals, a sort of community-consciousness, or public spirit, not absolutely one and the same in different citizens, and yet not by any means independent in them." [61] I am taking conscience to be not the cause but—as Leslie A. White put it—the vehicle of ethical conduct. Let me try to state White's explanation of the nature of what we call our conscience. It is not, let me quickly say, what Hamlet said made cowards of us all. On the contrary, quite on the contrary, for Hamlet meant introspection and inward doubt. White means and I mean what saves us from solitude and fright, the bond of solidarity and kinship with our fellows.

To White conscience is not any inborn physiological ability to tell right from wrong, as our ears give us a sense of balance and tell us when we start to sway out of the vertical. Conscience to White is the sense which makes us aware of cultural and social forces, as the canals in our ears make us aware of the forces of gravity. Or, for another analogy, White says that "the human organism lives and moves within an ethical magnetic field, so to speak." By our consciences, White declares, ". . . society not only succeeds in enlisting individuals in the cause of general welfare but actually causes them to work against their own interests—even to the point of sacrificing their own lives for others or for the general welfare." What's more, ". . . the individual is made to feel that it is *he* who is making the decision and taking the proper action, and, moreover, that he is perfectly 'free' in making his decisions and in choosing courses of action." White concludes as follows:

That conscience is a cultural variable rather than a psychosomatic constant is made apparent of course by a consideration of the great variation of definition of rights and wrongs among the various cultures of the world. What is right in one culture may be wrong in another. This follows from the fact that an act that will promote the general welfare in one set of circumstances may injure it in another. Thus we find great variety of ethical definition and conduct in the face of a common and uniform human organism, and must conclude therefore that the determination of right and wrong is social and cultural rather than individual and psychological. But the interpretation of conscience, rather than custom and mores, in terms of social and cultural forces serves to demonstrate once more that the individual is what his culture makes him. He is the utensil; the culture supplies the contents. Conscience is the instrument, the vehicle, of ethical conduct, not the cause. It is well, here as elsewhere, to distinguish cart from horse.[62]

III

Let me go back to the *Zorach* case and released time. I hope that I have convinced you that there and in the *McCollum* case the Court was dealing with immanent law.

In the *Zorach* case, six of the Justices, including three of the six who had held the released time in Illinois unconstitutional in the *McCollum* decision, refused to press that decision any farther, not even far enough to cover the release of school time without the release of classroom space. The other three Justices who had joined in the *McCollum* decision and who were still on the bench insisted that its principles should have been followed. Jackson said, "The distinction attempted between that case and this is trivial, almost to the point of cynicism. . . . Today's judgment will be more interesting to students of psychology and of the judicial processes than to students of constitutional law." [63] You see, the finger points at us too. Black said that he saw "no significant difference between the invalid Illinois system and that of New York here sustained," and said that he wanted "to reaffirm my faith in the fundamental philosophy expressed in *McCollum* and *Everson v. Board of Education*." [64] Frankfurter agreed with Black "that those principles are disregarded in reaching the result in this case." "Happily," he added, "they are not disavowed by the Court. From this I draw the hope that in future variations of the problem which are bound to come here, these principles may again be honored in the observance." [65]

Now Whitehead gave, as a fourth consequence of the doctrine of law as immanent, that "a reason can now be produced why we should put some limited trust in induction. For if we assume an environment largely composed of a sort of existences whose natures we partly understand, then we have some knowledge of the laws of nature dominating that environment." [66]

"Some limited trust." How much? How far may a court rely upon a principle which it has derived from an immanent order in our law? How far can a decision which it has reached in the immanent order be a precedent for a subsequent decision on a logically similar subject? Or does an immanent law speak only in particulars? Were Black and Frankfurter and Jackson justified in relying on the *McCollum* decision as a precedent, or should they have started afresh and looked to see if there was an immanent law relating to the release of school time unaccompanied by release of a schoolroom?

I suppose my queries resolve, as Whitehead's remark suggests, into the ancient and abiding question of the extent of the validity of inductive reasoning. Logically (but unjustifiably) you could argue that the principles to which these three Justices appealed would make the tax exemption of churches equally unconstitutional. President Grant's message to Congress, on which Frankfurter in part relied in the *McCollum* case, opposed tax exemption as well as direct aid.[67] Why would this reasoning be unjustified? I should say: because another immanent law permitted exemption from taxation. At any rate, I cannot think where else to stop the extension of an immanent law but at the point where another, different—I need not say conflicting or even inconsistent—immanent law begins.

Not only tax exemption, but also Bible reading, which is required by statute in a dozen states,[68] Christmas carols and a crèche and the three Wise Men approaching, free lunches, free textbooks, not to speak of the free school buses which were held valid in the *Everson* case,[69] all these "exceptions" make sense, if not logic, as soon as we recognize that we are dealing with an immanent law.

Only if all the things concerned have the requisite common character, Whitehead says, is exact conformation to an immanent law to be expected. It may be a pity, but I think it is true, that the development of the principles and the philosophy of the *McCollum* case will stand more securely on the observation and evocation of the presence of other immanent laws than on deductive reasoning. This is not to decry reason, but rather to couple it with observation, as the best way toward understanding how we behave as well as how the world behaves around us.

We lawyers are so used to thinking that our law is imposed upon us by the state that we are likely to neglect the other, and, as I believe, the larger component of our law which is of an immanent order. Here our laws are of the same nature as scientific laws, to be determined in the same way and valid to the same extent. "Laws," said Professor Dingle (speaking of the laws of science), "are valid just so far as they fulfil their purpose of rationalizing experiences, and no further." [70] This is no less true of the judicial or legislative statements of the immanent component of our laws. They are no more valid beyond the rationalization of the human behavior with which they deal. It is true that the experiences with which they deal are not so obstinately independent and incorrigible as the experiences with which the scientists are dealing. They are in some measure amenable to the very rationalization which expounds them. A good description can't help being in some degree normative. Moreover, courts and legislatures prefer to rationalize what seem to them to be the better patterns and not simply what appear to be the dominant patterns. But the better patterns of behavior are as susceptible of observation and statement as those which are dominant. The fact is, fortunately, they are easier. Anyhow, lawyers have to be better scientists than they think they are.

The doctrine of imposed law, Whitehead says in effect, conceives the character of each of the individuals who are the ultimate constituents of the community as its own private qualification. Each individual is understandable in complete disconnection from any other. The ultimate truth then is that each requires nothing but himself in order to live. But in fact there is imposed on each the necessity of entering into relationships with others. The imposed behavior patterns are the laws. Yet you cannot discover the natures of the individuals by any study of the laws of their relations. Nor, conversely, can you discover the laws by inspection of the natures of the individuals.[71]

Lawyers need no help, even from a philosopher, to understand law as an imposed order. Our hands are too deeply dyed in respect for authority, or else in pride of our skill in advising others how to obey, or sometimes how to roll with its punch, to understand at all readily any other doctrine.

The authority of Congress, or of any one in authority, from the Deity down to the founding fathers, works in an imposed, not in an immanent order. Whether "put out by a God on a mountain top, or by a Saint in a cave, or by a divine Despot on a throne, or at the lowest, by ancestors with a wisdom beyond later question. . . ."— these are Whitehead's words [72]—their rule is authoritarian and if it is accepted as authoritative, it is imposed upon us. Whitehead said that the doctrine of an imposed order "both suggests a certain type of Deism, and conversely it is the outcome of such a Deistic belief if already entertained." [73] Comparing our Hellenic and our Semitic heritages, he added that "the extremes of the two doctrines of Law lead on the one hand to the extreme monotheistic doctrine of God, as essentially transcendent and only accidentally immanent, and on the other hand to the pantheistic doctrine of God, as essentially immanent and in no way transcendent." [74]

In the immanent order, we are dealing with the more primitive component of our law, half as old as human time itself. No need to wonder, then, at the great head of pressure for its interpretation and expression. No wonder that this immemorial component, this elder sister in our law, meets her younger sister, the will of a majority, o. more than equal terms. What Marshall did was not simply to give the Court the function of declaring void and ignoring the acts and statutes of our imposed order which violated our Constitution. This was the least consequence of *Marbury v. Madison*. He opened the way for the Court to take upon itself the function of interpreting and declaring our immemorial immanent law.

The Court is quite aware that it is performing this function, but it is too discreet to boast about it. If the examples I have offered persuade us, we may be sure that the Court knows what it is doing. We find the Court taking evidence of the strength and character of these immanent patterns. A small example is the public-opinion survey on which the Commission and the Court in part relied when they found the music-as-you-ride radio was not unconstitutional.[75] Of the passengers polled, 76.3 per cent were in favor, 13.9 per cent didn't care, 3.2 per cent didn't know, 3.6 per cent said they would not oppose a majority. Only 3 per cent—exactly 3 per cent, if you add the others up—were "firmly opposed to the use of radios in transit vehicles."

A more convincing example is the Court's acceptance of the Brandeis factual brief. Even the old Court, fanatic ideologists though they were, listened; and what bearing did the facts which Brandeis' brief brought to the Court's attention have on due process of law except its immanent content? His brief was little or nothing more than a compendium of the numerous other such statutes, foreign as well as domestic, and nearly a hundred reports of committees, commissions, and factory inspectors. It was just such material as any anthropologist or social scientist would insist upon.

The Court said that these "expressions of opinion from other than judicial sources" are "significant of a widespread belief that woman's physical structure, and the functions she performs in consequence thereof, justify special legislation restricting or qualifying the conditions under which she should be permitted to toil. Constitutional questions, it is true, are not settled by even a consensus of present public opinion. . . . At the same time, when a question of fact is debated or debatable, and the extent to which a special constitutional limitation goes is affected by the truth in respect to that fact, a widespread and long-continued belief concerning it is worthy of consideration. We take judicial cognizance of all matters of general knowledge." [76]

True, the Court preferred its own economic theories, but its Spencerian theories were themselves nothing but evidence of another and countervailing immanent pattern. The Court read Spencer into the due process clause. We were reading our own patterns into it. Spencer had already made his patterns explicit and thereby the more persuasive. Brandeis was trying to make our patterns articulate.

We talk about the respect which the Court owes Congress and the great weight which the Court must give to legislation, so much weight that the Court must not hold a statute unconstitutional unless it appears to be so beyond a reasonable doubt. The respect is respect for the representatives of a majority which has the power to impose their law upon us. The doubt is doubt of the strength of our own immanent law.

We need both orders, an imposed as well as an immanent order.

We cannot do without either. The question is, how much of each shall we have. They are subcontraries, like oil and vinegar in a salad dressing. The more of one, the less of the other. I do not want my belief in the existence of an immanent order in our law to give the impression that I think an immanent law is always good and right and an imposed law always bad and wrong. The reluctance of Congress and most of our state legislatures to pass a compulsory FEPC bears witness to the respect we have for an immanent law which I believe bad and wrong, and which I call race prejudice. I believe this is an evil immanent law, and with the help of other and better immanent laws, whose aid may be invoked by expressing them, I believe that an imposed law can prevail.

Race prejudice is an immanent law prevalent among many of us, especially in one part of the country, where it has enough, but not too much, to feed on. Throughout most of the rest of the country a different and inconsistent immanent law prevails. When they conflict, and the adherents of neither are able to persuade the other, and one of them resorts to force, that is, judicial enforcement, does their immanent law become a law of an imposed order? I suppose this is one way of describing it, but it does not thereby lose its quality of immanence except in the particular case in which it is enforced and in such similar cases that we must suppose it was enforced by threat of force.

The distinction may rest upon the use or non-use of force, but this is not the best way to tell the two components apart. There is a difference in the kind of force each uses—pains and penalties, fines, and imprisonment by the imposed law, a posse of public opinion by the immanent. This may be the radical distinction, but it is a mistake to regard either kind of force as greater or more effective than the other. They are not even as different as they appear to be, except to lawyers.

The best way to tell an immanent from an imposed component lies in the way each is expressed, between the two subcontraries, particularity and generality. Law as an imposed order consists in commands, do this and don't do that. To be effective, a command must be particular, not as a matter of theory, but by reason of practical necessity. For the more general the terms in which it is couched, the more

vague they are, then the more they melt into an extension or delegation of discretion to the enforcing agency or to our good will and
acceptance. The best test, therefore, of how much a law belongs to an
imposed order is the possibility of expressing it with definiteness and
particularity. On the other hand, an immanent law can be expressed
only with a certain degree of vagueness and imprecision.

A statute can be so indefinite that it offends the requirement of
due process. Such a statute does not "sufficiently apprise those bent
on obedience." [77] It offends, not because the words lack the necessary precision of meaning, but because the generality of the word or
phrase lacks an immanent content.

Take, for example, the *International Harvester* case [78] where the
Court held that a provision in a Kentucky statute was so vague that it
was unconstitutional. It had been construed by the Kentucky Court
of Appeals "to be taken to make any combination for the purpose of
controlling prices lawful unless for the purpose or with the effect of
fixing a price that was greater or less than the real value of the
article." In another decision, the Court of Appeals had declared that
the real value of an article is "its market value under fair competition,
and under normal market conditions." [79] Justice Holmes said for the
Supreme Court, "We have to consider whether in application this is
more than an illusory form of words. . . ." Then he remarked "how
impossible it is to think away the principal facts of the case as it exists
and say what would have been the price in an imaginary world." [80]
The Court held the Kentucky statute unconstitutional, and Holmes
concluded,

> But if business is to go on, men must unite to do it and must
> sell their wares. To compel them to guess on peril of indictment
> what the community would have given for them if the continually
> changing conditions were other than they are, to an uncertain
> extent; to divine prophetically what the reaction of only partially
> determinate facts would be upon the imaginations and desires of
> purchasers, is to exact gifts that mankind does not possess.[81]

Here is a statute dealing with a subject in which by its very nature
there was no pertinent immanent law. The price of things is a matter
of rational observation. The Court was quite right to regard the stat-

ute as an illusory form of words, but the language itself is no more illusionary and no more indefinite than, say, the Sherman Act or the phrase "due process of law." [82]

Take another example which is recent and controversial, the case in which the banning of the movie "The Miracle" was held unconstitutional. In *Burstyn v. Wilson*,[83] three of the Justices concurred on the ground that the word "sacrilegious" was unconstitutionally vague, and, to be sure, it was. But is the word itself vaguer than "obscene," which is considered definite enough? If we were as thoroughly a Roman Catholic country (quite aside now from any established church) as we are sexually sanctimonious, would we then say that it was too indefinite? We have a sufficiently clear and common opinion as to what is "obscene." Should we not then have an equally clear, common, and generally satisfactory opinion of what is "sacrilegious"? In the *Winters* case,[84] which had to deal with "stories of deeds of bloodshed, lust or crime," the Court referred to "accepted standards of conduct," "the mores of the community." Frankfurter, Jackson, and Burton, who dissented, were impressed by the number of states which had such a law on their statute books. "That which may appear," Frankfurter said, "to be too vague and even meaningless as to one subject matter may be as definite as another subject matter of legislation permits, if the legislative power to deal with such a subject is not to be altogether denied." [85]

It's not the indefiniteness of the words, it's their emptiness, their lack of immanent content, which determines their constitutional status. For the medium through which our immanent order speaks is the general, vague word, and without an immanent content a vague word falls to the floor like an empty sack. It's not a carton. Vague language is nothing but a receptacle for immanent law.

When judges say, in their modesty, that they only find the law, and deny, sometimes with a certain heat, that they make it, there is, as Cardozo suggests, no need to rely on "the ancient dogma that the law declared by its courts had a Platonic or ideal existence before the act of declaration, in which event the discredited declaration will be viewed as if it had never been, and the reconsidered declaration as law from the beginning." [86] What the courts find is simply the patterns of our immanent law. There is nothing ideal or metaphysical about them. They are factual, implicit in our common behavior. They are there to be seen by anyone who will look for them.

I am not willing to admit that Learned Hand is ever wrong, but sometimes he can be only half right. He is an eloquent man with a command of rhetoric, and he was seldom more eloquent—few have been—than when he spoke on I Am An American Day, in Central Park in 1944. He said:

> *I often wonder whether we do not rest our hopes too much upon constitutions, upon laws and upon courts. These are false hopes; believe me, these are false hopes. Liberty lies in the hearts of men and women; when it dies there, no constitution, no law, no court can save it; no constitution, no law, no court can even do much to help it. While it lies there it needs no constitution, no law, no court to save it. And what is this liberty which must lie in the hearts of men and women? It is not the ruthless, the unbridled will; it is not freedom to do as one likes. That is the denial of liberty, and leads straight to its overthrow. A society in which men recognize no check upon their freedom soon becomes a society where freedom is the possession of only a savage few; as we have learned to our sorrow.*[87]

Judge Hand is only half right. Though liberty does indeed lie in our hearts, and it is indeed true that if it die there the Constitution cannot save it, it is not true that our liberties do not need a bill of rights.

Madison made the same mistake, at first, when he opposed, or was at least indifferent to, the inclusion of a bill of rights in the Constitution. He saw nothing more than "parchment barriers" in it. But then he changed his mind, agreed with Jefferson, and became the sponsor of the Bill of Rights in the first Congress. Professor Cahn has told us why Madison changed his mind, and for what reasons, right ones indeed in my humble opinion.[88] Madison wrote to Jefferson on October 17, 1788:

> *Wherever the real power in a Government lies, there is the danger of oppression. In our Governments the real power lies in the majority of the Community, and the invasion of private rights is*

chiefly to be apprehended, not from acts of Government contrary
to the sense of its constituents, but from acts in which the Government is the mere instrument of the major number of the Constituents. This is a truth of great importance, but not yet sufficiently
attended to; and is probably more strongly impressed on my mind
by facts, and reflections suggested by them, than on yours which
has contemplated abuses of power issuing from a very different
quarter. Wherever there is an interest and power to do wrong,
wrong will generally be done, and not less readily by a powerful
and interested party than by a powerful and interested prince. . . .
What use then may be asked can a bill of rights serve in popular
Governments? I answer the two following which, though less essential than in other Governments, sufficiently recommend the precau-
tion: 1. The political truths declared in that solemn manner acquire
by degrees the character of fundamental maxims of free Government, and as they become incorporated with the national sentiment,
counteract the impulses of interest and passion. 2. Altho. it be
generally true as above stated that the danger of oppression lies in
the interested majorities of the people rather than in usurped acts
of the Government, yet there may be occasions on which the evil
may spring from the latter source; and on such, a bill of rights will
be a good ground for an appeal to the sense of the community.[89]

Our hopes do not rest on the Constitution, nor on the law, nor on
our courts.[90] Our hopes rest on something among us, which we have
made articulate only in part. They are false hopes only if they are not
evoked and expressed, only when they have not been explained,
rationalized, understood, and acknowledged. We must carry them
across the dark gap between the implicit and the explicit. What we
sense but darkly must be said clearly for our salvation.

This, it seems to me, is what John Marshall did for us in the case of
Marbury v. Madison. He snatched from the majority and offered to
our courts, the function of rendering our political decencies and
aspirations into immanent law. What we owe to Marshall is the
opportunity he gave us of combining a reign of conscience with a
republic.

NOTE ON THE CONTRIBUTORS

RALPH F. BISCHOFF, Assistant Dean of New York University School of Law, is the author of the chapter on "Constitutional Law and Civil Rights" in *Annual Survey of American Law*.

EDMOND CAHN, Professor of Law at New York University School of Law, is the author of *The Sense of Injustice*.

CHARLES P. CURTIS, of the Massachusetts Bar, is the author of *Lions under the Throne*.

JOHN P. FRANK, Associate Professor of Law at Yale Law School, is the author of *Mr. Justice Black*.

PAUL A. FREUND, Charles Stebbins Fairchild Professor of Law at Harvard Law School, is the author of *On Understanding the Supreme Court*.

WILLARD HURST, Professor of Law at University of Wisconsin Law School, is the author of *The Growth of American Law*.

NOTES

1 *The Words of Justice Brandeis* 26 (Goldman ed. 1953).
2 Cahn, "Madison and the Pursuit of Happiness," 27 N.Y.U.L. Rev. 265 (1952).
3 My comments are based on the second draft, adequately excerpted in 1 Chafee, *Documents on Fundamental Human Rights* 111–9 (1951).
4 2 *The Federal and State Constitutions, Colonial Charters, and Other Organic Laws of the United States* 1518–20 (B. P. Poore ed., 2d edition 1878).
5 *Id.* at 1548.
6 *The Federalist,* No. 85.
7 They might have been amazed to hear it contended, only a generation ago, that the scope of amendability under Article V was subject to implied limitations. National Prohibition Cases, 253 U.S. 350 (1920); Leser v. Garnett, 258 U.S. 130 (1922). This contention is still advanced vigorously by Continental scholars. Paolo Barile, *La Costituzione come Norma Giuridica* 76 (Florence 1951).
8 It is easy to be misled as to Jefferson's attitude at the time: his famous letter to Madison dated December 20, 1787 was unenthusiastic in tone. [6 *The Writings of Thomas Jefferson* 385 (Bergh ed. 1907, which will be cited hereinafter as "Bergh")]. He had been optimistic about the work of the Convention before he saw its product (Letter to M. Dumas, September 10, 1787 in 6 Bergh 294) and by 1789 was willing to say that the Constitution was "unquestionably the wisest ever yet presented to men" (Letter to Colonel Humphreys, March 18, 1789 in 7 Bergh 319, 322). The correspondence reflecting his gradual approval of ratifying first and amending later was summarized in his Autobiography (2 Bergh at 118). This was certainly his view as early as his letter to William Carmichael, May 27, 1788 (7 Bergh 26, 29).

9   For a superb account of this convention, see 2 Mays, *Edmund Pen-dleton 1721–1803: A Biography* cc. XIII–XVI (1952). Mr. Mays has graciously read this chapter in manuscript in order to safeguard me from historical inaccuracy. Of course, he is in no sense responsible for my interpretations of the data.

10   Letter to Jefferson, October 17, 1788, 5 *The Writings of James Madison* 269, 272–3 (Hunt ed. 1904); also in *The Federalist*, No. 48.

11   *Bentham's Handbook of Political Fallacies* 67–8 (Larrabee ed. 1952).

12   1 Mays, *op. cit. supra* note 9, at 170.

13   1 Cranch 137, 180 (U.S. 1803).

14   Locke, *Second Treatise of Civil Government* c. XIX.

15   See 1 Beveridge, *The Life of John Marshall* cc. V–VI (1916) where, however, no notice is taken of the events here recapitulated and their probable impact on Marshall.

16   Commonwealth v. Caton, 4 Call 5 (Va. 1782). The case is excellently narrated in 2 Mays, *op. cit. supra* note 9, c. XI. Judge Mercer's views are not separately reported by Call, but are stated here on the basis of Pendleton's notes, which Mr. Mays summarizes.

17   Commonwealth v. Caton, 4 Call 5, 8 (Va. 1782). By way of fairness to Wythe's text, I have eliminated many of the commas with which the reporter sprayed it. Also, I have changed "english" to "English," which is Call's usage elsewhere in his Reports.

18   Concerning Marshall's whereabouts at the time, Mr. Mays recapitulates the evidence in a letter to me dated March 12, 1953, as follows:

"I was never able to find any reference stating specifically that Marshall was in Richmond during the argument or at the time the opinion was rendered in the case. However, he had just been elected to the House of Delegates of Virginia and it was the practice there, especially until a quorum could be attained, to call the roll frequently and to have the lists of the absentees certified to the sergeant-at-arms so that they would be brought into the House in custody. The roll was called on October 28th, the day before the case was heard, and again on November 2nd, the day the opinions were rendered. On neither day was Marshall listed among the absentees. It seems extremely unlikely that a mistake as to him would have happened twice in so short a period of time. I think it safe to say, therefore, that Marshall was in Richmond during the entire time the case was heard, and unless he was sick, I am pretty sure he was present during the whole proceeding."

19   1 Cranch 137, 176 (U.S. 1803).

20   1 Warren, *The Supreme Court in United States History* c. V (rev. ed. 1932).

21 Letter to Mrs. John Adams, September 11, 1804 in 11 Bergh 49. See also the letter to her, July 22, 1804 in 11 Bergh 42.

22 In the Marbury opinion, Marshall had exonerated himself from any pretension to jurisdiction over "Questions in their nature political, or which are, by the constitution and laws, submitted to the executive. . . ." 1 Cranch 137, 165–6, 169–70 (U.S. 1803).

23 1 *The Papers of Thomas Jefferson* 337, 347, 356 (Boyd ed. 1950 and subsequent years, which will be cited hereinafter as "Boyd").

24 For the Virginia constitution as adopted, see 1 Boyd 377.

25 This appears in 6 Boyd 294 (1952).

26 *Id.* at 304.

27. For his later philosophy of government, see Letter to Samuel Kercheval, July 12, 1816 in 15 Bergh 32. That he remained faithful to the doctrine of "appeal to the people" is attested by his Letter to Major John Cartwright, June 5, 1824 in 16 Bergh 42. Indeed, Jefferson's correspondence advocating periodic amendatory conventions may have been the indirect and entirely innocent source of Bentham's impression that our Constitution actually contained a provision to that effect. *Op. cit. supra* note 11 at 60. As early as 1776, Bentham had begun to form a picture of the implications of judicial review; of course, he did not see them in an American focus. Bentham, *A Fragment On Government* c. IV, xxx, p. 220 *et seq.* (F.C. Montague ed. 1891).

28 Professor Douglass Adair's scholarly argument for attribution to Madison, though impressive, does not entirely dispel my doubts. Adair, "The Authorship of the Disputed Federalist Papers," 1 W. & M.Q. (3d ser.) 97 (April 1944), 235 (July 1944). For one thing, the position is still clouded by the memorandum (6 Boyd 308) which Madison prepared as a commentary on Jefferson's draft and forwarded to John Brown in October 1788, this memorandum bearing no resemblance in tone or approach to the 49th *Federalist*. In any case, assuming the question is at all material for present purposes, our concern is not with the *true* authorship of Nos. 49 and 50 but only with the *belief* John Marshall may have held on the subject at the time he prepared his Marbury opinion. And in that special perspective, Publius would almost certainly be Hamilton, for one of Hamilton's final dispositions before his fatal duel the following year consisted in listing the numbers that he attributed to his collaborators and claiming authorship of all the remainder, which included Nos. 49 and 50. The Hamilton list was not publicly challenged on Madison's behalf until 1817. Adair *supra* at 102–4.

29 Like other progressives, Bentham suffered agonies whenever he ran into the fallacy of "too good to be practicable." He remarked,

"There is a particular kind of grin—a grin of malicious triumph with a dash of concealed foreboding and trepidation at the bottom of it—which forms the natural accompaniment of this fallacy when it is vented by any of the sworn defenders of abuse." *Op. cit. supra* note 11, at 201, 202.

30 Barron v. Baltimore, 7 Pet. 243, 250 (U.S. 1833).

31 In 1792, Jefferson recorded an anecdote which, if true, would show that at the 1787 Convention the less discreet conservatives like Gouverneur Morris were already attempting by hook or crook to restrict the people's role under Article V. The Anas, September 30, 1792 in 1 Bergh 314.

32 Letter to James Monroe, February 15, 1801 in 10 Bergh 201. See also Letter to James Madison, February 18, 1801 in 10 Bergh 202. I am at a loss to understand how, in the face of the statements in these letters (written by Jefferson himself, on the scene and in the very vortex of the contest), Claude G. Bowers could assert that Jefferson's plan to resort to a convention was communicated only to the addressees of the letters. Mr. Bowers apparently accepted the version contained in a letter written by Albert Gallatin forty-seven years after the event, when Gallatin was eighty-seven years old and in failing health. Moreover, Henry Adams, whose biography of Gallatin was Mr. Bowers' cited source, warned his readers that Gallatin's first-hand information had been incomplete and that his testimony was not wholly disinterested. Bowers, *Jefferson and Hamilton* 500 (1925), citing Adams, *The Life of Albert Gallatin* 247–51 (1879).

CHAPTER II

1   1 Cranch 137 (U.S. 1803).

2   1 Wheat. 304 (U.S. 1816).

3   Ashwander v. Tennessee Valley Authority, 297 U.S. 288, 341 (1936) (concurring opinion).

4   Adler v. Board of Education, 342 U.S. 485, 501 (1952) (dissenting opinion).

5   Doremus v. Board of Education, 342 U.S. 429 (1952).

6   262 U.S. 447 (1923).

7   342 U.S. 485 (1952); 342 U.S. 429 (1952); 343 U.S. 306 (1952).

8   330 U.S. 75 (1947).

9   318 U.S. 44 (1943).

10 Lederman v. Board of Education, 196 Misc. 873, 875, 95 N.Y.S.2d 114, 116 (Sup. Ct. 1949).

11 Massachusetts v. Mellon, 262 U.S. 447, 487, 489 (1923).

12 Sevilla v. Elizalde, 112 F.2d 29, 32 (D.C. Cir. 1940).

13 Z. & F. Assets Realization Corp. v. Hull, 114 F.2d 464, 468 (D.C. Cir. 1940).
14 Sevilla v. Elizalde, 112 F.2d 29, 33–4 (D.C. Cir. 1940).
15 United States v. City and County of San Francisco, 310 U.S. 16 (1940).
16 Caven v. Clark, 78 F. Supp. 295 (W.D. Ark. 1948).
17 7 How. 1 (U.S. 1849).
18 3 Dall. 199 (U.S. 1796).
19 Reprinted at Frankfurter & Shulman, *Cases on Federal Jurisdiction* 36 (1937).
20 12 Wheat. 19 (U.S. 1827).
21 Post, *The Supreme Court and Political Questions* 98–124 (1936).
22 315 U.S. 203 (1942).
23 Application of Yamashita, 327 U.S. 1 (1946).
24 318 U.S. 578 (1943); and see similarly Sullivan v. State of Sao Paulo, 122 F.2d 355 (2d Cir. 1941).
25 See Coleman v. Miller, 307 U.S. 433 (1939).
26 223 U.S. 118 (1912).
27 307 U.S. 433, 453–4 (1939).
28 328 U.S. 549 (1946).
29 333 U.S. 103 (1948).
30 Dennis v. United States, 171 F.2d 986 (D.C. Cir. 1948).
31 Coleman v. Miller, 307 U.S. 433 (1939).
32 Colegrove v. Green, 328 U.S. 549, 556 (1946).
33 Post, *op. cit. supra* note 21, at 112 *et seq.*
34 Fergus v. Marks, 321 Ill. 510, 152 N.E. 557 (1926).
35 Colegrove v. Green, 328 U.S. 549, 553 (1946).
36 114 F.2d 438, 442 (2d Cir. 1940).
37 See also MacDougall v. Green, 335 U.S. 281 (1948); South v. Peters, 339 U.S. 276 (1950).
38 See Chicago & Southern Airlines v. Waterman S.S. Corp., 333 U.S. 103, 111 (1948).
39 333 U.S. 103 (1948).
40 335 U.S. 160 (1948).
41 *Id.* at 178 (dissenting opinion of Black, J.).
42 342 U.S. 580 (1952).
43 *Id.* at 589.
44 Norris v. Alabama, 294 U.S. 587 (1935).
45 Cf. Knight, *Freedom and Reform* 12 (1947).
46 ["Probably the most notable contribution to the lawyer's technique in constitutional cases was the so-called Brandeis brief submitted in the Oregon hours-of-labor-for-women case. It drew on reports of public investigating committees, books and articles by medical authori-

ties and social workers, and the practice of legislatures here and abroad. This type of brief has been in fairly common use ever since. . . . The presumption of constitutionality need not be lost sight of; but even a court which relies on the presumption in sustaining a statute does so more confidently and more comfortably if some factual foundation has been established for the validity of the law." Freund, *Understanding the Supreme Court* 86–7 (1951).—Editor's footnote.]

47 Engineers Pub. Serv. Co. v. SEC, 138 F.2d 936 (D.C. Cir. 1943), vacated as moot, 332 U.S. 788 (1947).

48 South Carolina State Highway Dept. v. Barnwell Bros., 303 U.S. 177 (1938); Southern Pac. Co. v. Arizona, 325 U.S. 761 (1945).

CHAPTER III

1   96 U.S. 1, 9 (1877).
2   252 U.S. 416 (1920).
3   *Id.* at 433–4.
4   253 U.S. 221 (1920).
5   *Id.* at 227.
6   170 U.S. 343 (1882).
7   *Collected Poems* 173 (1952).
8   Scott v. Sandford, 19 How. 393, 410, 426 (U.S. 1857).
9   On June 26, 1857. *Speeches and Letters of Abraham Lincoln* 65–6 (Roe ed. 1923).
10 Hilder v. Dexter, [1902] A.C. 474, 477–8.
11 Haines, *The American Doctrine of Judicial Supremacy* 288 (1914); quoted by Brandeis at the end of his dissent in Eisner v. Macomber, 252 U.S. 189, 238 (1920).
12 Quine, "Two Dogmas of Empiricism," 60 Philosophical Review 20, 22 (1951). I am grateful to Professor Quine for this paragraph, which is the mainspring of my paper, not to speak of my recurrent gratitude for his clear counsel; but if you will read on in his article you will find that he does not approve of leaving even this remnant of Aristotelian essentialism in the notion of meaning. This, however, is a question in which we need not get involved.
13 252 U.S. 189 (1920).
14 *Id.* at 207, 208, 211.
15 *Id.* at 219.
16 See Marshall in Brown v. Maryland, 12 Wheat. 419, 441 (U.S. 1827).
17 1 Cranch 137 (U.S. 1803).
18 Bentham, 4 *Rationale of Judicial Evidence* 35–7, 422 (1827).

19 News-Week, Feb. 23, 1935, p. 7, col. 1.
20 304 U.S. 64 (1938); 16 Pet. 1 (U.S. 1842).
21 306 U.S. 466 (1939); 4 Wheat. 316 (U.S. 1819).
22 312 U.S. 100 (1941); 247 U.S. 251 (1918).
23 322 U.S. 533 (1944); 8 Wall. 168 (U.S. 1869).
24 Smith v. Allwright, 321 U.S. 649, 670 (1944) (dissenting opinion).
25 Youngstown Sheet & Tube Co. v. Sawyer, 343 U.S. 579 (1952).
26 Brown v. Allen, 344 U.S. 443 (1953).
27 Cardozo, *The Nature of the Judicial Process* 20 (1928).
28 Girouard v. United States, 328 U.S. 61 (1946), overruling United States v. Schwimmer, 279 U.S. 644 (1929), United States v. MacIntosh, 283 U.S. 605 (1931), and United States v. Bland, 283 U.S. 636 (1931).
29 Minersville School District v. Gobitis, 310 U.S. 586 (1940).
30 Jones v. Opelika, 316 U.S. 584 (1942).
31 West Virginia State Board of Education v. Barnette, 319 U.S. 624 (1943).
32 Everson v. Board of Education, 330 U.S. 1 (1947).
33 McCollum v. Board of Education, 333 U.S. 203 (1948).
34 343 U.S. 306 (1952).
35 Youngstown Sheet & Tube Co. v. Sawyer, 343 U.S. 579, 596 (1952) (concurring opinion).

CHAPTER IV

1 Dicey, *Introduction to the Study of the Law of the Constitution* 170–6 (8th ed. 1915).
2 See, e.g., Atty. Gen. B. C. v. Atty. Gen. Can., [1937] A.C. 368.
3 See Frankfurter, "A Note on Advisory Opinions," 37 Harv. L. Rev. 1002 (1924); Notes, 45 *id.* 1089 (1932), 62 *id.* 787, 867–74 (1949).
4 For Canada, see the thoughtful discussion in Laskin, *Canadian Constitutional Law* 102–3 (1951); for Australia, Atty. Gen. Vict. v. Comm., 71 C.L.R. 237 (1945).
5 McWhinney, Note, in 30 Can. Bar Rev. 832 (1952).
6 Laski, "The Obsolescence of Federalism," The New Republic, May 3, 1939, pp. 367–8.
7 Loewenstein, "The Value of Constitutions in Our Revolutionary Age," in *Constitutions and Constitutional Trends Since World War II* 211–2 (Zurcher ed. 1951).
8 Pound, "Law and Federal Government," in *Federalism as a Democratic Process* 23 (1942).
9 McCulloch v. Maryland, 4 Wheat. 316, 415 (U.S. 1819).

10 Marshall, C. J., in Gibbons v. Ogden, 9 Wheat. 1, 194 (U.S. 1824); Hughes, J., in Minnesota Rate Cases, 230 U.S. 352, 398 (1913).

11 Scott v. Sandford, 19 How. 393 (U.S. 1857); see Hughes, *The Supreme Court of the United States* 50–4 (1928).

12 "It is the irony of fate that for three-quarters of a century the accepted conception of Roger Brooke Taney has been based upon the occasion when, yielding to the temptation, always disastrous, to save the country, he put aside the judicial self-restraint which was his great contribution to the law and custom of the Constitution." Dean Acheson, "Roger Brooke Taney: Notes Upon Judicial Self Restraint," 31 Ill. L. Rev. 705 (1937).

13 109 U.S. 3 (1883).

14 United States v. Reese, 92 U.S. 214 (1876); see also James v. Bowman, 190 U.S. 127 (1903). The activities of the Department of Justice in this period are described in Cummings and McFarland, *Federal Justice* c. XII ("Peace to this House") (1937).

15 See the excellent study by Robert K. Carr, *Federal Protection of Civil Rights: Quest for a Sword* (1947).

16 Pollock v. Farmers' Loan and Trust Co., 157 U.S. 429, on rehearing 158 U.S. 601 (1895).

17 United States v. E. C. Knight Co., 156 U.S. 1 (1895).

18 See Twiss, *Lawyers and the Constitution* 208 (1942).

19 Winkelman, *John G. Johnson* 244 (1942).

20 Hammer v. Dagenhart, 247 U.S. 251 (1918).

21 Carter v. Carter Coal Co., 298 U.S. 238 (1936).

22 A full account is given in a series of articles by Robert L. Stern: "The Commerce Clause and the National Economy, 1933–1946," 59 Harv. L. Rev. 645, 883 (1946); "The Problems of Yesteryear—Commerce and Due Process," 4 Vand. L. Rev. 446 (1951).

23 United States v. Women's Sportswear Mfrs. Ass'n, 336 U.S. 460, 464 (1949).

24 Elkison v. De Liesseline, 8 Fed. Cas. 493, No. 4,366 (C.C.D.S. Car. 1823); see Morgan, "Mr. Justice William Johnson and the Constitution," 57 Harv. L. Rev. 328, 338 (1944). As this is being written, we are on the eve of argument in the Supreme Court on behalf of South Carolina in the public school segregation cases, where echoes of the cries of panic which assailed Johnson are likely to be heard.

25 Compare the use of the commerce clause to invalidate the California "Okie" law, Edwards v. California, 314 U.S. 160 (1941); for a discussion of the practical differences between the use of the commerce clause and the privileges and immunities clause or equal pro-

tection clause of the Fourteenth Amendment, see Antieau, "Equal Protection Outside the Clause," 40 Calif. L. Rev. 362, 371 (1952).

26 Collins v. Hardyman, 341 U.S. 651, 657–8 (1951).

27 Dissenting (with Mr. Justice Douglas) in Panhandle Eastern Pipe Line Co. v. Michigan Pub. Serv. Comm'n, 341 U.S. 329, 340 (1951).

28 Crossman v. Lurman, 192 U.S. 189 (1904); Baldwin v. Seelig, 294 U.S. 511 (1935).

29 Foster-Fountain Packing Co. v. Haydel, 278 U.S. 1 (1928).

30 Kansas Southern Ry. v. Kaw Valley District, 233 U.S. 75, 79 (1914).

31 Dean Milk Co. v. Madison, 340 U.S. 349 (1951).

32 Baldwin v. Seelig, *supra* note 28.

33 Henneford v. Silas Mason Co., 300 U.S. 577 (1937).

34 Mintz v. Baldwin, 289 U.S. 346 (1933).

35 See Taylor, Burtis, and Waugh, *Barriers to Internal Trade in Farm Products* 93 (U.S. Dept. of Agric., 1939).

36 Gallagher v. Lynn, [1937] A.C. 863, 870.

37 In Hood & Sons v. Du Mond, 336 U.S. 525, 551 n. 2 (1949), Mr. Justice Black, dissenting, explained his position: "State legislation which patently discriminates against interstate commerce has long been held to conflict with the commerce clause itself. The writer has acquiesced in this interpretation, Adams Mfg. Co. v. Storen, 304 U.S. 307, 331–332, although agreeing with the views of Chief Justice Taney that the commerce clause was not intended to grant courts power to regulate commerce even to this extent. The equal protection clause would seem to me a more appropriate source of judicial power in respect to such discriminatory laws."

Justices Frankfurter and Douglas at one time appeared to be attracted to this self-denying canon, when they joined with Mr. Justice Black in dissenting in McCarroll v. Dixie Greyhound Lines, 309 U.S. 176, 183 (1940).

38 Morgan v. Virginia, 328 U.S. 373 (1928).

39 See Sutherland and Vinciguerra, "The Octroi and the Airplane," 32 Cornell L. Q. 161 (1946). Compare also the call for a congressional survey, uttered in the dissenting opinion in the McCarroll case, *supra* note 37 at 189.

40 The trends are analyzed and the commentaries collected in the valuable article by Barrett, "State Taxation of Interstate Commerce 'Direct Burdens,' 'Multiple Burdens,' or What Have You?" 4 Vand. L. Rev. 496 (1951).

41 Cf. Interstate Busses Corp. v. Blodgett, 276 U.S. 245 (1928); but cf. Spector Motor Service, Inc. v. O'Connor, 340 U.S. 602 (1951).

42 United States Glue Co. v. Oak Creek, 247 U.S. 321 (1918).

43 Central Greyhound Lines, Inc. v. Mealey, 334 U.S. 653 (1948); but cf. Joseph v. Carter & Weekes Stevedoring Co., 330 U.S. 422 (1947). See Lockhart, "Gross Receipts Taxes on Interstate Transportation and Communication," 57 Harv. L. Rev. 40 (1943).

44 Cf. Ford Motor Co. v. Beauchamp, 308 U.S. 331 (1939) (sustaining a Texas tax measured by such proportion of the total capital, surplus, and undivided profits of the corporation as the gross receipts of its Texas business bear to gross receipts from its entire business); see Powell, "The Current Current of the Commerce Clause and State Taxation," Proc. Nat. Tax Ass'n 1940, pp. 274, 275, 310–2 (1940).

45 See Multiple Taxation of Air Commerce, H. R. Doc. No. 141, 79th Cong. 1st Sess., 43–60, 84 (1945).

46 Cf. the Spector case, *supra* note 41.

47 Cf. the Carter & Weekes case, *supra* note 43.

48 Fisher's Blend Station, Inc. v. State Tax Comm'n, 297 U.S. 650 (1936) (holding invalid an occupation tax, measured by the gross receipts from radio broadcasting from stations within the state).

49 Cf. Cream of Wheat Co. v. County of Grand Forks, 253 U.S. 325 (1920).

50 Abel, "The Commerce Power: An Instrument of Federalism," 35 Iowa L. Rev. 625, 658 n. 187 (1950) and 25 Ind. L. J. 498, 527 n. 187 (1950).

51 E.g., Curry v. McCanless, 307 U.S. 357 (1939); Graves v. Schmidlapp, 315 U.S. 657 (1942); State Tax Comm'n v. Aldrich, 316 U.S. 174 (1942).

52 Jackson, "Full Faith and Credit: The Lawyer's Clause of the Constitution," 45 Col. L. Rev. 1, 16, 17 (1945).

53 John Hancock Mut. Life Ins. Co. v. Yates, 299 U.S. 178 (1936).

54 Bradford Elec. Light Co. v. Clapper, 286 U.S. 145 (1932).

55 Yarborough v. Yarborough, 290 U.S. 202 (1933).

56 Exodus, XXIII, 3.

57 E.g., Pacific Employers Ins. Co. v. Industrial Accident Comm'n, 306 U.S. 493 (1939); Griffin v. McCoach, 313 U.S. 498 (1941); cf. Home Ins. Co. v. Dick, 281 U.S. 397 (1930); Order of United Commercial Travelers of America v. Wolfe, 331 U.S. 586 (1947).

58 See the critical discussion of the double domicile problem in Chafee, "Federal Interpleader Since the Act of 1936," 49 Yale L. J. 377, 382–93 (1940).

59 See Note, "Escheat of Corporate Dividends," 65 Harv. L. Rev. 1408, 1410–1 (1952).

60 Hoopeston Canning Co. v. Cullen, 318 U.S. 313 (1943); see also International Ticket Scale Corp. v. United States, 165 F.2d 358

(2d Cir. 1948); Coleman, "Corporate Dividends and the Conflict of Laws," 63 Harv. L. Rev. 433 (1950).

61 In other federations, notably Australia and Canada, these problems are resolved by the Supreme Court as an ordinary appellate tribunal for the state courts, without having to find constitutional bases for reversal. For the Swiss practice, see Schoch, "Conflict of Laws in a Federal State: The Experience of Switzerland," 55 Harv. L. Rev. 738 (1942).

62 Clark Distilling Co. v. Western Md. Ry., 242 U.S. 311 (1917).

63 Steward Machine Co. v. Davis, 301 U.S. 548 (1937).

CHAPTER V

1   Warren, *Congress, the Constitution, and the Supreme Court* 273–301 (1925).

2   261 U.S. 525 (1923).

3   Callan v. Wilson, 127 U.S. 540 (1888); United States v. Evans, 213 U.S. 297 (1909); United States v. Moreland, 258 U.S. 433 (1922).

4   Rassmussen v. United States, 197 U.S. 516 (1905).

5   319 U.S. 463 (1943).

6   United States v. Cohen Grocery Co., 255 U.S. 81 (1921).

7   116 U.S. 616 (1886).

8   142 U.S. 547 (1892).

9   4 Wall. 333 (U.S. 1867).

10 Wong Wing v. United States, 163 U.S. 228 (1896).

11 Carlson v. Landon, 342 U.S. 524 (1952).

12 United States v. Lovett, 328 U.S. 303 (1946).

13 Scott v. Sandford, 19 How. 393 (U.S. 1857).

14 92 U.S. 214 (1876).

15 106 U.S. 629 (1883).

16 109 U.S. 3 (1883).

17 This does not ignore, but rather puts aside, rare and minute utterances such as Joint Anti-Fascist Refugee Committee v. McGrath, 341 U.S. 123 (1951), and Lovett's case, *supra* note 12.

18 Holmes, "Law and the Court," in *Collected Legal Papers* 295 (1920).

19 Burton, "The Cornerstone of Constitutional Law: The Extraordinary Case of Marbury v. Madison," 36 A.B.A.J. 805, 882 (1950).

20 Harno, Letter to U. of Ill. Alumni (1952) (private pamphlet).

21 Martin v. Hunter's Lessee, 1 Wheat. 304 (U.S. 1816); Cohens v. Virginia, 6 Wheat. 264 (U.S. 1821).

22 The form of this reaction is described in 1 Warren, *The Supreme Court in United States History* 526 et seq. (1924).

23   283 U.S. 697 (1931); 301 U.S. 242 (1937); 303 U.S. 444 (1938).
24   Youngstown Sheet & Tube Co. v. Sawyer, 343 U.S. 579 (1952).
25   4 Wall. 2 (U.S. 1866).
26   317 U.S. 1 (1942).
27   Duncan v. Kahanamoku, 327 U.S. 304 (1946).
28   Gitlow v. New York, 268 U.S. 652 (1925).
29   4 Wall. 277 (U.S. 1867).
30   250 U.S. 616 (1919).
31   54 Stat. 670, 671 (1940), 18 U.S.C. §§10, 11, 13 (1946); H.R.
     9766, 76th Cong., 3d Sess. (1940); 61 Stat. 146 (1947), 29 U.S.C.
     §159(h) (Supp. 1951); 64 Stat. 987 (1950), 50 U.S.C. §781
     (Supp. 1952).
32   Marbury v. Madison and the Dred Scott decision are the sole in-
     stances of judicial review (in the sense used here) up to 1865.
33   Chafee, Book Review, 62 Harv. L. Rev. 891, 894 (1949).
34   Minersville School Dist. v. Gobitis, 310 U.S. 586 (1940). Post-
     decision consequences are recounted in Rotnem and Folsom, "Recent
     Restrictions Upon Religious Liberty," 36 Am. Pol. Sci. Rev. 1053,
     1061-2 (1942).
35   The *ex cathedra* status of such memoranda is based on a composite
     of impressions from the bills under discussion. The most striking
     example, however, is furnished by McCarran Act debate, in which
     the brief of the ABA "Standing Committee on Bill of Rights," re-
     printed in Hearings before House Committee on Un-American
     Activities on H.R. 3903 and H.R. 7595, 81st Cong., 2d Sess. 2311–9
     (1950), played a leading role in upholding assertions of the act's
     constitutionality. In reporting the bill favorably to the Senate, the
     Committee on the Judiciary reprinted the memo in full. Sen. Rep.
     No. 1358, 81st Cong., 2d Sess. 35–43 (1950).
36   See, for example, the reception accorded the lengthy legal statements
     of a dozen witnesses appearing in opposition to the McCarran bill.
     Hearings before House Committee on Un-American Activities on
     H.R. 3903 and H.R. 7595, 81st Cong., 2d Sess. 2162–2305 (1950).
     Most briefs received no countering constitutional argument at all;
     some, a few offhand remarks.
37   See, e.g., *id.* at 2136.
38   See, e.g., 96 Cong. Rec. 14299, 15254–8 (1950).
39   277 U.S. 274 (1928).
40   Louisville Joint Stock Land Bank v. Radford, 295 U.S. 555 (1935).
41   The new Frazier-Lemke Act, drafted to overcome the objections of
     the Radford case, was upheld in Wright v. Vinton Branch of the
     Mountain Trust Bank, 300 U.S. 440 (1937).

42 The latest survey of content analysis repeatedly stresses that only a measurement of the content of verbal communication is ordinarily attempted with the new method, and that it "is not normally done directly in terms of the latent intentions which the content may express nor the latent responses which it may elicit." Berelson, *Content Analysis in Communication Research* 16 (1952).

43 Hearings before Senate Committee on Labor and Public Welfare on S. 55 and S.J. Res. 22, 80th Cong., 1st Sess. 1476 (1947).

44 93 Cong. Rec. 3626–9, 3633–4 (1947).

45 54 Stat. 670, 671 (1940), 18 U.S.C. §§10, 11, 13 (1946).

46 84 Cong. Rec. 10359, 10452 (1939).

47 86 Cong. Rec. 8344–5 (1940).

48 84 Cong. Rec. 10452 (1939).

49 93 Cong. Rec. 4875–6 (1947).

50 "I cannot believe the Supreme Court would uphold such a law. [Reads entirely irrelevant excerpts from Jones & Laughlin and J. I. Case.] No, Mr. Chairman; I do not believe the Supreme Court would uphold H.R. 3020." 93 Cong. Rec. 3650 (1947).

51 Hearings before House Committee on Education and Labor, 80th Cong., 1st Sess. 3592 (1947).

52 86 Cong. Rec. 8213 (1940). Other examples of this approach are: In hearings on the McCarran Act, Rep. Harrison: "Even if such legislation as this were struck down by a divided decision of the Court, wouldn't the enactment of it and subsequent decisions have a salutary effect on public opinion in directing the attention of the rank and file of the people to the Communist menace?" Hearings before Committee on Un-American Activities on H.R. 3903 and H.R. 7975, 81st Cong., 2d Sess. 2154. Or testimony of Omar B. Ketcham, witness for the Veterans of Foreign Wars, *id.* at 2144: ". . . no one can say such a law is unconstitutional until it has been interpreted by the Supreme Court of the United States."

Buck-passing is equally apparent in matters outside the area of basic liberties. In opposing an alteration of the union shop provision of the Taft-Hartley Act, Sen. Taft submitted a memorandum which held that the proposed change would violate the due process clause of the Fifth Amendment. Sen. Malone, sponsor of the amendment, answered that he had a memo which held otherwise. But there was no need to "spend time in debating the question," Sen. Malone concluded, since the separability clause of the entire act insured that "there can be no serious harm done in either case." 86 Cong. Rec. 8213 (1940).

53 86 Cong. Rec. 8205 (1940).

54 *Id.* at 8345.

55 *Id.* at 8183.

56 *Id.* at 8200.

57 *Id.* at 8201.

58 Sen. Rep. No. 2031, 76th Cong., 3d Sess. (1940).

59 H.R. Rep. No. 2980, 81st Cong., 2d Sess. 5 (1950). This position was foreclosed for many Republicans since Governor Dewey had said in the 1948 campaign that he opposed outlawing the Communist Party, ". . . because it is a violation of the Constitution of the United States and of the Bill of Rights, and clearly so." Quoted in 96 Cong. Rec. 15698 (1950).

60 H.R. Rep. No. 994, 76th Cong., 1st Sess. 5 (1939).

61 For discussion, see Sen. Rep. No. 2369, Part 2, 81st Cong., 2d Sess. 7 (1950) (minority report).

62 64 Stat. 1019 (1950), 50 U.S.C. §§811–26 (Supp. 1952).

63 96 Cong. Rec. 14548 (1950). See also the statement of Sen. Ferguson, *id.* at 14585: "Mr. President, the substitute bill would wipe out . . . every known constitutional provision for the protection of the rights and liberties of the people of the United States, including the right to be tried by due process of law and by a jury of one's peers."

64 64 Stat. 1021–8 (1950), 50 U.S.C. §§813–20 (Supp. 1952).

65 96 Cong. Rec. 14548, 14551 (1950).

66 64 Stat. 1022, 1023, 1025, 1026 (1950), 50 U.S.C. §814 (d), (f), §819 (c), (g) (Supp. 1952).

67 96 Cong. Rec. 14548, 14578, 14593 (1950). Outrage over this threat to constitutional liberties invoked extremes of oratorical fury. The hearing officers of the Kilgore substitute, for whom the McCarran Act also provides, were termed "commissars" (*id.* at 14578); the closed proceedings, a "star chamber session" (*id.* at 14551); and the entire bill was continually classified as a "concentration camp" measure (see, e.g., *id.* at 14547). Sen. Ferguson claimed that "This is the first time in the history of America that an attempt has been made in the Congress to infringe the constitutional rights of citizens" (*id.* at 14585), and that "never in the history either of American jurisprudence or of the British common law was it ever contended that a man could be tried for his mere capacity to commit a crime" (*id.* at 14586). "We know," he continued, "that Russia has concentration camps today. We despise them" (*id.* at 14591).

68 64 Stat. 1022, 1023, 1025, 1026 (1950), 50 U.S.C. §814 (d), (f), §819 (c), (g) (Supp. 1952).

69 See, for an outstanding example, impeachment proceedings in the Senate against Federal District Judge James H. Peck, reported fully in Stansbury, *Report of the Trial of James H. Peck* (1833). Peck

had invoked the contempt power against editorial criticism of one of his decisions; the resulting trial treated Congress to a brilliant discussion of First Amendment limitations.

70 For a description of the sectional nature of the vote, see 1 Wilson, *History of the Rise and Fall of the Slave Power in America* 432 (1872).

71 Warren, *Congress, the Constitution, and the Supreme Court* 91–3 (1925).

72 1st Cong., 1st Sess., June 8, 1789. Quoted in Warren, *supra* note 71, at 93.

73 Jefferson to Dr. Priestly, June 19, 1802, in 5 A *Documentary History of the Constitution* 259 (1905). Mr. Curtis' chapter in this symposium shows that Madison came to share this view.

74 Pollock v. Farmers' Loan & Trust Co., 157 U.S. 429 (1895).

75 198 U.S. 45 (1905).

76 Harisiades v. Shaughnessy, 342 U.S. 580 (1952).

77 Hirabayashi v. United States, 320 U.S. 81 (1943).

78 330 U.S. 75 (1947). I would like to express agreement with views expressed on the Mitchell case by Davis, "Standing, Ripeness and Civil Liberties: A Critique of Adler v. Board of Education," 38 A.B.A.J. 924 (1952), [and on the point of a softening of the standing rules where First Amendment rights are concerned, by] Bernard, "Avoidance of Constitutional Issues in the United States Supreme Court: Liberties of the First Amendment," 50 Mich. L. Rev. 261 (1951).

79 United States v. Carolene Products Co., 304 U.S. 144, 152–3 n.4 (1948).

80 Cf. Schneider v. State, 308 U.S. 147 (1939); Thomas v. Collins, 323 U.S. 516 (1945).

81 American Communications Ass'n v. Douds, 339 U.S. 382 (1950); Dennis v. United States, 341 U.S. 494 (1951); Beauharnais v. Illinois, 343 U.S. 250 (1952).

82 Carr, *The House Committee on Un-American Activities* 439 (1952).

83 *Id.* at 438.

84 Jackson, J., in Harisiades v. Shaughnessy, 342 U.S. 580, 594 (1952).

85 Article 39: "No freeman shall be taken or imprisoned, or disseised, or outlawed, or banished, or any ways destroyed, nor will we pass upon him, nor will we send upon him, unless by the lawful judgment of his peers, or by the law of the land."

86 Whitney v. California, 274 U.S. 357, 372 (1927).

87 Chafee, Book Review, 62 Harv. L. Rev. 891, 901 (1949).

88 Meiklejohn, *Free Speech and Its Relation to Self-Government* 39 (1948):

"Individuals have . . . a private right of speech [*i.e.*, ". . . argument, or inquiry, or advocacy, or incitement which is directed toward our private interests, private privileges, private possessions . . . ," p. 94] which may on occasion be denied or limited, though•such limitations may not be imposed unnecessarily or unequally. So says the Fifth Amendment. But this limited guarantee of the freedom of a man's wish to speak is radically different in intent from the unlimited guarantee of the freedom of public discussion [*i.e.*, ". . . speech which bears, directly or indirectly, upon issues with which voters have to deal . . . ," p. 94], which is given by the First Amendment. . . . With regard to [this latter right], Congress has no negative powers whatever."

89 Joint Anti-Fascist Refugee Committee v. McGrath, 341 U.S. 123, 142 (1951); Dennis v. United States, 341 U.S. 494, 579 (1951); Breard v. Alexandria, 341 U.S. 622, 649 (1951); Beauharnais v. Illinois, 343 U.S. 250, 267 (1952); Wieman v. Updegraff, 344 U.S. 183, 192 (1952).

90 Trupiano v. United States, 334 U.S. 699 (1948).

91 Harris v. United States, 331 U.S. 145 (1947).

92 Weeks v. United States, 232 U.S. 383 (1914).

93 Olmstead v. United States, 277 U.S. 438, 470 (1928) (dissenting opinion).

94 On Lee v. United States, 343 U.S. 747 (1952).

95 United States v. On Lee, 193 F.2d 306, 317 (2d Cir. 1951) (dissenting opinion).

96 338 U.S. 25 (1949).

CHAPTER VI

1 Though there has been a great volume of writing about constitutional history in the United States, it has been written within a narrow definition of the subject. American legal history, at least from 1790 on, is still an almost unexplored field. The articles and monographs which should supply authoritative underpinning for many statements in this essay thus are yet unwritten. It would be tedious for the reader, to repeat this cautionary qualification at every relevant point in the text. Let me here sum up by saying that we presently have no history of (1) the reshaping of the legislative product by the courts through the process of statutory interpretation (see Parts II, III, V of this chapter), (2) legislative or executive response to what the Court has said and done in the name of the Constitution (Parts II and III), (3) judicial policy to curb pressure groups, through equal protection doctrine (Part II); (4) the "presumption of constitutionality" in

action (Part III); (5) the Court's influence over executive practice and procedure through its superintending power over lower federal courts as this affects rules of evidence in criminal proceedings (Part III). I have expressed judgments on these matters in this essay, based on my best appraisal of materials known to me. These judgments are not advanced dogmatically, but as hypotheses; I hope that the literature of the field may grow to the point where they may be tested.

2 6 Cranch 87 (U.S. 1810).

3 20 Wall. 655, 662 (U.S. 1875).

4 243 U.S. 188 (1917).

5 United States v. Butler, 297 U.S. 1, 78 (1936).

6 49 Cong. Rec. 4291–2 (1913).

7 79 Cong. Rec. 13449 (1935).

8 See discussion of the second Frazier-Lemke Act, in Wright v. Vinton Branch of the Mountain Trust Bank, 300 U.S. 440 (1937).

9 1 Cranch 137 (U.S. 1803).

10 E.g., Luther v. Borden, 7 How. 1 (U.S. 1849); Mississippi v. Johnson, 4 Wall. 475 (U.S. 1867); Field v. Clark, 143 U.S. 649 (1892).

11 Civil Rights Cases, 109 U.S. 3 (1883); New York Central R.R. v. White, 243 U.S. 188 (1917).

12 See Ohio Life Insurance and Trust Co. v. Debolt, 16 How. 416, 435 (U.S. 1853); cf. Charles River Bridge v. Warren Bridge, 11 Pet. 420 (U.S. 1837).

13 Compare the policy overtones of Carter v. Carter Coal Co., 298 U.S. 238 (1936); Schwegmann Brothers v. Calvert Distillers Corp., 341 U.S. 384 (1951).

14 Compare Associated Press v. National Labor Relations Board, 301 U.S. 103 (1937), with United States ex rel. Milwaukee Social Democratic Publishing Co. v. Burleson, 255 U.S. 407 (1921), and Near v. Minnesota ex rel. Olson, 283 U.S. 697 (1931).

15 United States v. Classic, 313 U.S. 299 (1941); Smith v. Allwright, 321 U.S. 649 (1944).

16 See Brandeis, J., concurring, in Ashwander v. Tennessee Valley Authority, 297 U.S. 288, 341 (1936).

17 See Haines, *The American Doctrine of Judicial Supremacy* 541–72 (2d ed. 1932).

18 Youngstown Sheet & Tube Co. v. Sawyer, 343 U.S. 579 (1952).

19 Scott v. Sandford, 19 How. 393 (U.S. 1857).

20 Schechter Poultry Corp. v. United States, 295 U.S. 495 (1935).

21 Hayburn's Case, 2 Dall. 409 (U.S. 1792); Mississippi v. Johnson, 4 Wall. 475 (U.S. 1867).

22 7 How. 1 (U.S. 1849).

23 Adkins v. Children's Hospital, 261 U.S. 525, 546 (1923); contrast with United States v. Carolene Products Co., 304 U.S. 144 (1938).

24 See Frankfurter, J., concurring, in Dennis v. United States, 341 U.S. 494, 517, 526–7 (1951).

25 Field v. Clark, 143 U.S. 649 (1892); cf. Norwegian Nitrogen Products Co. v. United States, 288 U.S. 294 (1933); Townsend v. Yeomans, 301 U.S. 441 (1937).

26 7 How. 1 (U.S. 1849).

27 Pacific States Box & Basket Co. v. White, 296 U.S. 176, 185–6 (1935).

28 Martin v. Mott, 12 Wheat. 19 (U.S. 1827); Terlinden v. Ames, 184 U.S. 270 (1902).

29 See United States v. Morgan, 313 U.S. 409, 422 (1941).

30 2 Richardson, *Messages and Papers of the Presidents* 581–2 (1896).

31 Panama Refining Co. v. Ryan, 293 U.S. 388 (1935); Schechter Poultry Corp. v. United States, 295 U.S. 495 (1935).

32 National Labor Relations Board v. Jones & Laughlin Steel Corp., 301 U.S. 1 (1937).

33 Scott v. Sandford, 19 How. 393 (U.S. 1857).

34 Pollock v. Farmers' Loan and Trust Co., 157 U.S. 429, on rehearing 158 U.S. 601 (1895).

35 Railroad Retirement Board v. Alton R.R., 295 U.S. 330 (1935); Schechter Poultry Corp. v. United States, 295 U.S. 495 (1935); Louisville Joint Stock Land Bank v. Radford, 295 U.S. 555 (1935); United States v. Butler, 297 U.S. 1 (1936); Carter v. Carter Coal Co., 298 U.S. 238 (1936).

36 295 U.S. 602 (1935).

37 See Youngstown Sheet & Tube Co. v. Sawyer, 343 U.S. 579, concurring opinions of Jackson, J., 635–49, and Frankfurter, J., 611–3 (1952).

38 Champion v. Ames, 188 U.S. 321 (1903) (lottery case); Clark Distilling Co. v. Western Maryland Ry., 242 U.S. 311 (1917) (Webb-Kenyon); Hammer v. Dagenhart, 247 U.S. 251 (1918) (child labor).

39 Pollock v. Farmers' Loan and Trust Co., 157 U.S. 429, on rehearing 158 U.S. 601 (1895).

40 Civil Rights Cases, 109 U.S. 3 (1883); United States v. Harris, 106 U.S. 629 (1883).

41 See note 6 *supra*.

42 McNabb v. United States, 318 U.S. 332 (1943).

43 Steele v. Louisville & Nashville R.R., 323 U.S. 192 (1944).

44 242 U.S. 470 (1917).

45 4 Wall. 2 (U.S. 1866).

46 Hirabayashi v. United States, 320 U.S. 81 (1943); Korematsu v.

United States, 323 U.S. 214 (1944); cf. *Ex parte* Endo, 323 U.S. 283 (1944).

47   See United States v. Bryan, 339 U.S. 323 (1950); United States v. Fleischman, 339 U.S. 349 (1950).

48   Helvering v. Davis, 301 U.S. 619 (1937); United States v. Darby, 312 U.S. 100 (1941).

49   157 U.S. 429 (1895).

50   Hammer v. Dagenhart, 247 U.S. 251 (1918); Bailey v. Drexel Furniture Co., 259 U.S. 20 (1922).

51   See note 35 *supra*.

52   See note 31 *supra*.

53   Standard Oil Co. v. United States, 221 U.S. 1 (1911).

54   Massachusetts v. Mellon, 262 U.S. 447 (1923).

55   Steward Machine Co. v. Davis, 301 U.S. 548 (1937); Helvering v. Davis, 301 U.S. 619 (1937).

56   Pollock v. Farmers' Loan and Trust Co., 157 U.S. 429, on rehearing 158 U.S. 601 (1895).

57   Youngstown Sheet & Tube Co. v. Sawyer, 343 U.S. 579 (1952).

58   1 Farrand, *The Records of the Federal Convention of 1787* 65 (1911).

59   United States v. Curtiss-Wright Export Corp., 299 U.S. 304 (1936).

60   See note 37 *supra*.

61   See United States v. Trans-Missouri Freight Ass'n, 166 U.S. 290 (1897); Wright v. Vinton Branch of the Mountain Trust Bank, 300 U.S. 440 (1937).

62   103 U.S. 168 (1881).

63   273 U.S. 135 (1927). But cf. Tenney v. Brandhove, 341 U.S. 367, 378 (1951).

64   Compare Davis, *Administrative Law* 135 (1951).

65   See Jones, *Life, Liberty and Property* 323, 332–4 (1941).

CHAPTER VII

1   Fairman, *American Constitutional Decisions* 24–5 (1948).

2   28 U.S.C. §342 (1946). The whole Code was revised in 1948 and all writs are now covered in 28 U.S.C. §1651 (Supp. 1952).

3   Brandeis' concurring opinion in Ashwander v. Tennessee Valley Authority, 297 U.S. 288, 347 (1936), reprinted in Fairman, *op. cit. supra* note 1, at 31.

4   See Thayer, *John Marshall* 78 (1901).

5   *Id.* at 79, referring to Marshall's opinion, 5 Cranch 137, 170 (U.S. 1803).

6   13 How. 40 (U.S. 1851). Fairman, *op. cit. supra* note 1, at 29.

7   4 The Record, Association of the Bar of the City of New York 321–58 (1949); Curtis, "A Better Theory of Legal Interpretation," 3 Vand. L. Rev. 407–37 (1950); and, in large part, in Cook, *Legal Drafting* 104–33 (1951).

8   Benedict, *Patterns of Culture* 252 (1934).

9   Cahn, *The Sense of Injustice* 121 (1949).

10 *Id.* at 112–3.

11 Ehrlich, *Fundamental Principles of the Sociology of Law* 74 (Moll transl. 1936).

12 *Ibid.*

13 *Id.* at 173–4. "*Verschulden*," for our purposes, is the equivalent of "negligence."

14 Letter to Wu, July 1, 1929, in Holmes, *Book Notices and Uncollected Letters and Papers* 201 (Shriver ed. 1936); that this was the book appears in a letter to Pollock, "I thought his *Grundlegung der Soziologie des Rechts* the best book on legal subjects by any living continental jurist that I knew of." 2 *Holmes-Pollock Letters* 34 (Howe ed. 1946).

15 Holmes, *Book Notices, loc. cit. supra* note 14.

16 Henry M. Hart, Jr. pointed out this dualism in Holmes' thinking. He referred to the first part of Holmes, "The Path of the Law," reprinted in *Collected Legal Papers* 167–79 for the positivistic part, and to pp. 179–202 for the other part. See Hart, "Holmes' Positivism—An Addendum," 64 Harv. L. Rev. 929 (1951). I agree with Mark Howe, who wrote a brief rejoinder, pp. 937–9, that the two parts are a consistent whole. It is my thesis that both are mingled in the law itself.

17 Kluckhohn, "Manners and Morals: A.D. 1950," The New Republic, June 12, 1950, p. 11.

18 Carter v. Carter Coal Co., 298 U.S. 238, 327 (1936).

19 National Mutual Insurance Co. v. Tidewater Transfer Co., 337 U.S. 582, 646 (1949) (dissenting opinion).

20 Curtis, *Lions Under the Throne* 275 *et seq.* (1947). Here let me correct an error in the account: It was not the Illinois but the Minnesota legislature which was involved in the great case of the Chicago, Milwaukee, and St. Paul, 134 U.S. 418 (1890).

21 See our round table in Chapter III *supra*.

22 1 Annals of Cong. 758 (1789).

23 333 U.S. 203 (1948).

24 Book Review, 63 Harv. L. Rev. 729, 731 (1950).

25 333 U.S. 203, 212 (1948).

26 *Id.* at 213 *et seq.* (concurring opinion).

27 Compare *id.* at 222 with Jefferson's report which Reed quotes in his dissent, *id.* at 245 n.11.

28 Muller v. Oregon, 208 U.S. 412 (1908). See Professor Freund's discussion in Chapter II *supra*.

29 333 U.S. 203, 231–2 (1948) (concurring opinion).

30 *Id.* at 237–8 (concurring opinion).

31 *Id.* at 244–8, 250, 255, 256.

32 American Federation of Labor v. American Sash Co., 335 U.S. 538, 550 (1949) (concurring opinion).

33 Montaigne, *L'Apologie de Raymond Sebond* 237–8 (Porteau ed. 1937). The translation is mine.

34 Zorach v. Clauson, 343 U.S. 306 (1952).

35 *Id.* at 315.

36 Cummings v. Missouri, 4 Wall. 277, 323 (U.S. 1867).

37 328 U.S. 303 (1946). I am going to borrow from my article, "A Modern Supreme Court in a Modern World," 4 Vand. L. Rev. 427, 442–3 (1951), the following account of this case, as indeed I did for much of my account of the McCollum case.

38 H.R. Doc. No. 264, 78th Cong., 1st Sess. (1943).

39 Lovett v. United States, 66 F. Supp. 142, 144 (Ct. Cl. 1945).

40 See 89 Cong. Rec. 4482–7, 4546–56, 4581–4605 (1943) (House); 89 Cong. Rec. 5023–4 (1943) (Senate).

41 United States v. Lovett, 328 U.S. 303 (1946).

42 *Id.* at 314, 316.

43 *Id.* at 318, 319, 321 (concurring opinion).

44 341 U.S. 716 (1951).

45 *Id.* at 725 (separate opinion).

46 Cummings v. Missouri, 4 Wall. 277 (U.S. 1867); *Ex parte* Garland, 4 Wall. 333 (U.S. 1867).

47 The current seems to have taken some time starting. Five years after Marbury v. Madison, the constitutionality of the Embargo Laws of 1807 and 1808 was argued before the U.S. District Court of Massachusetts. Samuel Dexter, the leader of the Massachusetts Bar, represented *The William*, a ship which had been seized. He contended that the Embargo Laws were unconstitutional, and that the court had the duty to declare them so. None less than Joseph Story, who went to Congress that fall, and who went on the Supreme Court three years later, was of counsel with the United States Attorney. Dexter, I may add, had been appointed Secretary of the Treasury by President Adams near the end of his term, in January of 1801, and had held that office into Jefferson's administration until January 1802, when he was succeeded by Gallatin. He had been in Washington, therefore, at the very time when Marbury's appointment was with-

held. He had a case of his own in the Supreme Court which was decided in the very term, the February Term of 1803, when Marbury v. Madison was decided. It is Hodgson v. Dexter, reported in 1 Cranch 345, in the same volume in which Marbury's case is reported on page 137. Yet curiously, and to me inexplicably, Dexter did not cite Marbury v. Madison to the District Court, although he insisted so strongly upon the duty of the court to ignore an unconstitutional act that he argued the point to the jury even after Judge Davis had ruled that these acts were constitutional, and in spite of Judge Davis' warning that he would hold him in contempt if he persisted. Judge Davis wrote a learned opinion, in which he cited Hayburn's case, 2 Dall. 409 (U.S. 1792), and Hylton v. United States, 3 Dall. 171 (U.S. 1796), and three others, and yet he too failed to cite Marbury v. Madison on what disturbed him most, whether he had the power to declare an Act of Congress unconstitutional. Judge Davis said, "Finding no direct judicial authority on the point, I shall next adduce opinions and reasonings, from a less authoritative source, but still highly respectable"; and he then had recourse to *The Federalist*. Judge Davis concluded that "the power to declare them [legislative acts] void exists, only, in cases of contravention, opposition or repugnancy, to some express restrictions or provisions contained in the constitution. The examples and the argument apply only to cases of legislative action, which their powers forbid; not to those, which their powers may be supposed not to authorize." United States v. The William, 28 Fed. Cas. 614, 618, 619 (1808).

I am still asking myself why Dexter did not cite Marbury v. Madison, why Story did not draw it to the attention of the court, and why Judge Davis did not find it. Warren notices these curious facts in 1 *History of the Supreme Court*, in a footnote on pp. 345–6, but he suggests no explanation.

48 And again I borrow from my article in 4 Vand. L. Rev., *op. cit. supra* note 37, at 437.

49 American Communications Ass'n v. Douds, 339 U.S. 382, 419 (1950) (concurring opinion).

50 Public Utilities Commission v. Pollak, 343 U.S. 451 (1952).

51 *Id.* at 467 (dissenting opinion).

52 For the presence of an immanent order in our law, let me refer to my article, "Ethics in the Law," 4 Stan. L. Rev. 477, 487 *et seq.* (1952); and to my article, "The Trial Judge and the Jury," 5 Vand. L. Rev. 150, 163–4 (1952).

53 Whitehead, *Adventures of Ideas* 142–3 (1937).

54 Thoreau, "Walden," *Walden and Other Writings* 290 (Atkinson ed. 1937).

55 Emerson, *Journal* 419 (1911).

56 Thoreau, *op. cit. supra* note 54, at 646, 650.

57 G. E. Fasnacht, *Acton's Political Philosophy* 29 (1952).

58 *Id.* at 32 n.4.

59 *Id.* at 24; see also at 46.

60 *Id.* at 55–6; this is a condensation of four letters which Acton wrote in 1861–2, and which were published by Cardinal Gasquet in his *Lord Acton and his Circle* 245–56 (1906).

61 *The Philosophy of Peirce* 47 (Buchler ed. 1940).

62 The foregoing summation and quotations are from Leslie A. White, *The Science of Culture* 156–8 (1949).

63 Zorach v. Clauson, 343 U.S. 306, 325 (1952) (dissenting opinion).

64 *Id.* at 316, 317–8 (dissenting opinion).

65 *Id.* at 322–3 (dissenting opinion).

66 *Adventures of Ideas* 143 (1937).

67 See Rutledge's dissent in Everson v. Board of Education, 330 U.S. 1, 61 n.56 (1947); Sutherland, "Due Process and Disestablishment," 62 Harv. L. Rev. 1306, 1337–8 (1949).

68 Sutherland, *id.* at 1338 n.97.

69 Everson v. Board of Education, 330 U.S. 1 (1947).

70 Herbert Dingle, *The Scientific Adventure* 250 (1952).

71 Whitehead, *Adventures of Ideas* 144 (1937).

72 *Id.* at 374.

73 *Id.* at 144.

74 *Id.* at 154.

75 Public Utilities Commission v. Pollak, 343 U.S. 451, 459–60 (1952).

76 Muller v. Oregon, 208 U.S. 412, 419–21 (1908). See Freund, *On Understanding the Supreme Court* 88 (1949).

77 Burstyn v. Wilson, 343 U.S. 495, 532 (1952) (Frankfurter concurring opinion); cf. Winters v. New York, 333 U.S. 507, 524 (1948) (Frankfurter dissenting opinion).

78 International Harvester Co. v. Kentucky, 234 U.S. 199 (1914).

79 *Id.* at 221.

80 *Id.* at 222.

81 *Id.* at 223–4.

82 See also United States v. Cohen Grocery Co., 255 U.S. 81, 86 (1921), where it was held unconstitutional to make it a crime "to make any unjust or unreasonable rate or charge in handling or dealing in or with any necessaries"; and A. B. Small Co. v. American Sugar Refining Co., 267 U.S. 233 (1925).

83 343 U.S. 495 (1952).

84 Winters v. New York, 333 U.S. 507 (1948).

85 *Id.* at 525 (dissenting opinion). See also SEC v. Chenery Corp., 318 U.S. 80 (1943), 332 U.S. 194 (1947).

86 Great Northern Ry. v. Sunburst Co., 287 U.S. 358, 365 (1932).

87 Hand, *The Spirit of Liberty* 189–90 (Dilliard ed. 1952).

88 See Cahn, "Madison and the Pursuit of Happiness," 27 N.Y.U.L. Rev. 265, 276 (1952).

89 5 *The Writings of James Madison* 269, 272–3 (Hunt ed. 1904); the *Oxford Dictionary* gives as one of the definitions of "sentiment": "6. What one feels with regard to something; mental attitude (of approval or disapproval, etc.); an opinion or view as to what is right or agreeable. Often pl. with collective sense."

90 This has already been said, and well said, by Paul Freund in his "The Supreme Court and Civil Liberties," 4 Vand. L. Rev. 533, 552 (1951).

LIST OF CASES

A. B. Small Co. v. American Sugar Refining Co., 267 U.S. 233 (1925)
    Curtis: 223
Abrams v. United States, 250 U.S. 616 (1919)
    Frank: 118
Adams Mfg. Co. v. Storen, 304 U.S. 307 (1938)
    Freund: 209
Adkins v. Children's Hospital, 261 U.S. 525 (1923)
    Frank: 110; Hurst: 148
Adler v. Board of Education, 342 U.S. 485 (1952)
    Bischoff: 27, 29, 31; Frank: 32
American Communications Ass'n v. Douds, 339 U.S. 382 (1950)
    Curtis: 222; Frank: 134
American Federation of Labor v. American Sash Co., 335 U.S. 538 (1949)
    Curtis: 221
Ashwander v. Tennessee Valley Authority, 297 U.S. 288 (1936)
    Bischoff: 26; Curtis: 219; Hurst: 217
Associated Press v. National Labor Relations Board, 301 U.S. 103 (1937)
    Hurst: 217
Atty. Gen. B. C. v. Atty. Gen. Can., [1937] A.C. 368
    Freund: 207
Atty. Gen. Vict. v. Comm., 71 C.L.R. 237 (1945)
    Freund: 207

Bailey v. Drexel Furniture Co. (Child Labor Tax Case), 259 U.S. 20 (1922)
    Hurst: 159
Baldwin v. Seelig, 294 U.S. 511 (1935)
    Freund: 209
Banco de Espana v. Federal Reserve Bank, 114 F.2d 438 (2d Cir. 1940)
    Frank: 40

Herndon v. Lowry, 301 U.S. 242 (1937)
    Frank: 116, 118
Hilder v. Dexter, [1902] A.C. 474
    Curtis: 206
Hirabayashi v. United States, 320 U.S. 81 (1943)
    Frank: 215; Hurst: 218
Hodgson v. Dexter, 1 Cranch 345 (U.S. 1803)
    Curtis: 222
Home Ins. Co. v. Dick, 281 U.S. 397 (1930)
    Freund: 210
Hood & Sons v. Du Mond, 336 U.S. 525 (1949)
    Freund: 209
Hoopeston Canning Co. v. Cullen, 318 U.S. 313 (1943)
    Freund: 210
Hot Oil case, see Panama Refining Co. v. Ryan
Humphrey's Executor v. United States, 295 U.S. 602 (1935)
    Hurst: 151
Hylton v. United States, 3 Dall. 171 (U.S. 1796)
    Curtis: 222

Income Tax Cases, see Pollock v. Farmers' Loan & Trust Co.
International Harvester Co. v. Kentucky, 234 U.S. 199 (1914)
    Curtis: 195
International Ticket Scale Corp. v. United States, 165 F.2d 358 (2d Cir. 1948)
    Freund: 210
Interstate Busses Corp. v. Blodgett, 276 U.S. 245 (1928)
    Freund: 209

J. I. Case Co. v. National Labor Relations Board, 321 U.S. 337 (1944)
    Frank: 213
James v. Bowman, 190 U.S. 127 (1903)
    Freund: 208
John Hancock Mut. Life Ins. Co. v. Yates, 299 U.S. 178 (1936)
    Freund: 210
Joint Anti-Fascist Refugee Committee v. McGrath, 341 U.S. 123 (1951)
    Frank: 133, 211, 216
Jones v. Opelika, 316 U.S. 584 (1942)
    Bischoff: 81
Joseph v. Carter & Weekes Stevedoring Co., 330 U.S. 422 (1947)
    Freund: 210

Kansas Southern Ry. v. Kaw Valley District, 233 U.S. 75 (1914)
    Freund: 209
Kilbourn v. Thompson, 103 U.S. 168 (1881)
    Hurst: 164
Korematsu v. United States, 323 U.S. 214 (1944)
    Hurst: 218

Mintz v. Baldwin, 289 U.S. 346 (1933)
    Freund: 209
Mississippi v. Johnson, 4 Wall. 475 (U.S. 1867)
    Hurst: 217
Missouri v. Holland, 252 U.S. 416 (1920)
    Hurst: 56, 57, 58
Morgan v. Virginia, 328 U.S. 373 (1928)
    Freund: 209
Muller v. Oregon, 208 U.S. 412 (1908)
    Curtis: 179, 223

National Labor Relations Board v. Jones & Laughlin Steel Corp., 301 U.S. 1 (1937)
    Frank: 213; Hurst: 218
National Mutual Insurance Co. v. Tidewater Transfer Co., 337 U.S. 582 (1949)
    Curtis: 220
National Prohibition Cases, 253 U.S. 350 (1920)
    Cahn: 201
Near v. Minnesota *ex rel.* Olson, 283 U.S. 697 (1931)
    Frank: 116; Hurst: 217
New York Central R.R. v. White, 243 U.S. 188 (1917)
    Hurst: 142, 217
Norris v. Alabama (Scottsboro case), 294 U.S. 587 (1935)
    Freund: 205
Norwegian Nitrogen Products Co. v. United States, 288 U.S. 294 (1933)
    Hurst: 218

Ohio Life Insurance and Trust Co. v. Debolt, 16 How. 416 (U.S. 1853)
    Hurst: 217
Olmstead v. United States, 277 U.S. 438 (1928)
    Frank: 216
On Lee v. United States, 343 U.S. 747 (1952), affirming 193 F.2d 306 (2d Cir. 1951)
    Frank: 138
Order of United Commercial Travelers of America v. Wolfe, 331 U. S. 586 (1947)
    Freund: 210

Pacific Employers Ins. Co. v. Industrial Accident Comm'n, 306 U.S. 493 (1939)
    Freund: 210
Pacific States Box & Basket Co. v. White, 296 U.S. 176 (1935)
    Hurst: 218
Pacific States Tel. & Tel. Co. v. Oregon, 223 U.S. 118 (1912)
    Frank: 38
Panama Refining Co. v. Ryan (Hot Oil case), 293 U.S. 388 (1935)
    Hurst: 61, 218
Panhandle Eastern Pipe Line Co. v. Michigan Pub. Serv. Comm'n, 341 U.S. 329 (1951)
    Freund: 209

INDEX

ABEL, ALBERT S.
  on state taxation of interstate commerce, quoted by Freund, 103–4
ACTON, LORD
  on liberty and self-government, quoted by Curtis, 187–8
ADMINISTRATIVE AGENCIES
  construction of Constitution by, 68, 70
  curbs on investigations by, 165
  judicial review and growth of, 150, 160–1, 163
  judicial review of procedure, 149, 151, 163, 166
  proposed, to regulate state taxation affecting commerce, 101–5
  regulations of, presumed constitutional, 148
  validity of delegations to, 150, 160–1, 163
ALIENS
  Communism as retroactive basis for deportation of, 42–3, 132, 134–5
  "concentration camp" provisions of McCarran Act, 127–8
  deportation of, as criminal punishment, 134–5
  Harry Bridges, congressional attempt to deport, 119, 124–6

  naturalization, oath to bear arms, 80
  policy toward, as political question, 42–3, 132
  procedural rights, 111, 127–8
AMENDMENT CLAUSE (ARTICLE V), see also Constitutions
  adoption of, 9–12
  as abandonment of immutability, 9
  as necessary for ratification, 11–12
  Hamilton, views on, 11
  immediate exercise of, 12, 23–4
    effect on Marshall, 23–4
  Jefferson and, 11
  Madison, views on, 11
  sufficiency of, for adaptability, 12, 19, 74
  The Federalist Nos. 43 and 85, 11, 22–3
  use of referendum in amending process, 56
ARISTOTLE
  concept of essence in constitutional construction, 68–71
  mentioned, 4, 76
ARTICLES OF CONFEDERATION, 8–9, 12

BENEDICT, RUTH
  on relation of law and custom, quoted by Curtis, 173–4

237